TROUBLING CONFESSIONS

TROUBLING
CONFESSIONS

Speaking Guilt in Law & Literature

PETER BROOKS

THE UNIVERSITY OF CHICAGO PRESS

CHICAGO & LONDON

The University of Chicago Press, Chicago 60637
The University of Chicago Press, Ltd., London
© 2000 by The University of Chicago
All rights reserved. Published 2000
Paperback edition 2001
Printed in the United States of America

09 08 07 06 05 04 03 02 01   2 3 4 5
ISBN: 0-226-07585-0 (cloth)
ISBN: 0-226-07586-9 (paperback)

Library of Congress Catologing-in-Publication Data

Brooks, Peter.
     Troubling confessions : speaking guilt in law and literature / Peter Brooks.
          p.   cm.
     Includes bibliographical references and index.
     ISBN 0-226-07585-0 (cloth : alk. paper)
     1. Confession in literature.   2. Confession.   3. Confession (Law)   I. Title.
PN56.C67B76   2000
809´.93353—dc21

                                                                99-059060

for Sophie and Sam, Nick and Phoebe

CONTENTS

ACKNOWLEDGMENTS

My thinking about the problem of confession began in teaching a course on "narrative and rhetoric in the law"—reading legal texts in the perspective of literary analysis—and the first debt of gratitude to be acknowledged is to Paul Gewirtz, professor at Yale Law School and originally my coteacher in the course. What I learned from him, in preparing and teaching the course, was immeasurably enriching, and his keen analysis has saved me from many an error. Other colleagues from Yale Law School have also lent their help, especially Owen Fiss, John Langbein, Kenji Yoshino, Guido Calabresi, and Anthony Kronman (the last two as Deans were notably hospitable to an enterprise marginal to their curriculum). Judge Barry Schaller has ever been a helpful friend. Robert Weisberg was an expert tutor in criminal procedure during the very pleasant semester I spent at Stanford Law School, at the kind invitation of Dean Paul Brest, where I was instructed also by Margaret Jane Radin, Kathleen Sullivan, Janet Halley, Thomas Grey, and William Simon. Some of my original interest in my subject arose from a faculty seminar I taught many years ago at Georgetown Law Center, at the invitation of my friend Norman Birnbaum, where I learned particularly from dialogue with Michael Louis Seidman and William Eskridge. In the field of religion, I have been helped by Katherine Gill and Lamin Sanneh. Conversation and correspondence with J. M. Coetzee have been illuminating. And in general, I have, as always, benefited from the comradeship of Michael Holquist, Juliet Mitchell, Richard Sennett, Toril Moi, and Robert J. Lifton. I had splendid research assistance for a time by Susan Schmeiser, who as a student jointly for the J.D. and the Ph.D., understood perfectly what I needed. And John Witt, another J.D./Ph.D. student, expertly checked my legal arguments and references. Todd Shuster and Lane Zachary also gave good advice on the manuscript. I have also profited from a number of occasions when I lectured from some of this material and was forced to revise my thinking in response to hard questions and pertinent comments. The two readers of the manuscript for University of Chicago Press—Patricia Meyer Spacks and Janet Halley—provided me with remarkably thoughtful and thorough comments. And Alan G. Thomas was the most expert and helpful editor one could have.

Parts of three of my chapters were published previously, in preliminary form: some of chapter 1 in *Yale Journal of Law and Humanities* (spring 1996) and then in the book I edited with Paul Gewirtz, *Law's Stories* (New Haven: Yale University Press, 1996); some of chapter 3 in *Representations* no. 64 (where I had an expert reading by Robert Post, professor at Boalt Hall); a portion of chapter 5 in *Diacritics* (fall 1995) (where it benefited from a critical reading by Jonathan Culler), and a shorter piece of that chapter in *Trauma and the Self*, a volume of the Robert Jay Lifton *festschrift* edited by Charles B. Strozier and Michael Flynn. My thanks to the editors of these journals and volumes for their hospitality and for permission to reuse the material.

Finally, my warm thanks to Rosa Ehrenreich, with whom dialogue on these as on all questions is ever animating and illuminating, and whose friendship is a buoyantly sustaining medium.

INTRODUCTION

"Contrition without Confession": so reads the title of the lead editor-ial in the *New York Times* of December 12, 1998. That editorial, like much media talk around the impeachment of President Clinton, was a plea for Clinton "to say the words"—that he had lied under oath—that would, according to the *Times,* bring a resolution to the stand-off. By this point in the protracted matter of Monica Lewinsky, everyone knew what Clinton had done. If his testimony under oath said he never had sexual relations with Monica Lewinsky, the sex he did have with her was known in the greatest detail. What was at issue was the name to give this sex. Many Americans appeared to take the position that the name didn't much matter, that Clinton's attempts to evade detection constituted standard behavior where sex is concerned, that he had admitted enough and should be allowed to continue in office. But the *Times* editorial stressed the other view: that there could be no true contrition, and thus no pardon and no reconciliation, until Clin-ton said "the words," until he explicitly gave public utterance to the statement: "I lied."

How strange this is: that faced with full revelation of the deeds done—documented over thousands of pages of the Starr Report and its annexes—and the admission that they were done, one should nonetheless feel the need for his affirmative statement—in his own words—that his prior (evasive) testimony constituted a lie. Strange, and yet familiar, in that the imperative to 'fess up, to take verbal responsibility for one's acts, is deeply ingrained in our culture, in our pedagogy, even in our law. Children are daily told that they must confess to their misdeeds, that confessing will be seen as possible grounds for mitigating punishment, that the refusal to confess will on the contrary aggravate the sanction, and—perhaps even worse—prevent reintegration into the community of parental affection. Confession of wrongdoing is considered fundamental to morality because it constitutes a verbal act of self-recognition as wrongdoer and hence provides the basis of rehabilitation. It is the precondition of the end to ostracism, reentry into one's desired place in the human community. To refuse confession is to be obdurate, hard of heart, resistant to amendment. Refusal of confession can be taken as a defiance of one's judges (apparently the view of the *Times* editorialist), whereas confession allows those judges to pass their sentences in security, knowing that the guilty party not only deserves and accepts but perhaps in some sense wants punishment, as the penance that follows confession.

Reflecting on the value we attach to the spoken confession of sin, crime, and error, we may become aware of how close we still are to the year 1215, when the Roman Catholic Church, in the Fourth Lateran Council, made annual confession obligatory for all the faithful. Lateran IV also issued for the first time a profession of the dogma— what a Christian is to believe—and established an inquisition for the extirpation of heresy. When one considers how the requirement of confession intersects with the definition of orthodox belief and the war on heresy, it begins to be apparent that confession plays a crucial role in moral cleansing and also in moral discipline: it works both to console and to police. It offers articulation of hidden acts and thoughts in a form that reveals—perhaps in a sense creates—the inwardness of the person confessing, and allows the person's punishment, absolution, rehabilitation, reintegration. The confessional model is so powerful in Western culture, I believe, that even those whose religion or nonreligion has no place for the Roman Catholic practice of confession are nonetheless deeply influenced by the model. Indeed, it permeates our culture, including our educational practices and our law. The image of the penitent with the priest, in the intimate yet impersonal, private and protected space of the confessional, represents a potent social ritual that both its friends and its enemies over the centuries have recognized as a shaping cultural experience.

Another image, though, is more regularly represented in our entertainments: the criminal suspect locked into the interrogation room, face to face with police detectives in a Spartan and sordid space where his confession of guilt arises not from the spontaneous contrition of the aggrieved conscience but from relentless interrogation. Only confession, the suspect is told, can bring release from interrogation. The interrogators are sure of his guilt. Denial will only make things worse. The process of rehabilitation and reintegration—if by way of punishment and expiation—can only begin when the suspect says those words, "I did it."

The demand that Clinton offer a full confession partook of both the legal and the religious models; Clinton himself seemed more willing to proclaim himself a sinner (and in fact assembled a group of clergy to help him return to the path of righteousness) than to admit to the legal fault of perjury, which was the demand of his censors. While we know there are vast differences in religious and legal confessions, precisely in the uses to which they are put, there is also a large cultural overlap. There are good historical reasons for this, since the religious model and the legal model emerge simultaneously, in a reciprocal influence, and, I believe, have continued to coexist with a certain accepted cultural blurring of the distinctions between them. If confessing to a priest is good for you, are we to say that confessing to a police interrogator is not? Certainly most would argue that it is good for society as a whole.

I contend in this book that our social and cultural attitudes toward confession suffer from uncertainties and ambivalences. And that these uncertainties and ambivalences should indicate that confession is a difficult and slippery notion to deal with. We worry about the trustworthiness of confessions because the speech-act that begins with the words "I confess" seems to be marked by contradictory intentions and subject to contradictory uses by those receiving this most personal of utterances. We want confessions, yet we are suspicious of them. The law has seen the necessity of attempting to regulate and police confessions: it has tried to establish conditions of the confessional act that guarantee that it has been "voluntarily" made, all the while authorizing kinds of pressure to confess that run counter to voluntariness. And the law still today—as in medieval times—tends to accept confession as the "queen of proofs." Meanwhile, Western culture, most strikingly since the Romantic era to our day, has made confessional speech a prime mark of authenticity, par excellence the kind of speech in which the individual authenticates his inner truth. In a contemporary culture that celebrates the therapeutic value of getting it all out in public, confession has become nearly banal, the everyday business of talk shows, as if the ordinary person could claim his individual identity only in the act of confessing. We appear today to live in a generalized demand for transparency that entails a kind of tyranny of the requirement to confess. When this demand intersects with the law—when, for instance, psychotherapeutically derived truth enters the courtroom—a confusion of realms can result, along with a reaction against the proliferation of unwanted confessions.

My intention here is to cross-cut between confession according to the law and confession according to literature—which will mean saying something also about the religious tradition of confession and about its large place in our culture as a whole. It is my notion that using different confessional practices one with another—one against another, at times—can be illuminating about the kinds of cultural work we ask confession to do, and whether we are, or should be, entirely comfortable with the results.

Judges, lawyers, and legal scholars (including Clinton and his legal team) have tended to treat the procedures and the language of the law as if they were fully hermetic. Thus if confession and voluntariness, for instance, are seen purely as terms of legal art, they don't necessarily have to pass muster according to our common uses of these terms. Interpretation in the law, it has often been assumed, can proceed on unchallenged assumptions about "intention" and "meaning" and how they line up with one another and how they are to be determined. But a result of the recent cross-disciplinary infiltration of interpretive theory from literary studies into legal studies has been a questioning of the law's internal definitions of some of its terms of art: a challenge to the notion that any act of interpretation is unproblematic, that it can refer to any principles that are not themselves products of acts of interpretation, that it does not reveal preferences, exclusions, unexamined assumptions that need testing against ordinary language and belief.

To do its job—to pass judgment—the law needs to insist upon

traditional notions of responsibility, including responsibility for acts of confession. Yet what we learn about confession from literature, from the religious tradition, and from the psychotherapeutic culture, suggests that where confession is concerned, the law needs to recognize that its conceptions of human motivation and volition are particularly flawed, even perhaps something of a fiction. Hence its heavy reliance on confessions in criminal justice creates a certain unease. If we have been taught that confession, the self-examination and the inwardness that confession both reflects and maybe creates, is essential to our psychic and moral health and our very definition as unique individuals, are we sure that we want the law to be able to use the confessional gesture so freely as it does? The Supreme Court of the United States has worried about this problem and sought to erect procedural safeguards against the coerced confession, yet it is not clear that in the day-to-day administration of justice—pursued in the police precinct, not the Court's marble chambers—these safeguards make much difference. Even so, they remain controversial: the famous "*Miranda* warnings" had to overcome a direct challenge to their constitutional status as recently as 2000.

The Fifth Amendment to the U.S. Constitution states that "No person . . . shall be compelled in any criminal case to be a witness against himself." This is clearly a rejection of the inquisitorially extracted confession, but what else is it? The phrase continues to elicit contentious interpretive reactions, such that neither its history nor its intent, its rationale nor its scope, can be said to be clear. Along with the "due process" clause of the Fourteenth Amendment, it has fostered debate on the permissible place and space of confession in the law, and it provokes reflection on how society wants to conceive the criminal suspect and defendant before the law. It is not only a question of the rights of accused, but of our whole conception of human dignity: of the extent to which we want to reduce the accused to a state of abjection, all the while maintaining that they must be unfettered to exercise their free will in acts of rational choice.

Nothing touches on these difficult issues more than the problem of confession. The requirement of confession imposed by the Church in the thirteenth century both reflects and instigates the emergence of the modern sense of selfhood and the individual's responsibility for his or her actions, intentions, thoughts—and for the acts of speech that lay them bare. With gathering momentum through the

5

Renaissance and Romanticism up to our time, confessional speech becomes more and more crucial in defining concepts—sincerity, authenticity—that we are supposed to live by. Our contemporary fascination with—though perhaps simultaneously revulsion from—the public, televised confession demonstrates the banalization of confessional practices. Tell-all confessional literature sells well. Magazines are devoted to nothing but the revelations of celebrities' private lives. With far more at stake, in South Africa, a nation is attempting to heal the wounds of its tragic past through a kind of generalized plea-bargain: a full confession of guilt to the Truth and Reconciliation Commission is supposed to result in amnesty, not conviction. On the other hand, every day in police stations across the United States, criminal suspects are warned of the dangers that may issue from confession—and then are subjected to every trick in the interrogator's manual in order to elicit their confession.

Confessant and confessor (to use the significant language of the Church) engage in a fateful dialogue. The bond between them, like that of suspect and interrogator, patient and analyst, urges toward speech. When it produces a confession, the confessor, and society as a whole, are reassured that they can pass judgment in good conscience. Yet the motives of confessing are often far from determinate: confessions activate inextricable layers of shame, guilt, contempt, self-loathing, attempted propitiation, and expiation. Unless the content of the confession can be verified by other means, thus substantiating its trustworthiness, it may be false—false to fact, if true to some other sense of guilt. The law records many instances of false confessions—and no doubt many have gone unrecorded. What is the truth of confession? Doesn't the requirement to confess suggest that there is always more than enough guilt to go around—since indeed once initiated, confession produces guilt as well as dissipating it? You may find yourself confessing to something else, something other than the supposed referent of your confession. You may damn yourself even as you seek to exculpate yourself.

We have become in Western culture what Michel Foucault calls "confessing animals," and the pages that follow ask how we may think about that and how we should treat confession. In my juxtapositions of different kinds of confessional speech, and my repeated return to the problem of confession in the law, I am not trying to formulate legal or social policy, but to provoke reflection, to ask difficult questions, and to suggest that more clarity about what we want confessions to be and to do would benefit our thinking and our treatment of those placed in accusation by the state. How we demand that confession take place, and what we do with the results, engages ethical issues about the state's power in relation to the individuals on whose behalf it exercises power. These issues lie in the background of my efforts to understand what it means to speak confessionally.

To map briefly what follows: chapter 1 focuses primarily on the Supreme Court's attempts to deal with the problem of confession, notably in *Miranda v. Arizona,* and pursues its discussion of this kind of confession in cross-reference to Rousseau, whose *Confessions*—in so many ways inaugural of the modern sensibility—are indeed a repeated point of reference throughout the book. Chapter 2 then considers the bond of confessor and confessant in various kinds of confessions, and eventually brings discussion to bear on Dostoevsky's *The Brothers Karamazov.* Chapter 3 returns to the law, with a close reading of the problem of "voluntariness" in one of *Miranda*'s important predecessor cases, *Culombe v. Connecticut.* Chapter 4 fills in some of the background to the modern problem of confession in the religious tradition, set in relation to the emergence of the "modern" sense of identity and selfhood. Chapter 5 concerns the law's difficulties in dealing with psychoanalytic versions of confessional "truth" and with the claims to hearing of victims. Chapter 6 dwells on motives to confession and reveries of the literary imagination on the requirement or the self-imposed compulsion to confess.

I

STORYTELLING WITHOUT FEAR?

THE CONFESSION PROBLEM

*Mea culpa belongs to a man and his God. It is a plea that
cannot be exacted from free men by human authority.*

Abe Fortas

*I have only one thing to fear in this enterprise; that isn't to
say too much or to say untruths; it's rather not to say
everything, and to silence truths.*

Jean-Jacques Rousseau

In Manchester, Vermont, in 1819, the disappearance of the can-
tankerous Russell Colvin led to an accusation that his feuding
neighbors, Stephen and Jesse Boorn, had murdered him. The Boorn
brothers declared their innocence throughout their trial, which
nonetheless ended in their conviction. Then, while awaiting execution in the local jail, where they were visited by fellow townspeople
urging that they clear their consciences before going to the gallows,
they did confess to the murder. Meanwhile, their attorney had put
notices in area newspapers seeking information about Colvin—for
the body had never been found—which led to the discovery that
Colvin was not in fact dead, but had merely gone to live in Schenec-
tady, New York. The subtitle of a narrative of the events gives the essential information: "A Full and Veracious Account of the Amazing
Events in Vermont: How Stephen and Jesse Boorn, two Brothers,
were Accused, Arrested, Indicted, Tried, Convicted and Sentenced
to die by Hanging for the Wilful Murder of Russell Colvin of
Manchester, Having confessed the Crime; how, while the Condemned Men Languished in Prison, it was Proved that Colvin had
not been Murdered, but was Alive and in Good Health and how He

Returned to Manchester and Saved the Unfortunate Doomed Men from a Terrible Fate."[1]

Confession has for centuries been regarded as the "queen of proofs" in the law: it is a statement from the lips of the person who should know best. Yet as the case of the Boorn brothers shows, confession can be untrue. The false confession is the extreme example that urges us to pose the more general question: how do we know a true confession? What are its marks? Is it a matter of the circumstances in which it is produced? Are there clear markers that allow us to judge that a confession has been freely and reliably given? And what is the relation between "freely" and "reliably"? Does the latter necessarily depend on the former? One begins to understand how confession and its contexts have long been a problem to the law.

Yet confession is considered to bear a special stamp of authenticity. From the thirteenth century, when the Roman Church began to require annual confession from the faithful, it has become in Western culture a crucial mode of self-examination; from the time of the early Romantics to the present day, confession has become a dominant form of self-expression, one that bears special witness to personal truth. In an increasingly secularized culture, truth *of* the self and *to* the self have become the markers of authenticity, and confession—written or spoken—has come to seem the necessary, though risky, act through which one lays bare one's most intimate self, to know oneself and to make oneself known. Psychoanalysis, one of the most conspicuous inventions of the twentieth century, offers a secular version of religious confession: it insists on the work of patient and analyst—comparable to confessant and confessor—toward the discovery of the most hidden truths about selfhood.

How can we understand this cultural urge toward confession on the one hand and our suspicion of confession on the other? What is it about confessional speech that appears to make it the vehicle of the most authentic truth, yet capable of the most damaging, sometimes self-destructive, untruth? If contemporary culture appears to insist on a generalized transparency, in which each of us is fully open to all others without dissimulation, doesn't the generalized confessional requirement also constitute a tyranny, a policing of the very privacy that selfhood requires? And if confession implies a penitential state that may involve disgrace, even abjection, doesn't it often appear a violation of human dignity? We need to ask, in all cases, what purpose is served by confession, what response it solicits, and what the person or persons who receive the confession are supposed to do with it.

The law adjudicates. When it accepts and uses a confession, it needs to know how the confession is made and what truth it represents. Thus it speaks an authoritative language about the conditions and nature of the confessional act, though it is dealing in what I think is one of the most complex and obscure forms of human speech and behavior. In the law's pronouncements on confession (how it is to be protected, authenticated, entered into the dispensation of justice), we can begin to grasp much about how we conceive the individual in relation to society and the troublesome role of confessional speech in that relation. The first step will be to look at the most prominent attempts of the United States Supreme Court to deal with these issues.

Miranda v. Arizona

In *Miranda v. Arizona* (1966),[2] the Supreme Court, in a 5–4 decision, issued its most far-reaching and controversial ruling on the place and use of confessions in the criminal law. The Court indeed established rules for determining what might be considered a "true confession"—rules that immediately entered the popular consciousness as the "Miranda warnings," familiar from arrests in almost any TV cop show: You have the right to remain silent; any statement you do make may be used as evidence against you; you have the right to the presence of an attorney; if you cannot pay for an attorney, one will be appointed to represent you. In establishing these "prophylactic standards" (as it later termed them) for confession, the Court was attempting to create for itself and for the police stations of the nation a set of guidelines that would permit a judgment of whether a confession had been given "voluntarily" or had been "compelled" or "coerced."[3]

The Court's major test of the admissibility of a confession at trial had long been whether it was voluntary or compelled. But the "due-process voluntariness test"—the requirement that all the circumstances of the case demonstrate that the suspect freely and knowingly confessed without coercion—had proved very problematic in its application. Five years before *Miranda,* Justice Felix Frankfurter produced a sixty-seven-page "treatise" on the subject without reaching a clear resolution on the characteristics by which the voluntary confession can be known, in *Culombe v. Connecticut*.[4] The Court found it-self presented with more and more petitions for review of individual cases contesting the voluntariness of confessions admitted at trial. With *Massiah v. United States* and *Escobedo v. Illinois*, both decided in 1964, the Court began to move toward more specific rules—primar-ily, the right to counsel in custodial pretrial questioning—governing the situation in which confessions could be said to be voluntary rather than coerced.[5] *Miranda* takes a leap forward, in specifying those con-ditions without which no confession will be admitted as voluntary. A cynical interpretation of the Court's decision in *Miranda* would say that the Court cut the Gordian knot of the problem of voluntariness by saying to the police: if you follow these forms, we'll allow that the confession you obtained was voluntary. And there is much post-*Miranda* evidence indicating that the police quickly learned to play by the new rules and that they produced as many confessions as before. A more generous interpretation would see the Court's decision as a well-intentioned if not entirely adequate attempt to deal with a prob-lem as old as the history of criminal prosecution. What are the criteria that allow us to know that a confession has been voluntarily made—and therefore that it may be accepted on its face as reliable, a confes-sion of the truth? Behind this question may lie another one, implicit rather than explicit in the Court's statements on confession: what is it about confession that makes it such a difficult and slippery notion to deal with? Why do we worry about confessions and their truth value, not only in the law but in literature and in daily life?[6]

Chief Justice Earl Warren, writing for the majority, claims that the rules and warnings established by *Miranda* "enable the defendant under otherwise compelling circumstances to tell his story without fear" (384 U.S. 436, 466). To this ideal of "storytelling without fear"—an unconstrained context for confession—stands opposed Justice Byron White's comment, in his dissenting opinion, that "it is by no means certain that the process of confessing is injurious to the accused. To the contrary it may provide psychological relief and enhance the prospects for rehabilitation" (538). I detect here two fundamentally opposed views of how confession works, and how it is to be valued—as well, no doubt, as two incompatible views of human nature and volition. White exaggerates only slightly when he argues, "The obvious underpinning of the Court's decision is a deep-seated distrust of all confessions" (537), which he finds in excess of the Fifth

Amendment injunction against compelling someone to bear witness against himself. The issue joined here turns on the question as to whether "storytelling"—in the confessional mode—should and even can take place "without fear."

Justice John Marshall Harlan, in his dissenting opinion, allows that the context of custodial questioning never can be wholly without fear.

> The atmosphere and questioning techniques, proper and fair though they be, can in themselves exert a tug on the suspect to confess, and in this light [here he quotes Justice Robert Jackson, dissenting in *Ashcraft v. Tennessee*], "[t]o speak of any confessions of crime made after arrest as being 'voluntary' or 'uncoerced' is somewhat inaccurate, although traditional." . . . Until today, the role of the Constitution has been only to sift out *undue* pressure, not to assure spontaneous confessions. (515)[7]

Justice Jackson's view of the "inaccurate but traditional" view of confession as voluntary or uncoerced will need further meditation. To stay with Harlan's opinion, that "tug" on the suspect to confess needs juxtaposition to one of the most effective moments of Warren's opinion: the moment when he invents what one might call the "story of the closed room."

Warren begins by founding this story on its inherent resistance to telling. It is essential, he says, to understand what has gone on when the defendant was questioned by police officers, detectives, or the prosecuting attorney "in a room in which he was cut off from the outside world" (445). But: "The difficulty in depicting what transpires at such interrogations stems from the fact that in this country they have largely taken place incommunicado." After reviewing earlier examples of police use of "third degree" tactics—including beating, hanging, whipping, and prolonged incommunicado interrogation—in order to extort confessions, Warren allows that in modern interrogation physical brutality has largely given way to psychological coercion:, then cites *Blackburn v. Alabama* to the effect that "the blood of the accused is not the only hallmark of an unconstitutional inquisition" (448).[8] He continues: "Interrogation still takes place in privacy. Privacy results in secrecy and this in turn results in a gap in our knowledge as to what in fact goes on in the interrogation rooms." Privacy produces secrecy that produces a gap in our knowledge. As literary scholars know, especially from the work of Wolfgang Iser, a "gap" [*Leerstelle*] demands to be filled and activates the interpreter's ingenuity.[9]

To fill in the gaps, Warren as ingenious interpreter turns to police interrogation manuals, especially Fred E. Inbau and John E. Reid, *Criminal Interrogation and Confessions* (1962) and Charles E. O'Hara, *Fundamentals of Criminal Investigation* (1956), works which at the time of *Miranda* had attained a circulation of over forty-four thousand copies (and in their revised editions continue to be widely used). The tactics preached by these manuals are as chilling as one might imagine. They recommend that interrogation take place in private, so that the suspect, isolated from all familiar surroundings, "be deprived of every psychological advantage"; that the interrogators assume from the outset that the suspect's guilt is a fact and that all they are after is an elaboration of a story the police already know; that interrogation create "an oppressive atmosphere of dogged persistence," that there be "no respite from the atmosphere of domination"; that interrogators use the "Mutt and Jeff," good-cop bad-cop routine to scare the suspect and suggest possible leniency if he cooperates; that they establish a context of dependency, so that the suspect feels he must throw himself on their mercy; that tricks be used, such as fake lineups with the accused identified by fictitious witnesses. The idea, says Warren, is to get the suspect to confirm "the preconceived story the police seek to have him describe" (455). At this point, one must ask of the confession made: whose story is it? If confession is in theory the most intimate and personal of statements by a subject, how can this story be supplied by his listener? And in fact, most confessions by criminal suspects traditionally take the form of a statement written by the interrogators and signed by the suspect.[10] As Warren concludes, the "interrogation environment is created for no purpose other than to subjugate the individual to the will of his examiner." From here, he argues the "intimate connection" between custodial interrogation and the Fifth Amendment privilege against self-incrimination.

I have sketched only in brief outline how Warren uses the secrecy of interrogation to create a dramatic story of the closed room, and the dramas of humiliation, deception, and coercion played out behind the locked door, convincing us that compulsion is "inherent" in custodial interrogation (458). He has effectively responded to Frankfurter's resigned complaint in *Culombe* that "[w]hat actually happens to [suspects] behind the closed door is difficult if not impossible to ascertain" (*Culombe,* 573–74). The closed room—in American police stations, it is nicely labeled "the interview room"—may remind us of the sealed Paris apartment of Edgar Allan Poe's "The Murders in the Rue Morgue," the first detective story and model for the genre, where this very closure activates the detective Dupin's interpretive method. The enclosed, self-contained space, from the English country house to the California villa, becomes a *topos* in detective fiction precisely because, like that *alcôve* where the young Sigmund Freud was instructed by his mentor to seek the secrets of hysteria, it appears to offer the inner sanctum of a hidden truth. And custodial police interrogation as we know it—as *Miranda* attempts to deal with it—historically is consubstantial with the rise of the detective story. There could be no cop stories before the nineteenth century because there were no police forces in the modern sense. Police interrogation at the station house did not take place much before the end of the nineteenth century. Earlier, other venues—such as questioning in the suspect's home, or before a magistrate—were common, and the extension of the right against self-incrimination to the station house simply unnecessary (an historical evolution which the dissents in *Miranda* ignore). The story of the closed room of course has its historical precedents, especially in inquisitorial proceedings, but so far as custodial interrogation by the police is concerned, it is very much a product of modern, urban crime and the social response to it. It is as if the pathological closed and isolated space of the interrogation room had been created to match the closed and isolated pathological space of the crime scene. Warren's creation of the story of the closed room, his opening up to light of its isolation and privacy and secrecy, his filling in of the gaps in our knowledge, stands as an exemplary narrative. Where is voluntariness in such a story? What confession can be trusted?

Yet, since the purpose of police work is to convict suspects and thus protect society, one may feel some surprise, as well as admiration, at the creation of the counter-conviction that suspects should be freed of the obligation to confess. That there is a right *not* to confess doesn't seem self-evident. It runs counter to standard morality, which censures concealment and values the confession of wrong-doing.[11] In many a routine case, confession is necessary to breach concealment and uncover the true story. Commonsensically, we might assume that the evidence against the accused produced from his own mouth is always the most reliable evidence we can have. When someone confesses, his judges may proceed to condemn him with a good conscience.

The Court's anxiety of course has a history, one that is intricated with religious practices of confession and with the ecclesiastical courts, reaching back at least to the Fourth Lateran Council of 1215, which defined the Christian faith, enjoined once-a-year confession on the faithful, and instituted a vast inquisition of heresy, including use of the oath of *de veritate dicenda,* holding those under suspicion to answer truthfully, under oath, any question that might be posed. As the Holy Office gained power in the fight against heretics, it developed the doctrine that confession to heresy was necessary to save the heretic's soul and preserve the purity of the Church: one had to stand condemned by one's own word—even if that word had to be extracted by the rack and the pinion and other ghastly techniques of torture.

Confession and inquisition in fact have close historical links. When the Fourth Lateran Council declared the abolition of "ordeals" (such divine proofs of guilt or innocence as putting one's hand into the fire), continental Europe generally began to adopt rules of evidence—derived from Roman-canon law—that said that in a capital case only the testimony of two eyewitnesses or the defendant's confession constituted full proof, sufficient to condemn. Circumstantial evidence was only partial proof. If partial proofs—*indicia*—were abundant enough, this justified proceeding to seek full proof by way of torture, in order to produce a confession. A confession made under torture was supposed to be fully repeated a day later without torture in order to be valid (but if not so repeated, the suspect could be tortured again, until he agreed to make the "voluntary" confession).[12] In ordinary capital cases, confessions made under torture were also supposed to have their facts verified by independent means, where possible. In cases of religious inquisition—the inquiry into heretical beliefs—this was of course impossible, since the matter being confessed to was entirely internal. Hence the special problem of inquisitorial requirements of confession in cases of religious belief and deeply held personal conviction: there could be no other source of convicting evidence than that produced by defendant's own lips—however extracted from those lips.

In Elizabethan England, the Court of High Commission, which was the ecclesiastical equivalent of the Star Chamber, imposed what was known as the oath *ex officio*. Like the oath of the Inquisition, it required that even in the absence of any specific charge, one must give a full accounting for one's beliefs. Taking the oath put the religious nonconformist—who, at that time, could be either a Catholic or a Puritan—in a complete double bind. If you confessed to the charge of heretical belief, you were condemned. If you refused to confess, you were also condemned, because you were in violation of the oath. It is in the context of such inquisitorial proceedings concerning matters of deeply held religious beliefs and personal conscience that the accused, with greater and greater frequency under Elizabeth and then under the Stuarts, began to put forward the defense summed up in the Latin phrase *nemo tenetur seipsum prodere* ("no one is required to bear witness against himself"), which eventually became part of the Fifth Amendment to the Constitution: "No person . . . shall be compelled in any criminal case to be a witness against himself."[13] The *nemo tenetur* defense appears to be of ancient derivation, part of the medieval *ius commune*. It embodies a claim that there is a reserved domain, concerning matters of personal conscience and belief, on which persons cannot be required to speak in proceedings that could lead to their condemnation for this belief. Gradually, this right came to be established in English law, in some part thanks to the effort of lawyers associated with the Puritan cause to found the right in Magna Carta, that is, to see it as entailed by the basic rights of free subjects, in a government where even monarch and church are constrained by the law. By 1609, Lord High Justice Sir Edward Coke could write:

> the Ecclesiastical Judge cannot examine any man upon his oath, upon the intention and thought of his heart, for *cogitationis poenam nemo emeret* [no man may be punished for his thought]. And in cases where a man is to be examined upon his oath, he ought to be examined upon acts or words, and not of the intention or thought of his heart; and if any man should be examined upon any point of religion, he is not bound to answer the same; for in time of danger, *quis modus tutus erit* [how will he be safe] if everyone should be examined of his thoughts . . . for it hath been said in the proverb, *thought is free*."[14]

This privilege, relating originally to ecclesiastical courts and to questions of religious belief, came to be recognized as a fundamental right of the accused in any accusatorial criminal proceeding.

It can be argued—as indeed both Justice Harlan and Justice White argue in their dissents in *Miranda*—that the privilege against self-incrimination and the rule against coerced confessions have separate origins and separate histories. Coerced confessions were originally barred because they were perceived to be unfairly obtained, thus unreliable, untrustworthy—possibly false confessions. The privilege against self-incrimination, as I noted, arose essentially to protect beliefs and matters of conscience. Yet since the compulsion to self-incrimination could also produce confessions that were untrustworthy, and coerced confessions violated a suspect's right to refuse to answer under oath, there has come to be an indissoluble connection between the exclusion of coerced confession and the privilege against self-incrimination.[15] If the "trustworthiness" of a confession seems the more pragmatic and perhaps useful test, "voluntariness" may be the more probative one, since it relates not only to the "content" of the confession—its truth, which in some cases can be verified from other sources—but also to its "context," that is, how it was produced. This test insists that the involuntary can never be accepted as trustworthy: to coerce a mental state or psychological disposition (the choice to confess) is somehow paradoxical, a forced voluntariness.[16] Above all, to compel confession may be an ethical violation, somehow an invasion of human dignity. The proposed procedural safeguards of *Miranda* touch on the relation of individual rights to the state's power.

In *Miranda,* Chief Justice Warren briefly evokes the history of the Fifth Amendment privilege as part of the search for "the proper scope of governmental power over the citizen," to conclude that "our accusatory system of criminal justice demands that the government seeking to punish an individual produce the evidence against him by its own independent labors, rather than by the cruel, simple expedient of compelling it from his own mouth" (460). Compulsion, inquisition, and torture lie in the background of the Court's suspicion directed to confession. As Abe Fortas, soon to be a Justice of the Supreme Court, eloquently summed it up: "*Mea culpa* belongs to a man and his God. It is a plea that cannot be exacted from free men by human authority. To require it is to insist that the state is the superior of the individuals who compose it, instead of their instrument."[17] The *Miranda* warnings, then, are to set the conditions in which the voluntary confessional narrative can unfold—or fail to unfold. The point, as Warren puts it, is that "a knowing and intelligent waiver of these rights [cannot] be assumed on a silent record" (498–99). A "silent record" is another "gap" attributable to the "closed room." Henceforth, the record must speak, precisely of the accused's knowledge of the right not to say anything that might be self-incriminating.

Confessional Speech

The Court's debates about the contexts in which confession is allowable, in *Miranda* and other cases—and the continuing debate in legal scholarship about the scope and even the *raison d'être* of the privilege against self-incrimination—may point, beyond issues of specific legal doctrine, to a more general problem in our thinking about confession. Consider that the law as we know it has elaborated as a most basic right of the accused the protection against involuntary confession, while on the other hand, from early in the Romantic era onward, Western literature has made the confessional mode a crucial kind of self-expression that is supposed to bear a special stamp of sincerity and authenticity and to bear special witness to the truth of the individual personality. From Jean-Jacques Rousseau to Michel Leiris, from William Wordsworth to Philip Roth, the baring of one's innermost thoughts and desires has been held to be a business as necessary as it is risky. If psychoanalysis is perhaps the most characteristic development of modern thought in the "human sciences," it, too, appears to be predicated on the confessional act, in a secular reinterpretation of auricular confession. After imposing the requirement of annual confession in 1215, the Roman Catholic Church, responding to the Protestant critique of confessional practices, affirmed at the Council of Trent (1551) that confession is of divine origin and necessary for one's spiritual salvation. And modern cultures have, in their literature and their therapies, adopted some version of this view. In a secularized world, the insistence has come to be placed on truth to oneself. And getting at this truth almost necessarily involves a confessional gesture, a claim to lay bare that which is most intimate in order to know oneself, or to make oneself known.

Jean-Jacques Rousseau is of course the symbolic fountainhead here. On the opening page of his *Confessions* he announces that he will present himself before his creator on the Judgment Day with this book in his hand. He captures in this manner the transition between religious confession and the secular writing of one's intimate self into a book. "I have unveiled my inner being as you have seen it yourself," he announces to his "sovereign judge."[18] But readers of Rousseau have long been aware that the act of confessing does not offer so straightforward or unproblematic an access to the inner being as one might assume. The problem may not be one of error, in any simple sense: study of any autobiographical and confessional text can usually detect some errors of fact, but that does not necessarily invalidate the confession of the "inner being," which has no referential verifiability other than the speech act that makes it known to us. But if that is the case, what is it that is being confessed to? In what sense is the confession true, if its apparent referent is false? What other kind of truth, what other place of truth, is involved? Herein lies the problem: what is the relation of the act of confessing to the reliability of what is confessed? If Rousseau, and other writers in the modern confessional tradition, are clearly making "voluntary" confessions—in that no other person is coercing them to confess—can we therefore trust the fruits of confession? Indeed, what must we conclude about the very notion of "voluntariness" in confession when we look at the circumstances of the confessional speech act?

A good instance for making an approach to these questions is also a famous one: the episode of the "stolen ribbon" that closes book 2 of the *Confessions*. Briefly: following the death of Madame de Vercellis, in whose household the young Rousseau has been a servant, a ribbon is found to be missing. It is discovered among Rousseau's things. Summoned publicly by the Comte de la Roque (acting as executor), Rousseau is asked where he got it. He accuses the young kitchen maid Marion of having given it to him. When she denies this calumny, Rousseau persists in his accusation, and the Comte de la Roque, uncertain as to where the truth lies, dismisses them both, with the comment that the conscience of the guilty one will avenge the innocent. This, says Rousseau, has happened every day since the incident. He goes on to imagine the future fate of Marion, dismissed under suspicion of theft, no doubt unable to find another place, condemned to a probable future of prostitution. Rousseau, on the other hand, has continued to suffer nighttime hallucinations in which he stands accused of the crime as if it happened only yesterday. He has never been able to confess the crime, even to his most intimate friends. The weight of the crime on his conscience has been such that it has been a key motive in his decision to write his confessions.

Thus far, we seem to be close to Justice White's view that confession is good for one, that "it may provide psychological relief and enhance the prospects for rehabilitation." But we may have some doubts about this result as we read on. For now Rousseau moves from the narrative of what happened to the story of what he calls his *"dispositions intérieures,"* his inner feelings (86). And here he tells an entirely different story, one that stands in total contradiction to the external events. He tells us that in fact malice was never farther from his thoughts than in this "cruel moment." When he accused Marion, it is bizarre but true that his "friendship" for her was the cause. "She was present in my thoughts, I excused myself on the first object that came to hand." This seemingly random accusation is then further specified: "I accused her of having done what I wanted to do and of having given me the ribbon since my intention was to give it to her." Thus we have a problem in desire which, thwarted in its intent, gives way to its apparent opposite, the wish to punish. If only his accusers had given him time to repent, and the opportunity to confess privately, he would have told the truth. But public exposure, the risk of being publicly declared a thief and liar, is too strong for him to perform on the spot the confession he wants to make—and now makes so many years later. Over those years, Rousseau now says, he has been so persecuted that Marion has been well revenged. And he concludes with the request that he be allowed never to speak of this incident again—a conclusion violated when he returns to the stolen ribbon in the fourth of his *Rêveries du promeneur solitaire.*

Rousseau's telling of the story of the stolen ribbon is a stunning and troubling performance. Not only does it represent the emblematic confession, where the failure to confess on the spot becomes the motive for the very act of confessing as an accounting for one's life, it also suggests that confession as a speech act accomplishes something other than the simple revelation of a truth. Confession here permits the staging of a scene of exposure, guilt, and retribution that appears to be itself the very motive of confession. Paul de Man, in a classic essay on this episode, effectively underlines the issue: "What Rousseau *really* wanted is neither the ribbon nor Marion, but the public scene of exposure which he actually gets. . . . The more there is to expose, the more there is to be ashamed of; the more resistance to exposure, the more satisfying the scene, and especially, the more satisfying and eloquent the belated revelation, in the later narrative, of the inability to reveal."[19] In other words, this primal scene of exposure, shame, guilt, is absolutely necessary to the project of making a confession, and if the scene never occurred, one would have to invent something like it in order to motivate and perform the writing of the *Confessions*.

Qui s'accuse s'excuse, says the French proverb: self-accusation is a form of self-excuse. As de Man suggests, the speech act of confession is double. In the terms of J. L. Austin's famous distinction, there is a constative aspect (the sin or guilt to which one confesses) and a performative aspect, precisely the elusive and troubling *action* performed by the statement "I confess."[20] When one says "Bless me Father, for I have sinned," the constative meaning is: I have committed sins, while the performative meaning is: absolve me of my sin. The confessional performance of guilt always has this double aspect, and since it does, it opens the possibility that the performative aspect will produce the constative, create the sin or guilt that the act of confessing requires. That is, the verbal act that begins "I confess" entails guilt, which is already there in the act of confessing, so that the referent—this particular guilt—may merely be a by-product of the verbal act. The law furnishes a number of examples of signed confessions that have later been repudiated and sometimes discovered to have been false—as in Manchester, Vermont, in 1819—and there are no doubt many other instances where the truth never came to light.

How can someone make a false confession? Precisely because the false referentiality of confession may be secondary to the need to confess: a need produced by the coercion of interrogation or by the subtler coercion of the need to stage a scene of exposure as the only propitiation of accusation, including self-accusation for being in a scene of exposure. Or, as Talmudic law has recognized for millennia, confession may be the product of the death-drive, the production of incriminating acts to assure punishment or even self-annihilation, and hence inherently suspect because in contradiction to the basic human instinct of self-preservation. Or, as Freud would have it, unconscious guilt may produce crime in order to assure punishment as the only satisfaction of the guilt.[21] Guilt can in any event always be produced to meet the demand for confession, since there is always more than enough guilt to go around, and its concealment can itself be a powerful motive for confession. One might want to say that confession, even if compelled, is always in some sense "true" as a performative, indeed as a performance, but this does not guarantee that it is not false as a constative, as a relevant "fact."

Furthermore, the French proverb I cited can also be turned around: *Qui s'excuse s'accuse:* self-excuse serves to incriminate one. "Excuses generate the very guilt they exonerate," writes de Man (299). And again: "there can never be enough guilt around to match the text-machine's infinite power to excuse." From which de Man concludes—using, I believe, the term "cognitive" where I would use Austin's "constative": "Since guilt, in this description, is a cognitive and excuse a performative function of language, we are restating the disjunction of the performative from the cognitive: any speech act produces an excess of cognition, but it can never hope to know the process of its own production (the only thing worth knowing)" (299–300). That is, the performative aspect of the speech act is not itself the object of cognition.

To restate this in simpler terms: the confessional rehearsal or repetition of guilt is its own kind of performance, producing at the same time the excuse or justification of guilt (by the fact of confessing it) and the accumulation of more guilt (by the act of confessing it), in a dynamic that is potentially infinite. The more you confess, the more guilt is produced. The more the guilt produced, the more the confessional machine functions. The very act of confessing necessarily produces guilt in order to be functional. As a speech act, "I confess" implies and necessitates guilt, and if the guilt is not there in the referent, as an object of cognition, it is in the speech-act itself, which simultaneously exonerates and inculpates. A version of one typical way in which this doubleness of confession operates in criminal law is recorded in *Miranda*'s predecessor case, *Escobedo v. Illinois:* when suspect Danny Escobedo is told that his associate Benedict DiGerlando has pinned the shooting on him, then is taken to the room where DiGerlando is undergoing interrogation. He tells DiGerlando he's lying, exclaiming: "I didn't shoot Manuel, you did it."[22] Here Escobedo's attempt to exculpate himself involves an admission of direct knowledge of the shooting that inculpates him as at least an accomplice to the crime. By David Simon's detailed account of police interrogations in Baltimore, such self-incrimination through attempted self-exculpation would seem to be very common.[23] Rousseau's confession of the stolen ribbon is of course more complex, and more akin to the sins of conscience aimed at by inquisitorial proceedings, yet he, too, may inculpate himself while ostensibly seeking exculpation.

Rousseau's example is different also, it may be claimed, since he *wants* to confess. Yet his voluntary confession comes under the compulsion of writing his *Confessions,* in a generic constraint to reveal all his guilty secrets: indeed, he could not confess without this kind of matter, which the act of confession would have to invent (and may in fact invent) if it did not already exist. Conversely, can we be sure that suspects in criminal cases themselves don't want to confess, especially when they have been told, over hours, days and nights of intensive interrogation that it is only by confessing that they can be released from the obligation to confess—that their guilt is certain and its corroboration alone will release them from the extreme duress in which they find themselves? And told that their refusal to confess is itself an admission of guilt?[24] Confession alone will bring release from the situation of accusation and allow reintegration with normal social existence and community. We come back to some of the deep-seated suspicions of confession that Justice White detected, I think correctly, in the majority opinion in *Miranda.* There is something inherently unstable and unreliable about the speech-act of confession, about its meaning and its motives. You may, as in Rousseau's case, be confessing simultaneously to avoid punishment (to obtain absolution) and to assure punishment (to produce the scene of shame and guilt). Even without the oath *de veritate dicenda,* you may be in a situation of damning yourself if you do confess or if you don't confess. Or you may be confessing to the wrong crime, that is, producing what you think your interrogators want in order to avoid confessing to something for which you feel more guilty. Or, more generally, you may be confessing to *something else,* something other than what you think is the referent of your confession.

This brings us back to the question of "voluntariness." In what sense can we say that a confession is voluntary? In the case of *Brewer v. Williams*—of which more in a moment—Justice White, dissenting, writes: "Men usually intend to do what they do, and there is nothing in the record to support the proposition that respondent's decision to talk was anything but an exercise of his own free will."[25] In another dissent in the same case, Chief Justice Warren Burger states: "The human urge to confess wrongdoing is, of course, normal in all save hardened, professional criminals, as psychiatrists and analysts have demonstrated" (420).[26] While both White and Burger disagree with the Court's conclusion that suspect Williams did not confess voluntarily, they offer somewhat different views of confession. For White, statements are utterances from which one can generally infer the intention to make them. Intention and utterance line up in an unambiguous manner. For Burger, the intention of the confessional statement is slightly displaced; it lies elsewhere, in the "urge to confess"—which may, as Rousseau's case so well demonstrates, be aberrant, the product of a need for exposure and punishment, and which thus may not fully coincide with White's kind of intentionality, a point which the two Justices do not confront.

Let me try to press harder on this question of the kind of voluntariness at issue in confession. First, a citation from John Wigmore's classic treatise on evidence, concerning the decision whether or not to confess:

> The situation is always one of choice between two alternatives— either one disagreeable, to be sure, but still subject to a choice. . . . All conscious verbal utterances are and must be voluntary; and that which may impel us to distrust one is not the circumstance that it is involuntary, but the circumstance that the choice of false confession is a natural one under the conditions.[27]

This appears to confirm White's hard-headed doctrine that everything one says—if conscious, not under the influence of drugs, or whatever—is necessarily voluntary, though it does leave open the important and troubling escape-hatch that circumstances may make the confessional utterance false rather than true. Now, a citation from Justice Jackson, dissenting in *Ashcraft v. Tennessee* (already mentioned in Justice Harlan's dissent in *Miranda*):

> It probably is the normal instinct to deny and conceal any shameful or guilty act. Even a "voluntary confession" is not likely to be the product of the same motives with which one may volunteer information that does not incriminate or concern him. The term "voluntary" confession does not mean voluntary in the sense of a confession to a priest merely to rid one's soul of a sense of guilt. "Voluntary confessions" in criminal law are the product of calculations of a different order, and usually proceed from a belief that further denial is useless and perhaps prejudi-

cial. To speak of any confessions of crime made after arrest as being "voluntary" or "uncoerced" is somewhat inaccurate, although traditional.

A confession is wholly and uncontestably voluntary only if a guilty person gives himself up to the law and becomes his own accuser. The Court bases its decision on the premise that custody and examination of a prisoner for thirty-six hours is "inherently coercive." Of course it is. And so is custody and detention for one hour. Arrest itself is inherently coercive, and so is detention. (160)

Jackson's dissent from the finding that Ashcraft's confession was coerced unfolds as a narrative of how Ashcraft dug a hole for himself during his interrogation, attempting to implicate an accomplice in a way that eventually pointed to his own guilt, and obliged him to confess: again, inculpation by way of attempted exculpation. Jackson's seems to me one of the most honest and accurate statements on confession from the Supreme Court, even though he uses it, in my view, to support the wrong conclusions. He effectively evacuates the issue of "voluntariness" in our usual acceptation of the term. He makes us understand that if we can say, with Wigmore and White, that all confessional statements are somehow intentional, in another sense they are all unintentional—or rather, correspond to some intention other than that we usually associate with intentional statements. To be put in a situation where one is made dependent on one's interrogators and asked to confess—pressured to confess—would always seem to create the possibility that the motive of the confessional statement will be different from that of normal intentional statements. Its intentions will be aberrant which, at worst, may make it a false confession, or at least, a confession whose truth is not in its referent, is not constative but performative.

"Christian Burial" and Other Mousetraps

In *Brewer v. Williams,* the suspect's confession and what produces it are particularly interesting. Robert Williams, the suspect—a recent escapee from a mental hospital—has surrendered to the police in Davenport, Iowa, on the advice of the Des Moines lawyer whom he has telephoned, and has been charged with abducting a nine-year-old-girl in Des Moines. The girl is presumed dead, but the body has not been found. The Des Moines police set out to get Williams and bring him back to Des Moines, but not before agreeing with the Des Moines lawyer, in an arrangement confirmed by a Davenport lawyer, that Williams will not be interrogated during the ride in the police car—a ride from which the Davenport lawyer is excluded. During the drive, Detective Leaming does refrain from an "interrogation" of Williams, in the traditional sense. Instead, he makes him what has come to be known as the "Christian Burial Speech." Addressing Williams, whom he knows to be a deeply religious person, as "Reverend," he proceeds to evoke the weather conditions, the forecast of several inches of snow, the likelihood that the young girl's body will be buried and unlocatable. Since Williams must know where the body is, he could take the police officers to it—and then her parents could give her a decent Christian burial. "I want to give you something to think about while we're traveling down the road," Leaming says. And then:

> They are predicting several inches of snow for tonight, and I feel that you yourself are the only person that knows where this little girl's body is, that you yourself have only been there once, and if you get a snow on top of it you yourself may be unable to find it. And, since we will be going right past the area on the way into Des Moines, I feel that we could stop and locate the body, that the parents of this little girl should be entitled to a Christian burial for the little girl who was snatched away from them on Christmas [E]ve and murdered. . . . I do not want you to answer me. I don't want to discuss it any further. Just think about it as we're riding down the road. (430 U.S. 387, 392–93)

Williams eventually directs the police to a service station, where he claims to have left the girl's shoes, then to a rest area where he claims to have left a blanket in which the body was wrapped, and finally leads them to the body itself.

No one sitting on this case doubts for a moment that Williams is guilty of a horrible crime. His confession is certainly reliable, validated by a corpse. The issue is whether that confession has been obtained in violation of his rights. Warned of his right to remain silent and of his right to counsel—and his two lawyers have additionally obtained a promise from the police that he will not be interrogated in absence of counsel, during the drive—does Williams's confession in-dicate a knowing waiver of his rights, making his confession volun-tary, or an infringement of his rights, invalidating the confession? The Court, in another 5–4 split decision, reaches the conclusion that Williams's confession is invalid. It bases that decision not on *Miranda,* but on the earlier case, *Massiah v. United States,* which established that the right to counsel guaranteed by the Sixth Amendment applied during postcharge pretrial interrogation. The use of *Massiah* rather than *Miranda* as precedent may represent a choice to take the simplest applicable rule and perhaps also to avoid the controversies that con-tinue to swirl around the *Miranda* decision.[28]

Deciding whether Williams's confession was illegally obtained during interrogation in absence of counsel turns in part on judging whether or not the "Christian Burial Speech" was interrogation. To Chief Justice Burger, dissenting, the test of an interrogative seems to involve the commonsensical idea that it must be followed by a question mark. "I find it most remarkable," he writes, "that a mur-der case should turn on judicial interpretation that a statement be-comes a question simply because it is followed by an incriminating disclosure from the suspect" (419–20). Does a statement that elicits a response constitute a question? Burger characterizes Detective Leaming's speech as, not interrogation, but "'statements' intended to prick the conscience of the accused." The majority, on the other hand, claims that the Christian Burial Speech is "tantamount to in-terrogation" (400). "There can be no serious doubt," Justice Potter Stewart writes for the Court, "that Detective Leaming deliberately and designedly set out to elicit information from Williams just as surely as—and perhaps more effectively than—if he had formally interrogated him" (399). The "Christian Burial Speech" is in effect like the confession statement prepared by police interrogators for the suspect to sign: his confession written by another, to which, in this case, he responds, not with a signature, but with the revelation of a dead body. Justice Thurgood Marshall, in his concurring opinion, characterizes Leaming's speech as a "charade," adding, with a cita-tion from *Blackburn v. Alabama:* "The detective demonstrated once again 'that the efficiency of the rack and the thumbscrew can be matched, given the proper subject, by more sophisticated modes of "persuasion."'" For Marshall, there is torture in the air, whereas for the dissenters, as Justice Harry Blackmun puts it, "Persons in custody frequently volunteer statements in response to stimuli other than interrogation" (440).

Blackmun's dissent contains a sentence that strikes one as slightly curious in a Supreme Court opinion, and somehow characteristic of this strange case. He writes: "I am not persuaded that Leaming's observations and comments, made as the police car traversed the snowy and slippery miles between Davenport and Des Moines that winter afternoon, were an interrogation, direct or subtle, of Williams" (439). That evocation of the police car negotiating the icy highway, with Leaming and Williams engaged in their weird and fateful dialogue, seems almost to suggest a classic situation of storytelling on a winter's afternoon.[29] There is a kind of dreamy atmosphere to it, as if we could never quite recapture the motives of telling and listening, and the way that telling a story—as in the Christian Burial Speech—can elicit the profoundest, and most incriminating, responses from a listener. If Leaming's story is like Hamlet's "mousetrap," the play-within-the-play—"the play's the thing / Wherein I'll catch the conscience of the king"—who's to say whether such play (Marshall's "charade") is innocent or not, since it simply reveals a preexisting guilt? Since, indeed, it leads to a dead body. And yet, is "pricking conscience" an innocent act? Or a violative one?

Brewer seems to me such an interesting and troubling case precisely because the motive of the confessional act, in that closed police car traversing the snowy and slippery miles, remains so obscure. Why does Williams confess? Should we inquire so closely into the why? In the absence of the rack and the thumbscrew, should we be suspicious of the "charade," of the well-told story that pricks or traps its listener into self-implication, into signing-on to a confession prepared by another? Isn't this what many good stories attempt to do? Doesn't confessional literature of the type associated with Rousseau, with Dostoevsky, with Gide, precisely want to elicit a counter-confession in which the reader admits to complicity? And yet, in that case, whose story is it? Who is the author of the confession, Leaming or Williams? Hasn't the person who should be the listener to the story, Leaming, become its teller, and he who should be its teller, Williams, its listener? And what authority does the story then have? How can we authenticate a confession as "voluntary" when we know so little about its motives and intentions? And how can the law, which cannot remain within the ambiguities of literature, handle such elusive kinds of speech?

The Court has held, in a series of other cases, that it finds no problem with compelled *evidence:* a defendant may be compelled to surrender tax documents and bank records, to produce a handwriting sample, a voice sample, even to submit to a blood test.[30] In the case of the compelled blood test, *Schmerber v. California,* Justice William Brennan, writing for the Court, argues that the privilege against self-incrimination "protects an accused only from being compelled to testify against himself, or otherwise provide the State with evidence of a testimonial or communicative nature, and that the withdrawal of blood and use of the analysis in question in this case did not involve compulsion to these ends."[31] Brennan here cites Justice Oliver Wendell Holmes: "[T]he prohibition of compelling a man in a criminal court to be witness against himself is a prohibition of the use of physical or moral compulsion to extort communications from him, not an exclusion of his body as evidence when it may be material."[32] In dissent, Justice Hugo Black ripostes that the Court's finding that "compelling a person to give his blood to help the State convict him is not equivalent to compelling him to be a witness against himself strikes me as quite an extraordinary feat" (773). Blood, says Black, is indeed "testimonial." He continues: "It is a strange hierarchy of values that allows the State to extract a human being's blood to convict him of a crime because of the blood's content but proscribes compelled production of his lifeless papers" (775).[33]

One may be sympathetic to this view, and also to Justice William O. Douglas's dissent on privacy grounds (citing *Griswold v. Connecticut*) and Justice Fortas's protest that "As prosecutor, the State has no right to commit any kind of violence upon the person" (779).[34] And yet, Brennan—who normally of course staked out positions protective of the rights of the accused—may in his opinion lay bare a central distinguishing feature of Fifth Amendment history and jurisprudence. It is what a defendant may do with his lips—what may issue from his mouth—that is considered worthy of special protection. The body of the suspect or defendant is not protected by the Fifth Amendment. Confession is a verbal act, motivated by the "will" (a term that will need further study), a discourse proffered to a listener. In another case, the Court cites words written by Justice Burger when he was on the D.C. Circuit Court: "The proffer of a living witness is not to be mechanically equated with the proffer of inanimate evidentiary objects illegally seized. . . . The living witness is an individual personality whose attributes of will, perception, memory and volition interact to determine what testimony he will give."[35] It is as if the Court implicitly understood—without ever articulating it as such—that the problem of confession, its voluntariness or its compulsion, is one that concerns a speech act.

What I detect in cases such as *Miranda* and *Brewer* and in the long, complex history of the right against self-incrimination is the law's semi-conscious struggle to come to terms with the difficult, layered, perplexing notion of the speech-act that follows from the statement "I confess." Chief Justice Warren displays a certain awareness of this special aspect of confessions when, in *Miranda*, he notes of the Court's newly prescribed warnings: "a warning is a clearcut fact" (469). If a warning is a "fact," it is so in the mode of a speech act: "I warn you that . . ." constitutes a performative, whatever the content of the warning. It is as if this performative were striving to do justice to the performative conditions of confession. Possibly some of the contentiousness and uncertainty of the debate about the Fifth Amendment protection could be illuminated, if not resolved, by fuller recognition that confession involves a special, and especially complex, form of speech act.

Speech acts, Austin tells us, can "misfire" if the "felicity conditions" are not right. For instance, if you consent to marriage before a priest who is really not a priest at all but your seducer's best friend in priest's clothing (something played out in a number of Gothic novels), your "I do" has no standing. Yale Kamisar produces a hypothetical scenario for the law: the suspect asks for a priest, in order to make confession, and is sent a police officer disguised as a priest. What then is the status of his confession?[36] The outrageous example is not unrelated to *Brewer*, where Leaming addresses Williams as "Reverend," though there is no one present who merits that title. What are the "felicity conditions" in which the voluntary confession can be made and recognized as voluntary? What are the contexts in which Warren's "storytelling without fear" can go forward? Where confession is concerned, do these questions even make sense, or is the speech act so layered with contradictory intentions that one can never use the term "voluntary" in confidence, and thus never be wholly sure that confession and its intention line up in any unambiguous way?

The Court has continued to assert that the acceptable confession must be, in Justice Sandra Day O'Connor's phrase, "the product of a free and rational will,"—though it may have hedged this proposition when it accepted as voluntary the confession of a delusional schizophrenic.[37] Yet as Justice Frankfurter recognized in *Culombe,* "The notion of 'voluntariness' is itself an amphibian. It purports at once to describe an internal psychic state and to characterize that state for legal purposes" (605). Frankfurter's opinion—which will bear further discussion in a later chapter—offers a cautionary tale about why a traditional philosophical analysis of the problem of voluntariness, couched in terms of free will and responsibility, can never really reach the situation of confession, and why *Miranda,* in its turn, encounters difficulties "by transforming an intractable metaphysical doctrine into a bureaucratically administrable test," as Louis Michael Seidman puts it.[38] Rules governing the conditions of confession may never be wholly adequate to the problem: they address only the context, not the nature of confession. And they tend to create an infinite regress in our thinking about the problem: what, for instance, will be your rules for a recognizing a "knowing waiver" of the right not to confess?

"By the 1990's, a generation of police officers had come of age with *Miranda,* which they had grown to see as a manageable annoyance," according to a *New York Times* report on the legacy of the *Miranda* decision.[39] Some detectives are such good interrogators they report an 80 to 90 percent success rate in producing suspects' confessions. The courts, including the Supreme Court, have been lenient in interpreting the rules imposed on interrogators, so that many forms of trickery are permitted—including lies about evidence inculpating the suspect, fake confessions by confederates—and statements made before the suspect is "Mirandized" are often allowed on the grounds that the suspect was not yet subject to custodial interrogation or, if not allowed in the prosecution's "case in chief," nonetheless judged permissible for rebuttal, to allow impeachment of testimony, and even statements clearly taken in violation of *Miranda* rules may lead to "fruits" that are admissible into evidence.[40] Suspects continue to talk, to give confessions (including some later discovered to be wholly false) because the pressure to talk is too great to resist. As the *Times* reporter puts it, perhaps the best weapon in the hands of the police is "a belief embedded in the psyche: silence equals guilt." To the extent this is true, to the extent that the interrogator's questions more often than not elicit an answer rather than silence, an interlocutionary relation is established, which then leads to continued talk. And if the protocol of that talk is that only a confession will be acceptable to your interlocutors, a confession very often results.

As Abe Fortas seemed to suggest, in that eloquent line in which one hears an echo of Maimonides, confession may ultimately concern a truth of angels, not of men. Or at least, a truth whose use in the human arena is so fraught with complexities that it had better be set aside. A certain strain in modern literature, descending in direct line from Rousseau, has understood very well the disturbing power of the confession, whether autobiographical or fictional. Think of the self-abasing and self-aggrandizing confessional speeches of Dostoevsky's Karamazov, or Raskolnikov, or his Underground Man, the original instance of what Mikhail Bakhtin has called "the dialogic" because these monologues implicate the words and anticipated reactions of their listeners, so that listener, or reader, cannot escape scot-free from having listened to them. Think of a more recent instance, Albert Camus' *The Fall,* whose narrator tells his sordid tale to an unidentified listener in an Amsterdam bar precisely to pass on to that listener a taint of guilt, an implication in a story in which none of us can fully proclaim his or her innocence. These instances and a number of others—including the psychoanalytic model of confession and its pop versions, and the encounter of psychotherapeutic thinking with the law—will need exploration in the pages to come, where I shall probe further how it is that confession appears to be a mode of discourse capable of producing both the deepest truth and the most damaging untruth.

To reach a provisional conclusion on the dilemmas suggested by *Miranda,* one may wonder whether the Supreme Court's difficulties in dealing with the concept and the act of confession don't have something to do with a semi-conscious awareness of the problematic, double, perhaps even duplicitous nature of confession as a speech act. It may be that the only true confessions are involuntary, somehow coerced, if only by the fact that their truth is not there where it appears to be. So it is that confession may be inherently unreliable for purposes of the law and for the policing of society. The story of what goes on in that closed room, where interrogations lead to confessions, always leaves us uneasy, like so many modern narratives proffered by "unreliable narrators," narratives indeed that give us no basis for judging what "reliability" might mean. And in the case of confession, that unreliability can be contagious, since it suggests that the more the guilt confessed, the more guilt there will be to confess, since the act of confession produces further culpability. Justice Harlan may unintentionally make the point when he says in *Miranda* (once again citing Justice Jackson): "This Court is forever adding new stories to the temples of constitutional law, and the temples have a way of collapsing when one story too many is added" (526). The pun on "stories" as architecture and as narrative is no doubt involuntary, but it suggests a perception of the uncontrollable proliferation of narratives produced by confession.

Miranda, for all its ambiguities and unresolved problems, has nonetheless endured, and indeed gained firmer footing in legal doctrine. It survived a major challenge from its conservative detractors in *Dickerson v. United States,* in 2000.[41] In that case, the U.S. Court of Appeals for the Fourth Circuit—a notoriously conservative body—ruled that Charles T. Dickerson, charged with bank robbery, made a confession which, though "unwarned," was nonetheless "voluntary" according to the provisions of the 1968 Omnibus Crime Control Act, 18 U.S.C. § 3501. This section of the Omnibus Crime Control Act was expressly intended by Congress to overrule *Miranda,* to make specific warnings unnecessary, and to return determination of the "voluntariness" of a confession to the old "totality of the circumstances" analysis. Section 3501 had long remained a dead letter, since seven successive Justice Departments had judged it to be unconstitutional in the light of *Miranda.* But the Fourth Circuit—accepting the *amicus* brief of the conservative Washington Legal Foundation—decided that the *Miranda* warnings were not themselves constitutionally protected rights but merely a judicially created rule designed to protect the suspect's Fifth Amendment rights. If the warnings were merely a judicial rule, then Congress could overrule them legislatively. If, however, they were of "constitutional dimension," such legislation would be unconstitutional.

And so the Supreme Court ruled in *Dickerson v. United States,* in a 7–2 decision. The majority opinion was written by Chief Justice Rehnquist, in a striking demonstration that *Miranda* has become settled doctrine even for the Court's conservative wing—though the radical right wing, Justices Scalia and Thomas, dissented. Rehnquist concedes that the language of some post-*Miranda* Supreme Court opinions gave the impression that *Miranda* warnings were "prophylactic standards" and "not themselves rights protected by the Constitution" (see *Michigan v. Tucker,* 417 U.S. 433, 446, 443), but he reaches the conclusion that "*Miranda* announced a constitutional rule that Congress may not supersede legislatively" (at 2336). Whether or not the Court would create the rule in the precise form of the *Miranda* warnings were it addressing the issue in the first instance, Rehnquist argues, "the principles of *stare decisis* weigh heavily against overruling it now." In what may be the most interesting sentence of his opinion, Rehnquist claims that a kind of social and cultural *stare decisis* also mandates the affirmation of the *Miranda* warnings: "*Miranda* has become embedded in routine police practice to the point where the warnings have become part of our national culture" (at 2336).

Indeed they have. And as such, they have become a powerful symbol of individual liberties in relation to the power of the State. The mantra of the *Miranda* warnings have become the stuff of popular entertainment and the national cultural imagination because they seem in some primordial form to incarnate a sense of the citizen's rights, and the presumption of innocence until proven guilty. The symbol over time has come to appear a substantive right. The decision in *Dickerson* recognizes that such a symbol of rights, once granted, cannot be easily withdrawn. Nonetheless, *Dickerson* does nothing to resolve the ambiguities and limitations of *Miranda,* which following chapters will explore. The mantra recited when a suspect is arrested still does not reach the conditions under which, in the "interview room," most confessions are produced.

CONFESSOR AND CONFESSANT

da lui saprai di sè e de' suoi torti
[from him will you learn of himself and his sins]
                                        Dante, *Inferno* 19:36

*Because of the nature of consciousness, Dostoevsky
indicates, the self cannot tell the truth of itself to itself and
come to rest without the possibility of self-deception.*
            J. M. Coetzee, "Confession and Double Thoughts"

Interrogation and Confession

Directors of conscience in the religious tradition and police interrogators appear to share an understanding that the bond of confessant and
confessor often is crucial to the production of confession. It is an
affective bond, comparable to that of analysand and analyst in the
psychoanalytic transference. It contains, and activates, elements of dependency, subjugation, fear, the desire for propitiation, the wish to
appease and to please. It leads to the articulation of secrets, perhaps to
the creation of hitherto unrealized truth—or perhaps the simu-
lacrum of truth.

One of the most remarkable and horrible instances of how this
bond can work I find in the letter that Vsevolod Meyerhold, the great
Russian theatre director, sent to Vyatcheslav Molotov in protest at his
imprisonment and interrogation at the hands of the NKVD in 1939:

> Immediately after my arrest . . . I was cast into the deepest de-
> pression by the obsessive thought "This is what I deserve!" The
> government thought, so I began to convince myself, that the
> sentence I had received . . . was not sufficient for my sins . . . and

that I must undergo yet another punishment, that which the NKVD was carrying out now. "This is what I deserve!" I repeated to myself and I split into two individuals. The first started searching for the "crimes" of the second, and when they could not be found, he began to invent them. The interrogator proved an effective and experienced assistant and, working closely together, we began our composition.[1]

Another interrogation session, lasting fourteen hours:

When my fantasy started running out, the interrogators took over . . . they prepared and revised the depositions (some were rewritten three or four times).

Finally:

I could not think at all clearly because a Damoclean sword dangled over me: constantly the interrogator repeated, threateningly, "If you won't write (invent, in other words?!) then we shall beat you again, leaving your head and your right arm untouched but reducing the rest to a hacked, bleeding and shapeless body."

He signed everything. The result of his inventive collaboration with his interrogators was of course predestined: Meyerhold was executed in February 1940.

In setting this horrifying testimony against police interrogations of criminal suspects and examples of everyday and literary confessions, it is important to clear the decks of physical torture of the sort undergone by Meyerhold. Though "third degree" tactics were once countenanced in many an American police station, they no longer are, and have probably become infrequent (though the threat of violence often is very much present). With the landmark case of *Brown v. Mississippi* in 1936—where the "suspects" were hung from the limbs of a tree and whipped, and put over the backs of chairs and beaten with belts until they confessed to a crime that they clearly had not committed—the Supreme Court moved to setting constitutional limits to the means used in various states to extract confessions: "The State is free to regulate the procedure of its courts in accordance with its own conceptions of policy, unless in so doing it 'offends some principle of justice so deeply rooted in the traditions and conscience of our people as to be ranked as fundamental.'"[2] Any system of interrogation that forswears the use of physical torture is undoubtedly to be preferred to the likes of the NKVD, and one must keep in mind the measure of decency reflected in progress beyond physical coercion. Nonetheless, the kind of bond between confessant and confessor described by Meyerhold, and the kind of "creativity" in the confession of crimes it may lead to, operates even where torture is not involved. The coercion of interrogation itself may be all that is needed. This is of course especially true when it is a matter of custodial interrogation, which the suspect is not free to break off at will. Many clearly false confessions have been uncovered by researchers who have had access to taped interrogations—I shall look at some examples in later chapters—and it is safe to suppose that there have been many more in the annals of criminal justice never exposed.[3] Interrogation can be effectively coercive also in situations where the suspect allows questioning that he could legally refuse since there is not, or not yet, demonstrated "probable cause." And I want to suggest further that the bond of confessor and confessant can be productive of the confession of guilt even without the coercion that comes with the deprivation of freedom.

First, though, it may be useful to say something more about custodial interrogation as practiced in American police stations. The suspect is isolated in the euphemistically labeled "interview room," a typically Spartan space which he is not free to leave without permission, and is seated as far as possible from the door, which is locked. In his majority opinion in *Miranda v. Arizona,* Chief Justice Warren reconstructs the procedures followed in the interview room through readings from the interrogation manuals most used by police detectives, especially Charles E. O'Hara's *Fundamentals of Criminal Investigation* and Fred E. Inbau and John E. Reid's *Criminal Interrogation and Confessions.* For instance, Warren cites O'Hara:

> In the preceding paragraphs, emphasis has been placed on kindness and stratagems. . . . Where emotional appeals and tricks are employed to no avail, he [the interrogator] must rely on an oppressive atmosphere of dogged persistence. He must interrogate steadily and without relent, leaving the subject no prospect of surcease. He must dominate his subject and overwhelm him with his inexorable will to obtain the truth. . . . In a serious case, the in-

terrogation may continue for days, with the required intervals for food and sleep, but with no respite from the atmosphere of domination. It is possible in this way to induce the suspect to talk without resorting to duress or coercion. (384 U.S. at 451)[4]

In his conclusion to his review of the interrogation manuals, Warren states: "It is obvious that such an interrogation environment is created for no purpose other than to subjugate the individual to the will of his examiner" (457).

Reading these manuals, even in their post-*Miranda* revisions, one is indeed impressed by the acumen of professional interrogators in establishing a context of dependency, where confessing is made to appear the only way out, the only escape from interrogation itself. "The suspect . . . may tell his story more readily if he feels that the investigator understands his helplessness," says O'Hara.[5] "The principal psychological factor contributing to a successful interrogation is privacy—being alone with the person under interrogation. . . . [A] suspect or witness is much more apt to reveal any secrets in the privacy of a room occupied only by himself and the interrogator," write Inbau and Reid.[6] And they go on to detail the design of the interrogation room, the close proximity of the interrogator's chair in relation to the suspect's (providing even a diagram), the interrogator's clothing, his forms of address to the suspect (insist on calling a middle-class professional by his first name; on the contrary, call the lowlife suspect "Mr."), and the control of the narrative flow the interrogator must insist on. "The interrogator must always be in command of the situation. The strength of his personality must constantly be felt by the subject," says O'Hara.[7] The interrogator, again according to O'Hara, can be "Helpful Advisor" or "Sympathetic Brother"; he can suggest extenuating circumstances, imply the crime was morally justified, shift the blame to others; suggest that the subject "can't win"; bluff on knowledge he doesn't have; use, with a partner, the Mutt and Jeff, good cop/bad cop routine; and so on.[8]

Mutt and Jeff routinely offer the suspect, on the one hand, an attenuated version of his legal jeopardy—"you weren't centrally involved in the killing, you only drove the getaway car," etc.—and on the other hand an aggravated version—"you've got a prior conviction record, if we charge you with premeditated murder you'll get the gas chamber"—leading to what the suspect believes to be a plea to a lesser or even an anodyne charge, which very often simply proves the opening wedge to a more damning charge. It may come as something of a surprise to many of us that police interrogators not only lie frequently to suspects—claiming "proof" of guilt from fabricated polygraph tests, false eyewitness reports, false findings of fingerprints, hair, blood, semen at the crime scene: the list is extendible almost at will—but that they generally are allowed to lie by the courts. In *Frazier v. Cupp* (1969), the Supreme Court allowed a confession elicited when interrogators falsely informed the suspect that his co-suspect had confessed. In *State v. Kelekolio* (1993), the Hawaii State Supreme Court struggled to distinguish between what it called "intrinsic" lies—relating to evidence in the case, the story of the crime—which police detectives could validly use, and "extrinsic" lies—threats on nonexistent rules and punishments, promises of leniency following a confession—which should be barred.[9] The American legal system continues to assume that tricks and lies will not elicit a false confession from an innocent suspect, despite strong evidence to the contrary.

A recent article by two professional consultants on interrogation gives a useful summary of recommended, and legal, techniques:

1. State that the purpose for the interrogation is not to find out whether or not the suspect committed the crime but, rather, to determine what caused the suspect to commit it;
2. Express high confidence in the suspect's guilt;
3. Attempt to prevent the suspect from verbalizing denials by maintaining a monologue and urging the suspect to listen to the interrogator;
4. Sympathize with the suspect's position and express understanding as to why he committed the crime. In this regard the investigator may blame the victim for causing the suspect to commit the crime, minimize the impact of the crime on others, or blame psychological stress or intoxication for affecting the suspect's judgment;
5. Falsely tell the suspect about possible evidence implicating him in the commission of the crime;
6. Move physically close to the suspect to maintain his attention and interest.[10]

The assumption of the suspect's guilt is primordial; all the techniques of interrogation follow from this assumption and are designed to suggest that only confession will bring interrogation to an end.

The interrogator thus seeks to pattern the unfolding narrative according to a preconceived story. The qualities of the effective interrogator according to O'Hara in fact sound rather like those of the novelist:

> the investigator must develop intellectual curiosity and a keen sense of observation. He must cultivate a genuine interest in people and their problems, for such knowledge will help him in determining motives as he deals with many types of personalities in a variety of circumstances. It is highly desirable that he have a wide range of general knowledge concerning professional and technical matters, since his subjects represent nearly every phase of human activity.[11]

Above all, the good interrogator maintains control of the storytelling, so that the suspect is put in a position of denying or affirming—often, affirming through denials that lead to entrapment—the unfolding narrative that, one notes, is largely of the interrogator's own making, his "monologue." The following is a typical piece of interrogator storytelling from Inbau and Reid, based on a successfully completed interrogation in the case of the murder of an estranged wife:

> You went over to her apartment with the intention of talking to her about the marriage separation and money settlement like normal human beings, but she probably started an argument with you, and she got so mad and unreasonable that she even backed you up to the kitchen table. Now, if you were backed up to the kitchen table, and she was raising complete hell with you, and your hand accidentally rested on a knife, and you used it without thinking, I can understand that, and I can easily see how this could happen. That's one thing, but if you took the time to look into the drawer to find one and then you used it, that's different; if that's what happened, I don't want to talk to you further. However, if it was on the table and not in the drawer, and in backing up while she was sticking her finger in your face and screaming at you, and your hand then landed on it and you used it on her without thinking, I can well understand how this happened.[12]

Admission to the apparently extenuated version of "the knife on the table" of course thoroughly implicates the suspect, initiates the confession—and in this case eventually led to the admission that the knife was indeed in the drawer. The narrative either/ors of the interrogators offer choices that all are traps.

To Chief Justice Warren in *Miranda,* these interrogation techniques induce the suspect to confirm "the preconceived story the police seek to have him describe" and create a situation in which the individual surrenders his free will and makes statements contrary to his interest, perhaps even contrary to the truth. The Court must ban "all interrogation practices which are likely to exert such pressures upon an individual as to disable him from making a free and rational choice" (464–65). The language of the Supreme Court here—on other occasions it talks of the necessity for confessions to be the "product of a free and rational will" and of the danger of the suspect's will being "overborne"—may appear curiously archaic and in need of some specification in terms of our current understanding of "the will." But then, the whole conception of the human individual and his faculties reflected in legal language and concept may appear somewhat archaic to those nourished on Freud, Lacan, and Foucault, or more simply on Dostoevsky, George Eliot, and Stendhal.

What the lofty language of the Supreme Court translates into in practice is perhaps best described in David Simon's *Homicide,* subtitled *A Year on the Killing Streets,* an eyewitness account of a year in the life of the Baltimore, Maryland detective squad.[13] Despite the *Miranda* warnings, suspects waive their right to counsel and their right to silence. Suspects talk, and they appear to do so largely because the bond enforced by the interrogator and the state of dependency, including both offers of help and the menace of no escape, induces them to find an "out," that is, a statement that the suspect believes is exculpatory—but which inevitably proves the basis for self-inculpation. This "out," this window to crawl through, is, says Simon "as much the suspect's fantasy as the detective's mirage." Simon continues:

> The effect of the illusion is profound, distorting as it does the natural hostility between hunter and hunted, transforming it until it resembles a relationship more symbiotic than adversarial. That is the lie, and when the roles are perfectly performed, deceit surpasses itself, becoming manipulation on a grand scale and ultimately an act of betrayal. Because what occurs in an interrogation room is indeed little more than a carefully staged

drama, a choreographed performance that allows a detective and his suspect to find common ground where none exists. There, in a carefully controlled purgatory, the guilty proclaim their malefactions, though rarely in any form that allows for contrition or resembles an unequivocal admission. (209)

Simon's observation of how an adversarial relation becomes a symbiotic one, how common ground is found where none exists, strikes me as a profound comment on the conditions that must govern most criminal confessions. The affective bond of interrogator and suspect, confessor and confessant, interfused with elements of fear, subjugation, dependency, and attempted propitiation, leads to a fateful dialogue. As Simon further observes: "The fraud that claims it is somehow in a suspect's interest to talk with police will forever be the catalyst in any criminal interrogation. It is a fiction propped up against the greater weight of logic itself, sustained for hours on end through nothing more or less than a detective's ability to control the interrogation room" (213). Controlling an interrogation in this sense means imposing a controlling narrative, preventing a suspect's choice of silence—clearly the only intelligent choice, and that adhered to by experienced criminals—and maintaining the conditions in which speech will break forth.

"Mr. Apology"

So far, I have mentioned confessions produced under situations of clear constraint and coercion. I think we need to worry about such confessions—worry, in particular, whether Meyerhold's account of inventing what he thinks his interrogator wants, creating fictions of confession, doesn't in some number of cases apply as well to interrogations where the coercion is "merely" psychological rather than physical torture—and I shall return in later chapters to the issue of false confessions. But I want at this point to introduce the possibility that the confessor/confessant bond, that "symbiotic" relation observed by Simon, can take place even without constraint, indeed without interrogation in the normal sense, and without the locked door of the interview room. A striking example is provided in a *New Yorker* article by Alec Wilkinson entitled "The Confession," which concerns the experiments of a man who dubbed himself "Mr. Apology," who set up a tape recorder and advertised a phone number on posters taped to walls in Manhattan that invited people to record their confessions—and, at a later stage, to call in to listen to the confessions of others. "Get Your Misdeeds off Your Chest! Call APOLOGY (212) 255-2748" proclaimed the posters.[14] Mr. Apology's confession solicitation was designed to produce an exhibit, shown at the New Museum in 1981. (Mr. Apology wore a false beard to the show's opening, to disguise himself from the confessed criminals he thought might appear.) But after the exhibit was over, Mr. Apology kept his line open: "A number of people seemed to have become dependent on it, and, besides, Mr. Apology was still interested."

The main episode of "The Confession" concerns the messages from the caller who identifies himself as "Jumpin' Jim," who confesses to having finally turned on his nagging mother and killed her. Mr. Apology decides to "assemble a program featuring Jim's call along with one from a man who described a violent sexual escapade and one from a woman who had been forced as a child into sex by her brother" (163). This wholesome program leads to various call-in comments, including one from "Trevor," who comments that "Mr. A. generally likes to hear some kind of documentation of murders, some kind of evidence, before he'll believe that you killed somebody." When these comments become part of the program, Jim calls back, and asks Mr. Apology to phone him.

In a curious, possibly artful, elision, "The Confession" cuts from Jim's message requesting that Mr. Apology call him to "The first time Jim spoke to Mr. Apology. . . ." We are given no explicit statement of the motives that lead Mr. Apology to violate the anonymity and unidirectional protocol of the "Apology line" to enter into dialogue with Jim. But from here on, we have a tale of his strange interaction with Jim, as he attempts to determine whether his interlocutor is telling the truth. Mr. Apology even gives himself a name, "Chris"—whether real or fictive, the text doesn't say—in his dialogue with Jim, which promptly leads to Jim's invitation to a rendezvous, in the Alcatraz Bar: an invitation proposed, Jim says, because "I have this strange but very positive trust in you" (166). Mr. Apology asks time to think about this. A couple of days later, he calls to say he won't meet Jim. Then, that very night, following a party in the East Village, he stops in at the Alcatraz—which turns out to be a heavy-metal bar—at 3 A.M., but without any means of identifying Jim. The telephonic dialogue continues, with Mr. Apology more and more convinced that Jim is telling the truth, and seconding Trevor's request for proof of the murder, which Jim promises to provide. Then comes a call from Mr. Apology to Jim which is answered by a woman—who identifies herself as Jim's mother.

In subsequent conversations, Jim will deny that the woman on the phone was his mother and express resentment that Mr. Apology should accept her assertion that she was. "See, I don't want you to be like that," he complains, "I want you to say, 'Yes, he did kill his mother'" (170). Jim continues to promise proof of the murder, which Mr. Apology now must decline, since he doesn't want to be in the position of motivating a murder carried out to prove Jim's assertions. "I don't want you hurting anybody to create proof," he says, to which Jim replies, "I'm going to show it to you anyway. Just for the fact that you called me a liar" (171). Here, Mr. Apology's response is strangely equivocal. "If something shows up, I'll look at it, but I don't want to motivate you to create harm to someone to create some proof."

Perhaps it is the word "create" that causes Jim at this point to turn on Mr. Apology and to denounce the dynamic of their interaction:

> What do you mean "create"? You already created something when you called me. You already started something when you returned my call. So the damage, or whatever you want to call it, has been done. There's no stopping that. . . . Like I said, you're the one who started this. You're the one who returned my call. You didn't have to. If somebody told me they killed their mother and said they wanted to speak to me about it, I'm not going to call them back. This guy's nuts, you know, whatever, which I'm not crazy or anything like that, but, you know, I just wouldn't call them back. Provoke them more. No. (171)

One might say that at this point the confessant becomes his own confessor, perhaps even that he works his own "cure" by denouncing the confessional bond and the role played by Mr. Apology—somewhat in the manner that "Dora" turns on Freud, withdrawing from the transferential bond of psychoanalysis in a gesture that Freud interprets as vengeful but may also be a sign of returning health. In any event, in another phone call a few minutes after the one quoted above, Jim peacefully and, the reader is led to believe, definitively says goodbye to Mr. Apology.

Jim's accusation that Mr. Apology is "the one who started this" directs our attention to the layers of dependency and complicity apparent in "The Confession." If Mr. Apology's callers become dependent on his service, he appears to become equally dependent on them. His "interest" in his confessants—well beyond his original "exhibit" of them—comes to appear larded with bad faith and voyeurism; his composition of "programs" featuring the most lurid confessions suggests exploitation and a certain prurience to his interest; his relation to Jim has all the complicity of an alcoholic's codependent partner. As Jim himself perceives, Mr. Apology's choice to enter into dialogue with his arch-sinner "creates" something, "provokes" a situation, with the result that "the damage, or whatever you want to call it, has been done." The story may be read as an object-lesson in the transferential bond of confessor and confessant and in the "creative" proliferation of confession produced.[15] That the transferential space of confession between confessant and confessor in this instance appears to produce and initially to ratify a false confession, a fiction as invented as Meyerhold's, further points the lesson. How do you find truth in the confessional act? Where do you look for confessional truth: what is its status? What kind of truth is it? This is the elusive question I wish to pursue.

Confessional Truth

We take confession to be in the nature of a human urge or drive. As noted earlier in the words of Chief Justice Burger, dissenting in the "Christian burial case": "The human urge to confess wrongdoing is, of course, normal in all save hardened, professional criminals, as psychiatrists and analysts have demonstrated." (That Burger at this point refers us to Theodor Reik's *The Compulsion to Confess* is a bit strange, given the nature of Reik's analysis of the "urge to confess," of which more in a moment.) Confession of misdeeds has become part of the everyday pedagogy of Western societies, normally with the understanding that recalcitrance in confession will aggravate punishment, while full confession will both cleanse the soul and provide possible mitigation of sanctions. It was certainly part of the genius of the Roman Catholic Church to understand the uses of confession. It is suggestive to recall that the Fourth Lateran Council, in 1215, promulgated at the same time the Christian dogma—what the faithful had to profess—the obligation of confession at least once a year, and the institution of an inquisition to eradicate heresy. The urge to confess is thus put to work both toward the absolution of the sinner's individual conscience and toward the policing of religious orthodoxy. Confession is the way to contrition and to absolution, which permits a reintegration into the community of the faithful. There is, historically, a change in emphasis from the process of penance to the verbal act of confessing.

The model of absolution and reintegration no doubt plays a role as well in the kinds of confession under interrogation described by Meyerhold and by Simon: only confession will propitiate the interrogators, bring interrogation to an end, allow one to cease being the pariah called a "suspect." Theodor Reik's observations on the possible psychoanalytic meaning of confession may be pertinent here.[16] For Reik, confession expresses a desire for punishment, and to the extent that it is made to a father-figure—representative of the superego—it is perfectly consonant with the dependency model of both religious confession and police interrogation, and of course the Apology Line as well. Discussing "acting out" as a form of confession, Reik comments:

> This confession is often not an end in itself. It has the meaning of an appeal to the parents or their substitutes, which is what makes necessary the addition of a concluding sentence: "Please consider those weaknesses! Just because this is how I am, you must forgive me! Punish me, but love me again!" Thus the confession becomes an eloquent plea for absolution. (208)

To the extent that it is a plea for absolution, for reintegration into parental love, confession poses no problem to the Church, which is well-equipped for such tasks. It may present some problems for those interested in the rights of criminal suspects since, as Simon suggests, it constitutes a fraud, an implicit promise that will be exploited to the suspect's grief. Beyond that, confession as a plea for love redirects us to the status and nature of the truth involved in confessions—not only those that are compelled by interrogation or required by religious belief but those that are apparently freely offered, by Jumpin' Jim, by Jean-Jacques Rousseau, by Dostoevsky's Underground Man, and by a host of other confessants, real and fictive, whose discourses raise many important questions about their intent and the criteria of their evaluation, as well as suggesting troubling issues in the concept of the human subject on which so many of our social systems, and notably our law, is constructed.

One of the most thoughtful discussions of confession that I know is novelist and critic J. M. Coetzee's essay, "Confession and Double Thoughts: Tolstoy, Rousseau, Dostoevsky."[17] Coetzee worries about the kind of truth provided in confessions where what is explicitly confessed to does not appear to coincide with other implied, more ambiguous sorts of material that may reveal a deeper guilt—or may on the contrary reveal a self-satisfaction in confession. Without tracing the complexities of Coetzee's argument, and without discussing once again the famous episode of Rousseau's stolen ribbon and Paul de Man's analysis of it (an important part of Coetzee's discussion) since these were treated in the last chapter, let me cite the conclusion of his discussion of Rousseau:

> What I have written thus far indicates that the project of confession when the subject is at a heightened level of self-awareness and open to self-doubt raises intricate and, on the face of it, intractable problems regarding truthfulness, problems whose common factor seems to be a regression to infinity of self-awareness and self-doubt. It is by no means clear that these problems are visible to the Rousseau of the *Confessions* or the Tolstoy of *The Kreutzer Sonata*. But to trust that evidence of such an awareness must necessarily surface in the text, when it is precisely not in the interest of either writer to bear such awareness, would be incautious. (274)

The next "stage" in self-awareness and self-doubt is visible in Dostoevsky's Underground Man, who in confessing finds "behind every motive another motive, behind every mask another mask." The "ultimate motive," writes Coetzee, may be "the *motive for unmasking* itself," and thus a perverse truth, "a perverse choice made in accord with a design invisible to him though perhaps visible to others." Coetzee continues:

> We are now beyond all questions of sincerity. The possibility we face is of a confession made via a process of relentless self-unmasking which might yet be not the truth but a self-serving fiction, because the unexamined, unexaminable principle behind it may be not a desire for the truth but a desire to *be a par-*

ticular way. The more coherent such a hypothetical fiction of the self might be, the less the reader's chance of knowing whether it is a true confession. We can test its truth only when it contradicts itself or comes into conflict with some "outer," verifiable truth, both of which eventualities a careful confessing narrator can in theory avoid. (280)

This comment suggests, first of all, why compelling the confession of belief, of inward thoughts or convictions, has always posed a problem. In early modern Europe, I noted, confessions extorted under interrogation, including torture, were supposed to be verified from circumstantial evidence. But there is no circumstantial evidence about inner beliefs, which is why certain suspects put on trial for heresy began to make the argument that testimony as to inner beliefs, matters of conscience, could not be compelled—the defense that eventuated, for Americans, in the Fifth Amendment to the U.S. Constitution. Then, compelling confession may simply uncover layer upon layer of a truth that cannot be distinguished from fiction because there appears to be no endpoint for confession other than that "motive for unmasking itself," which has no truth value. Coetzee refers us to "such self-abasing breast-beaters as Marmeladov and Lebedev [in *The Idiot*], in whom the shamelessness of the confession is a further motive for shame, and so on to infinity" (290).

Coetzee sums up what he takes to be Dostoevsky's view:

The end of confession is to tell the truth to and for oneself. The analysis of the fate of confession that I have traced in three novels by Dostoevsky indicates how skeptical Dostoevsky was, and why he was skeptical, about the variety of secular confession that Rousseau and, before him, Montaigne attempt. Because of the nature of consciousness, Dostoevsky indicates, the self cannot tell the truth of itself to itself and come to rest without the possibility of self-deception. True confession does not come from the sterile monologue of the self or from the dialogue of the self with its own self-doubt, but ... from faith and grace. (291)

One more citation from Coetzee:

[T]here is no argument that will succeed in outflanking the underground man's assertion that self-consciousness works by its own laws, one of which is that behind each true, final position lurks another position truer and more final. From one point of view this is a fertile law, since it allows the endless generation of the text of the self exemplified by *Notes from Underground*. From another point of view, that of the hungerer after truth, it is sterile, deferring the truth endlessly, coming to no end. (292)

This is undoubtedly a correct characterization, both of the typical Dostoevskian confession, and of the ultimate solution to the problem envisioned by Dostoevsky: faith and grace. Such an "end" to confession is explicit in (to take an example not mentioned by Coetzee) Raskolnikov's choice of the confession that will bring on him punishment, penance, and ultimately—*Crime and Punishment* suggests—redemption. But what about a world, or a writer, for whom faith and grace are not viable concepts? Is the confessional discourse without faith and grace condemned to being nothing but the sterile, unending unmaskings of the underground "paradoxicalist"?

Where Coetzee's brilliant reading of Rousseau and Dostoevsky leaves me unsatisfied is in its traditional notion of "truth," which seems to me comparable to the Enlightenment concept of "Man" that is assumed by much American law. What may be indicated by the disturbing infinity of confessions (at least from Rousseau's onwards), their inability to reach an endpoint, and thus their inability to offer a principle for judging what, finally, is the *true* confession, is the need for other criteria of truth in thinking about confessions: criteria that make confession less useful for purposes of both law enforcement and absolution, but nonetheless may give a more accurate context for our thinking about how confessions work, the kind of "creativity" they generate, and the way in which they cohabit with both truth and lie.

Rousseau once again seems an inevitable point of reference. Here I will take an example from book 3 of the *Confessions,* one that fully displays the shame and the shamelessness of confession as an act of self-exposure, where a literal act of self-exposure is doubled by its narration, but to ends that disturbingly displace any unproblematic notion of the truth. The young Jean-Jacques is an adolescent in Turin, dreaming of finding a woman who would reproduce the scenes of childhood punishment which, starting from the spanking administered by Mlle. Lambercier, have determined his notion of sexual enjoyment. Too timid to ask directly for the object of his desire—asking indeed would defeat his passive aim—he instead seeks dark alley-ways where he can expose himself to women "in the state in which I would have wished to be in their company."[18] What he exposes, as predetermined by his early sensual awakening to spanking, is "not the obscene object" but rather "the ridiculous object": his backside, not his genitals. One day, he exposes himself in a courtyard where serving girls come to draw water from the well, having first assured himself that there are deep cellars leading off the courtyard in which he can take refuge. While he offers what he now, writing about the episode, calls "a spectacle more laughable than seductive," some of the girls are not amused and call for a man. This gives an unexpected in-flection to the story. Jean-Jacques retreats into the labyrinthine cellars. He is pursued. Then, instead of reaching the safety of deeper dark-ness, he comes out in a lighted portion of the cellar and is brought up short by a blank wall. His pursuers catch up with him. The man—"a big man wearing a big mustache, a big hat, a big sword," escorted by a number of the women—seizes him and demands an explanation. Pushed to the wall in this manner, Jean-Jacques has recourse to what he calls "*un expédient romanesque*": a novelistic invention, a fiction. He "confesses" that he is a young foreigner of high birth whose mind is deranged, that he has escaped from his father's house because he was going to be locked up, that he will be done for if his identity is made known, and that he can perhaps some day reward an act of grace. Contrary to his expectations, the fiction works: the man lets him go. A few days later, though, he encounters the "big man" in the street, and the man says to him: "I'm a Prince . . . I'm a Prince; and as for me, I'm a fool; but may his Highness not come back." The fictive identity, having done its work, is unmasked.

Self-exposure in this episode leads to a moment of constraint in which Jean-Jacques is obliged to confess—but gives a false confes-sion, a fictional "expedient." One that is not entirely unrelated to the truth, however. A foreigner he is, not of high birth, to be sure—but then, he is always imagining himself as in fact naturally superior to the situations in which he finds himself: repeatedly forced to be a ser-vant, he feels he is never "in his right place," and this displacement then serves to legitimate actions that seem out of place. For instance, his correct interpretation of the ancient motto of the House of Solar, which wins him the momentary admiration of the beautiful Mlle. de Breil, but affects him to the point that he pours water on her because his hands are trembling, constitutes an episode that Rousseau characterizes as "one of those too rare moments that re-place things in their natural order" (96). His mind is not quite "deranged" but often judged to be close to that condition. He has escaped from his father's house, not because he was to be locked up as a lunatic but because he couldn't stand the master to whom he was apprenticed. And so on. The fictional expedient is not necessarily a lie, in that its definition of the truth corresponds to the order of desire and self-conception.

What the episode of self-exposure in Turin may most forcefully indicate is how the self is bound up with the fictions it tells about itself—as much a product as a source of those fictions. When one further considers that the self gets into a scene of self-exposure because it is driven by childhood affects that have determined its sexual desires and identity and that are founded on imaginary scenarios of childhood satisfaction, it becomes difficult to say that the lying confession in the cellars of Turin is not some kind of truth. The setting and actions of the episode—exposure in the corner of a courtyard at the center of which is a communal well from which women draw water; retreat into dark cellars that end in light and a blocked passage; "discovery" superseded by the creation of a fictive identity and history—suggest a sexualized topography and an allegory of self-discovery as sexualized fiction. And the fictions engendered by human sexuality are always devious and "deviant," in that sexuality is not simply genital or reproductive utility but consubstantial with the imaginary and the phantasmatic. This is one of Freud's important lessons: that human sexuality is always, in Juliet Mitchell's term, "psychosexuality."[19] Rousseau in recounting this episode from the adolescence of Jean-Jacques tells us that self-exposure leads not to a simple or direct act of self-recognition, but to a deviated recognition of self in a wish-fulfilling fiction. In reexposing himself in the narration of the episode, Rousseau offers an allegory of the act of confessing as an act of self-exposure, with the implicit warning that confession is never direct, simple, straightforward, but rather a discourse whose relation to the truth takes the shape of a tangent, since it involves fantasies and fictions that are both gratuitous (pure inventions) and predetermined (by sexual orientation) and are in some sense (according to the dictates of desire) truer than what we might normally consider the truth. But then, what access do we have to the truth of such a confession other than the discourse, Rousseau's speech act, that proffers it? Is that where its truth lies? The act of self-exposure is undeniable, as an act, as a performance, indeed a performative, though always doubtable as a factual reference, as a constative.

Rousseau anticipates Dostoevsky's confessants in demonstrating that confession can suggest a potentially infinite regress. That is not Rousseau's stated intention, to be sure, since he believes that he is guided by the sincere desire to portray himself in his entirety, that is, to make his soul "transparent" to the reader's eye.[20] But this transparency never is a simple achievement. The more guilt or shame he finds to confess, the more guilt and shame he accumulates by the act of confessing, so that the distinction between the referent—a guilty or shameful act in the past now confessed to—and the speech act that confesses it becomes indeterminate. Exposing the scene of self-exposure in Turin produces a vertiginous doubling. I have argued that confession may be best conceived as a speech-act that has a constative aspect (the sin or guilt confessed to) and a performative aspect (the performance of the act of confessing), and that the performative aspect can producte the constative, creating guilt in the act of confessing it. Certainly Meyerhold's testimony and Mr. Apology's experience with Jumpin' Jim suggest that the constraint of a situation that requires or invites confession can itself produce proliferating confessions; the need or desire to confess leads to a performance of confession where the referent, in the guilty or shameful action, loses any referential stability—becomes, perhaps, simply what is required to get on with the business of confessing. Rousseau's constraint of confessing is self-imposed—the test he sets himself—but the results are much the same. Unlike Saint Augustine, who can stabilize his confessions in the discovery of revealed truth, Rousseau cannot come to rest in the speech-act that begins "I confess."

The most elaborated (one might say the most "professionalized") form of modern secularized confession that I can think of is psychoanalysis. The status of the "true confession" in psychoanalysis is of course complex. What the analysand confesses most easily—what he or she thinks is what needs confessing—is always an object of suspicion to the analyst, since the matter easily confessed is usually not what is causing the neurosis. Confessions by the analysand can serve many motives—shame, guilt, revenge, self-justification, self-abasement—but the deeper sources of shame and guilt are blocked from confession by repression and resistance. Psychoanalytic work must normally be directed not so much to confession as to the resistance to confession, working to uncover what the analyst—somewhat in the manner of the interrogator—knows the analysand knows, but knows only unconsciously. "Truth" is to be sought in those places that have been marked by censorship. It is not the voluntary confession that interests the analyst, but the involuntary—that which can be coerced from the analysand in the course of analytic work.

This means that the "truth" of psychoanalysis depends very much on the process of its articulation. Freud in the course of his career came to recognize more and more clearly that there is no final truth uncovered by this process—indeed, that psychoanalysis is inherently interminable, since the dynamics of the transference and the resistance to closure will always create new material to work on. The transferential bond between analysand and analyst is crucial here, as it is in the situation of police interrogation, and, I think, all confessional situations. In fact a bond comes into being even when the confessor is a simple tape recorder, and even when confessor and confessant are the same person (as with Rousseau and the Underground Man), since in the performance of confession they become double. Freud's self-analysis, inaugural of the discipline of psychoanalysis, is here the key gesture transforming the tradition of secular confession exemplified by Rousseau (a precursor of whom Freud was keenly aware) into "the impossible profession."

In one of his last papers on psychoanalytic technique, "Constructions in Analysis" (1937), Freud gives his most radical reading of transference and the kind of truth discovered by psychoanalysis. In this essay, Freud sets out to consider the roles played by analysand and analyst in constructing the story of the past. The analyst takes the raw material (the *Rohstoff*) provided by the analysand and attempts to construct it as story, feeding it back to the analysand to see what effect it will have. "The analyst," writes Freud, "finishes a piece of construction and communicates it to the subject of analysis so that it may work upon him; he then constructs a further piece out of the fresh material pouring in upon him, deals with it in the same way and proceeds in this alternating fashion until the end."[21] In such alternating, reciprocal work (*Abwechslung*) the analyst constructs parts of the story in order for the analysand to find more of the story—to produce a fuller confession. And what confirms that the analyst's constructions are the right ones is not a simple assent by the analysand. A "yes" from the analysand may have no value, says Freud, "unless it is followed by indirect confirmations, unless the patient, immediately after his 'Yes,' produces more memories which complete and extend the construction" (23:262). In other words, the real test of truth in constructing the analysand's confessional story is simply the production of more story.

In his case history of "Dora," Freud calls transferences "new impressions or reprints" and "revised editions" of earlier texts (7:116). Who is author of this revised edition is put into question by "Constructions in Analysis." Freud notes that while "the path that starts from the analyst's construction ought to end in the patient's recollection," this is not always the case:

> Quite often we do not succeed in bringing the patient to recollect what has been repressed. Instead of that, if the analysis is carried out correctly, we produce in him an assured conviction [*sichere Überzeugung*] of the truth of the construction which achieves the same therapeutic result as a recaptured memory. (23:265–66)

Thus it is that elements of the analysand's story may not in fact be produced by the person whose story it is but rather by the interlocutor, yet result in the conviction that these elements must be true. Freud of course repudiates the notion that these constructed story elements are merely "suggestion" on the part of the analyst that persuades the analysand to give credence to a fiction, or a lie. If the analysand accepts the construction, it is because it must in some profound sense be true. But that truth is not necessarily the truth of verifiable fact, the truth of event: it can be the truth of desire, of affect, of that which makes sense of things in an emotional register. Freud, one might say, is opting for the supplementation of realism by romance, famously defined by Henry James as "the things that . . . we never *can* directly know; the things that can reach us only through the beautiful circuit and subterfuge of our thought and our desire."[22] In this manner, the transferential bond of psychoanalysis, like that of interrogation, can produce matter that is undoubtedly "true" according to some measure of psychic need and desire, but not necessarily true in the world of outer events. In Freud's terms, it's a matter of "psychic truth" rather than "material truth."

I do not wish to be construed as equating Freud's constructions with those of the police interrogator. Where the production of confessions is concerned, everything depends on what use is made of them. David Simon calls our attention to the "fraud" that claims it is in a suspect's interests to confess to police interrogators, but it may well be in the interests of an analysand, or a religious confessant, to seek Rousseau's "transparency" of the soul with the analyst or confessor. Yet it is evident that the power of the transferential bond can be abused, not only in its use by totalitarian political régimes (as in Soviet psychiatry) but also in the unscrupulous or inept production of "recovered memories"—of child abuse, for instance—that may often in fact be constructions made by a therapist or interrogator and confirmed by a subject who feels rage or guilt, but whose guilt may be psychic rather than material (issues I shall discuss further in chapter 5). Confessions no doubt speak *of* guilt, but don't necessarily speak *the* guilt. As our examples from Meyerhold to Jumpin' Jim seem to indicate, confessions need to be marked "handle with care," since the status of confessional truth is delicate. There is probably something true in most confessions, but the kind and nature of that truth is not always evident—and not always evidence. At worst, it can be—as perhaps it sometimes is for Rousseau and Dostoevsky's paradoxicalists— the performance of confession in order to produce the guilt needed in order to confess.

Mitya's Confessions

My principal literary example must almost of necessity come from Dostoevsky's greatest novel, from a moment that seems to overlay or jumble criminal, religious, and psychotherapeutic confession. I have in mind the interrogation of Dimitri Fyodorovich Karamazov following the murder of his father Fyodor Pavlovich in *The Brothers Karamazov*.[23] Dimitri—Mitya—will of course be found guilty of a murder he did not commit, a murder in fact committed by Smerdyakov, who confesses to Ivan Fyodorovich but in such a form as to charge his confessor with the crime: Smerdyakov argues that since Ivan knew Smerdyakov was planning the murder and chose to absent himself rather than preventing it, he is truly responsible for it—a charge that cuts close enough to Ivan's guilty conscience toward his father that when Ivan produces Smerdyakov's confession as part of his own confession, it's in a manner that does not persuade the court. Since we are dealing here with the killing of the loathsome father of the Karamazov clan, psychic parricide—the wish if not the deed—abounds, and can be activated in any instance of interrogation or accusation to gain the effective power of the deed.

Mitya is arrested following his night of revels with Grushenka at the inn at Mokroye and charged as suspect in his father's murder and the theft of the three thousand roubles his father kept hidden as his gift to Grushenka should she come to him (father and son are rivals for her favors). In fact, Mitya turned away from the temptation of attacking his father, but in fleeing his father's house was intercepted by the old servant Grigory Vasiliev, whom he struck down with a pestle he had in his pocket. That pestle, and the missing 3,000 roubles—thought to be the funding of his revels in Mokroye—will weigh heavily against him, especially since he has never disguised his wish to see his father dead.

Mitya's interrogation—his "torment," the novel calls it—activates layers of guilt:

> "Wait, wait, write it down like this: 'Of violence—guilty; of inflicting a savage beating on a poor old man [Grigory Vasiliev]—guilty.' And then, within himself, too, inside, in the bottom of his heart, he is guilty—but there's no need to write that down," he turned suddenly to the clerk, "that is my private life, gentlemen, that doesn't concern you now, the bottom of my heart, I mean . . . But of the murder of his old father—not guilty! It's a wild idea! It's an utterly wild idea . . . ! I'll prove it to you and you'll be convinced immediately. You'll laugh, gentlemen, you'll roar with laughter at your own suspicion . . . !" (460)

On the one hand, Mitya appears to enter wholly into a transferential bond with his interrogators, insisting on seeing them as kind companions: "We are three noble men come together here, and let everything with us be on the footing of mutual trust between educated and worldly men, bound by nobility and honor. In any case, allow me to look upon you as my best friends in this moment of my life, in this moment when my honor is humiliated!" (467). On the other hand, his confessional discourse in response to these best friends/tormentors develops as a general assumption of shame. For instance, in regard to the competition with his father over Grushenka: "Of his jealousy he spoke ardently and extensively, and though inwardly ashamed at displaying his most intimate feelings, so to speak, 'for general disgrace,' he obviously tired to overcome his shame for the sake of being truthful" (469). "General disgrace" becomes Mitya's badge of truthfulness, abjection the guarantee of his full confession.

Yet the assumption of general disgrace also appears as a way to avoid articulating a particular disgrace of which he is more deeply ashamed: the source of the three thousand roubles the court believes he stole from his father when he murdered him, but which in fact were given to him by Katerina Ivanovna to send to her sister, and spent by him, in two equal portions, in revels with Grushenka. He would rather be thought guilty of killing and robbing his father than reveal his misappropriation of Katya's money on his drunken evenings with her disreputable rival in his affections. "I won't tell you, gentlemen, you've guessed right, you'll never know. . . . I keep silent, gentlemen, because it involves a disgrace for me. The answer to the question of where I got this money contains such a disgrace for me as could not be compared even with killing and robbing my father, if I had killed and robbed him. That is why I cannot speak. Because of the disgrace" (479–80). So that the production of shameful confessional statements nonetheless leaves in silence that which Mitya considers most shameful—his behavior toward Katya—but which has nothing to do with the issue of his legal guilt, on the murder charge. The inner understanding of what most resists confessing stands in a curious and debilitating relation to the confession the court seeks: debilitating, because guilt for the unavowable deed he did commit contaminates, in the eyes of the court, professions of innocence for the deed he did not commit. It is exculpatory evidence that he resists giving.

The source of the three thousand roubles indeed becomes a key presumption against Mitya; the prosecutor states that his "obdurate silence" on this point leaves them no choice but to believe in his guilt. "Try . . . to understand our position as well," pleads the prosecutor:

> Mitya was inconceivably agitated; he turned pale.
>
> "All right!" he suddenly exclaimed, "I will reveal my secret to you, reveal where I got the money . . . ! I will reveal my disgrace, so as not to blame either you or myself later on. . . ."
>
> "And you may believe, Dimitri Fyodorovich," Nikolai Par-

fenovich added, in a sort of tenderly joyful little voice, "that any sincere and full confession you make precisely at this moment, may afterwards contribute towards an immeasurable alleviation of your fate, and, moreover, may even . . ."

But the prosecutor nudged him slightly under the table, and he managed to stop himself in time. Mitya, to tell the truth, was not listening to him. (489)

On the one hand, then, the interrogators seize upon Mitya's sense of shame in order to foster and produce more confession, while on the other hand Mitya himself sinks into a kind of unlimited self-exposure to his "disgrace." When the prosecutors suggest he might simply have asked Katya to lend him the money, he repudiates the idea of such baseness—deliberately asking for Katya's money in order to spend it on Grushenka, rather than temporarily misappropriating money given to him for another purpose—then assumes the shame of having in fact contemplated such baseness, in a downward spiraling confession:

> "Oh, how base that would be! Gentlemen, you're torment-
> ing me, do you know that? As you wish, I'll tell you everything,
> so be it, I will now confess all my infernality to you, just to put
> you to shame, and you yourselves will be surprised at what base-
> ness a combination of human feelings can sink to. Know, then,
> that I already had that solution in mind, the very one you were
> just talking about, prosecutor! Yes, gentlemen, I, too, had that
> thought during this cursed month, so that I almost resolved to
> go to Katya, so base I was! But to go to her, to announce my be-
> trayal to her, and for that betrayal, to carry through that be-
> trayal, for the future expenses of that betrayal, to ask money (to
> ask, do you hear, to ask!) from her, from Katya, and immedi-
> ately run off with another woman, with her rival, with her hater
> and offender—my God, you're out of your mind, prosecutor!"
> (495)

Mitya's "infernality" is of the thought, not the deed, and concerns "baseness," not crime. "I've made a terrible confession to you," he adds. "Do appreciate it, gentlemen. And it's not enough, not enough to appreciate it, you must not just appreciate it, it should be precious to you, and if not, if this, too, goes past your souls, then it means you really do not respect me, gentlemen, I tell you that, and I will die of shame at having confessed to such men as you!" (495).

By this point, there is no possibility of communication between the kinds of confession proffered and those received. The confessant is deep within an inner world of shame and guilt and the disgrace brought by the public performance of shame and guilt, whereas the confessors simply seek confirmation of a crime. It's as if Mitya had mistaken his interrogators for ministers of the faith, to whom a confession should be a "precious" trust. The distinctions he makes between shameful thoughts, motives, psychological states and his innocence in fact are as blurred for his interrogators as Jumpin' Jim's confessions for Mr. Apology. And despite his assumption of the deepest shame, they don't believe the truth he tells. To the court, his many-layered confession merely demonstrates *mens rea,* the state of mind necessary to have committed the deed.

Mitya's confession is in some sense realized and completed by Ivan's some two hundred pages later in the novel—after we have learned of Ivan's visits to Smerdyakov (like Mitya's "torments," they are three in number) and Smerdyakov's confession of the murder, which is simultaneously an accusation that Ivan bears the ultimate responsibility for it, followed by his suicide. For whereas Mitya is forever making distinctions between thoughts and deeds, Ivan's confession thoroughly blurs them, offering Smerdyakov's deed as a version of his own thoughts, and indeed of *everyone's* thoughts. After handing the judge the three thousand roubles stolen by Smerdyakov from the murdered man, Ivan answers the judge's question about where he got the money:

> "I got it from Smerdyakov, the murderer, yesterday. I visited him before he hanged himself. It was he who killed father, not my brother. He killed him, and killed him on my instructions . . . Who doesn't wish for his father's death . . . ?"
>
> "Are you in your right mind?" inadvertently escaped from the judge.
>
> "The thing is that I am precisely in my right mind . . . my vile mind, the same as you, and all these . . . m-mugs!" he suddenly turned to the public. "A murdered father, and they pretend to be frightened," he growled with fierce contempt. "They pull faces to each other. Liars! Everyone wants his father dead.

Viper devours viper . . . If there were no parricide, they'd all get angry and go home in a foul temper . . . Circuses! 'Bread and circuses!' And me, I'm a good one! Is there some water? Give me a drink, for Christ's sake!" he suddenly clutched his head. (686)

Ivan continues to confirm that he is a murderer, but the court demands confirmation of his confession. It gains no credence. "Witness, your words are incomprehensible and impossible in this place," says the judge.

One might say that Ivan's confession is too true to be believed. Sweeping away his brother's distinctions between thought and deed, it posits as universal the wish for parricide, a level of guilt so deep and general that it almost makes the specific commission of the deed irrelevant—or at least, makes the commission of the deed the result of a collective wish, thus evidence of a collective guilt. Ivan simply assumes the deed from the wish, which has the effect of making Smerdyakov's factual guilt pale before the stark illumination of the wish. Ivan's confession in this manner completes and realizes Mitya's confession, endowing Mitya's guilty thoughts with their true importance and magnitude, but, insofar as he insists that he, Ivan, is the murderer, completes and realizes Mitya's confession as a factual lie.[24]

The court chooses to treat Ivan's confession as "incomprehensible and impossible in this place" and goes on to find Mitya guilty. Perhaps the most profound confessions elicit this result. Confessions, as Rousseau and Jumpin' Jim and a number of Dostoevskian confessants suggest, can be aggressive: they challenge the confessors to join in the confessional game, to recognize and articulate their own guilt. When that guilt is as deep and universal as the wish for parricide, the confessors will regularly throw up a barrier of resistance and repression: "incomprehensible and impossible in this place." The law in any event doesn't know what to do with such confessional guilt; it has no place for it. In Mitya's trial, it sets it aside for the more convenient definition of guilt, which in this case condemns an innocent man.

"The guilt of the subject is to be posited as a fact," notes Chief Justice Warren in his examination of police interrogation manuals in *Miranda v. Arizona*. When the confessant in return posits his guilt as universal, this fact is unusable. At this point, one might see another of Warren's observations on the results of interrogation come into play:

"He [the suspect] merely confirms the preconceived story the police seek to have him describe." Justice needs a stock story leading to conviction—a conviction that bears some kinship to Freud's constructed narrative, which may not be materially confirmable but nonetheless carries conviction. Mitya and Ivan together, as paired or twinned confessants, make the point of how the wrong kind of confession, from the law's point of view, leads to the imposition of the preconceived story. In *The Brothers Karamazov,* one can even say that the preconceived, and false, story carries a certain conviction even for the man falsely found guilty since he seeks suffering as purification. Mitya says at the end of his interrogation:

> I accept the torment of accusation and of my disgrace before all, I want to suffer and be purified by suffering! And perhaps I will be purified, eh, gentlemen? But hear me, all the same, for the last time: I am not guilty of my father's blood! I accept punishment not because I killed him, but because I wanted to kill him, and might well have killed him. . . . (509)

Mitya's judges can condemn him in good conscience, not because he is guilty but because he wants to be punished. This, too, is part of the logic of confession: there's always something punishable going around.

I offer one last example from fiction, from another writer for whom the confessional mode was a continuing preoccupation. In Stendhal's *Le Rouge et le noir,* Julien Sorel is tried for the shooting of Mme. de Rênal, and toward the close of his trial is asked if he has anything to say. At his point, he breaks his self-imposed silence as if despite himself. A "horror of contempt," he says, forces him to speak:

> Gentlemen of the jury,
> The horror of contempt, which I thought I would be able to face down at the moment of death, forces me to speak. Gentlemen, I don't have the honor of belonging to your class, you see in me a peasant who revolted against the baseness of his condition. . . .
> My crime is atrocious, and it was *premeditated.* Thus I have merited the death sentence, Gentlemen of the jury. But even if I were less guilty, I see men who, without considering what pity

my youth might warrant, will want to punish in me and set a stern example to that class of young people who, born to an inferior class and as it were oppressed by poverty, have the good fortune to obtain a good education and the effrontery to mix with what the pride of the rich calls society.

There is my crime, Gentlemen, and it will be punished with all the more severity in that, in fact, I am not being judged by my peers. I don't see in the jury box any enriched peasant, but only indignant bourgeois. . . .[25]

What is curious here is Julien's self-identification as a "peasant who has revolted against the baseness of his condition," as a plebeian who has sought to rise in society, and whose trial takes place before those representatives of middle-class society who are not his peers, but his class enemies. As the Abbé Frilair will say later, raising this issue of class warfare—the taboo topic that haunts post-Revolutionary Restoration France—Julien here virtually commits suicide. He has good grounds for pleading for mitigation: Mme. de Rênal has recovered from her wounds, he has powerful friends in high places, and he has been calumniated. But he chooses instead the identity that he has earlier described as "monstrous": that of the scheming, Tartuffe-like hypocrite who has used others, included the women who fell in love with him, to become something that he was not. He seems to accept that "preconceived story" his prosecutors would have him tell. The moment is disorienting for readers of the novel, since we have long since ceased to think of Julien as social usurper, have come to accept—as we thought he himself had—his natural belonging to the upper class and the ruling elite, whether or not this belonging should be thought of as legitimated by illegitimate fatherhood by an aristocrat, as the Marquis de la Mole, the Abbé Pirard, and even Julien at times seem to believe. In assuming the monster image of himself, Julien chooses the guillotine.[26] His confession provides an example of why Talmudic law, as I noted earlier, traditionally did not allow confessions from the accused: they appeared contrary to the instinct for self-preservation, something like a product of the death drive.

But "chooses" may be the wrong word. Julien's courtroom confession breaks forth as a nearly involuntary statement, compelled from him by his "horror of contempt." Like Dostoevsky's Mitya, his reaction to the situation of exposure and disgrace is to assume a confession that urges distinctions in kinds of guilt and that all the more effectively condemns him in the eyes of the court. Unlike Mitya, he accepts guilt for the deed and paints that deed as black as possible. Like Mitya, he is concerned with the degrees of abjection that characterize him. More than Mitya—more like Ivan—he gets it all wrong. The moment of confessional clarification—truth at the foot of the scaffold—obscures more than it illuminates.

The historical moment of Julien Sorel's speech to the jury is interesting. Stendhal, born in 1783, educated by a grandfather who was an ardent reader of Voltaire and a champion of enlightened ideas, is a late product of the French Enlightenment who lived through the Revolution, the Napoleonic epic, the reaction of the Restoration and the Holy Alliance, and the coming of the vast transvaluation of values we call Romanticism. Julien's confession, like so much else in this character who sees himself as motivated by self-imposed rational conceptions of man and society, sounds as a warning that the Enlightenment conception of man as a rational choice-maker endowed with free will may be too limited. Such a statement of course simplifies the Enlightenment far too much, since it understood the power of unreason and the inexplicable motive even as it deplored them. After all, it is a time that produced its great dissenter in Rousseau, and at the end of the Enlightenment stands Rousseau's deviant disciple, the Marquis de Sade.

Nonetheless, the image of "man" (and it traditionally is expressed in terms of the one gender) that underlies American law—and is embodied in the Constitution, very much an Enlightenment document—has this rationalistic cast. The Supreme Court has continued to assert that the legally acceptable confession must be the "product of a free and rational will." Everything we have observed in confessions, "real" or "fictional" (the borders tend to blur here) tends to suggest that confessions rarely are products of a free and rational will. They arise in situations of constraint, whether physical or psychological. They are motivated by inextricable layers of shame, guilt, disgrace, contempt, self-loathing, propitiation, and expiation. Their "truth" is often not straightforward but deviated from its apparent referent: a truth of performance and dialogue, a truth created by the bond of confessant and confessor and the confessional situation. To say this is not to argue that the law should embrace post-Freudian and post-Foucaultian notions of the individual, two versions that deconstruct the idea that we are masters in our own psychic abodes and suggest that rational free will is an illusion. To do its job, the law needs to insist upon traditional notions of individual responsibility, including responsibility for acts of confession. But where confession is concerned, I'd suggest, the law needs to recognize that its conceptions of human motivation and volition are particularly flawed, and indeed something of a fiction. Perhaps the only way to conclude is to caution would-be confessors, whether police interrogators or Mr. Apology, with something like Mitya's anguished words during his interrogation: this is a confession, handle with care.

3

THE OVERBORNE WILL — A CASE STUDY

*Neither the body nor mind of an accused may be twisted
until he breaks.*

Justice Frankfurter, in *Culombe v. Connecticut*

Five years before *Miranda v. Arizona,* the Supreme Court attempted
an earlier resolution of the problem of police interrogation and confession in *Culombe v. Connecticut,* a case in many ways more thoughtful and interesting than *Miranda* because of the sixty-seven-page
"treatise" written by Justice Felix Frankfurter in the opinion an-
nouncing the judgment of the Court. Frankfurter undertakes to solve
the longstanding problem of how we determine what constitutes a
"voluntary" confession by a criminal suspect under interrogation by
the police. In the absence of physical violence, are there forms of psychological pressure that make the confession coerced or compelled
rather than voluntary? Is the test of voluntariness a legal or a factual
matter, or an admixture of both? How does the characterization "voluntary" square with narratives of arrest and interrogation? Frankfurter's long and closely reasoned analysis of these questions lets us
focus discussion of the problematic status of confession on a concrete
case.[1]

    In his somewhat acid concurring opinion in this case, Chief Jus-
tice Earl Warren notes that the "general principles" enunciated by
Frankfurter are construed by the three dissenting Justices as "requir-

ing a result in this case exactly opposite from that reached by the author of the opinion," and therefore "it cannot be assumed that the lower courts and law enforcement agencies will receive better guidance from the treatise for which this case seems to have provided a vehicle." Warren calls for a better case: "I would prefer not to write on many of the difficult questions which the opinion discusses until the facts of a particular case make such writing necessary" (636). The better case would come with *Miranda,* where Warren will set forth what he hoped would be a clear-cut set of "rules" for judging the valid confession, admissible in evidence. *Miranda* establishes formal threshold conditions for voluntariness in its well-known "warnings." If the suspect thus forewarned does confess, his confession will be presumed voluntary; if the police fail to warn, the confession will be presumed coerced. Thus *Miranda* provides a ritual intended to cleanse confessions of the taint of coercion. One may have doubts, as I have already suggested, whether an approach by way of the formal conditions of confession can ever get to the essence of confession, its voluntariness or compulsion, especially since *Miranda* does not seem to have diminished the police's ability to induce suspects to talk.

One must, however, agree with Warren that Frankfurter's opinion in *Culombe* fails in its intention "of establishing a set of principles which could be easily applied in any coerced-confession situation." But despite (or perhaps because of) this failure, Frankfurter's treatise appears to me one of the most interesting and honest attempts to think through the problem of voluntariness versus compulsion or coercion in the production of a confession from a suspect. Frankfurter's careful, meditative narrative of Arthur Culombe's experience at the hands of the Connecticut State Police (and the New Britain police) and his attempt to match this narrative to normative as well as legal standards of the voluntary versus the coerced, make his opinion, for all its decorous sobriety, something that might not be disavowed by a Dostoevsky or a Céline.

We begin on December 15, 1956, at Kurp's Gas Station in New Britain, with two corpses: Edward Kurpiewski, the owner, and Daniel Janowski, a customer, both shot in the head. The perpetrator has vanished. The only surviving eyewitness, in Janowski's car parked at the pumps, is Janowski's daughter. She is unharmed. She is eighteen months old. The shootings at Kurp's were not the first in the area; they appeared to belong to a series of unsolved violent crimes, but the local and state police forces had made no progress in their investigations. There seemed to be no clues. Even when the investigation had begun to focus on Arthur Culombe and his pal Joseph Taborksy, it was only Culombe's eventual confession that would lead to indictment of the two men. Taborsky then also confessed. Their trial and conviction for first degree murder thus was entirely dependent on the confessions, the introduction of which at trial was objected to by defense counsel on the grounds that they were extracted from the defendants by police methods that violated the Fourteenth Amendment's due process voluntariness test.

Frankfurter goes at once to the heart of the matter when he notes the characteristic problem that these murders present: "offenses frequently occur about which things cannot be made to speak" (571). With no evidence and no witnesses, the only recourse of the police is to seek out those who know about the crime precisely because they are implicated in it—and to get them to confess. On the one hand, then, the questioning of suspects is recognized to be "indispensable to crime detection." On the other hand stands a society "strongly and constitutionally committed to the principle that persons accused of crime cannot be made to convict themselves out of their own mouths"—the rights entailed by the long and complex history of the privilege against self-incrimination. Frankfurter alludes rapidly to the fact that interrogation of suspects, in the United States today, has become a matter for the police (rather than, for instance, a committing magistrate) and that much police interrogation involves taking suspects into custody, a practice of dubious legality that has nonetheless become standard. "What actually happens to them [suspects] behind the closed door of the interrogation room is difficult if not impossible to ascertain" (573–74). Five years later, Warren's opinion in *Miranda* makes a concerted effort to pry open that closed door and to bring to light of day the dramas of fear, dependency, and psychological duress played out in the interrogation room, arguing the conclusion that custodial interrogation is "inherently" coercive.

Frankfurter's consideration of confession by suspects in custody proceeds by way of a kind of dialectical balancing. On the one hand, the suspect in custody, deprived of familiar surroundings and dependent on the will of his interrogator, comes to believe that the interrogator expects an answer, will not cease until there is an answer, and thus becomes "the unwilling collaborator in establishing his guilt" (575). On the other hand,

> a confession made by a person in custody is not always the result of an overborne will. The police may be midwife to a declaration naturally born of remorse, or relief, or desperation, or calculation. If that is so, if the "suction process" has not been at the prisoner and drained his capacity for freedom of choice, does not the awful responsibility of the police for maintaining the peaceful order of society justify the means which they have employed? (576)

Here are some curious terms to work with: an "overborne will," as opposed (by a process of echoing?) to "a declaration naturally born of remorse" (with the police as midwife); a "suction process" (Frankfurter here refers us in a footnote to his own opinion in *Watts v. Indiana* [1949]) that might drain one's "capacity for choice" (as if the will were a fluid). In the contest set up in the police versus the suspect, it is fairly obvious who the police are and what they want. It's much less clear who the suspect is, how he is to be conceived, what conception we are to have of his "will" and what we are to understand by his "freedom of choice."

What's so interestingly at stake in Frankfurter's *Culombe* opinion is our conception of the individual in the face of the law and the state and the analytic language we use to describe and define personhood in such a situation. The legal scholar Robert Weisberg has written:

> The jurisprudence of the Fifth Amendment directly raises the question raised indirectly by searches and seizures: What image of the autonomous human being do we believe in? . . . We have no coherent analysis of what it means to be autonomous in the face of the law, and we are left instead with shallow rationalizations about the psychology of volition, abetted in the Sixth Amendment area by hilarious rationalizations about the effects of the invisible formalities of state prosecution on the volition of a poor wretch of a subject.[2]

If Weisberg is right, we seem to have little basis on which to answer crucial questions. Frankfurter's opinion very much wants to answer these questions. It sets forth to do so with a conceptual armament including such items as the "overborne will," the "suction process," and "freedom of choice" and the admonition that, consistent with the Fourteenth Amendment, "neither the body nor mind of an accused may be twisted until he breaks" (584).[3]

We know what a body twisted until it breaks looks like. The body broken on the rack is our very emblem of inquisition, torture, coerced statement, of everything we believe American law abhors and disallows. What about a mind that is twisted until it breaks? How can we know that has happened? What is our test? "The ultimate test," writes Frankfurter, "remains that which has been the only clearly established test in Anglo-American courts for two hundred years: the test of voluntariness" (602). In glossing voluntariness, Frankfurter returns to the conceptual tools mentioned above:

> Is the confession the product of an essentially free and uncon-strained choice by its maker? If it is, if he has willed to confess, it may be used against him. If it is not, if his will has been over-borne and his capacity for self-determination critically im-paired, the use of his confession offends due process. . . . The line of distinction is that at which governing self-direction is lost and compulsion, of whatever nature or however infused, pro-pels or helps to propel the confession. (602; citation omitted)

Voluntariness thus means to Frankfurter the exercise of the will in an act of free, unconstrained choice. The admissible confession must be the willed confession, a speech act in which the choice to speak and the enunciation itself line up in an unambiguous way. If this is not the nature of the speech act—if free choice has been constrained or im-paired, the will overborne—then the confession is compelled. The line between voluntary and involuntary is to be sought where "gov-erning self-direction is lost" and then, in its place, some element of compulsion "propels" the confession. The only admissible confession, we might say, is that offered by an autonomous human agent uncon-strained in his or her choices—a very high standard, not only because Culombe is of limited mental capacity (considered in expert testi-mony to be a "high moron" with an IQ of sixty-four and a mental age of about nine) but because, as I have argued in previous chapters, con-fession rarely appears to occur without some form of constraint "pro-pelling" its utterance. The Court's standard of voluntariness—restated in 1985 that the confession must be the product of a "free and rational will"—is nobly high and, for that very reason, of difficult application to the realities of criminal justice, whose actors rarely seem to live up to the standards of autonomy and rationality enunciated here.

Frankfurter is aware that his high principles need translation into a discovery procedure for determining the presence or absence of voluntariness in a given instance. He sees the need for a "three-phased process": first, finding "the crude historical facts," that is, the external circumstances and events surrounding the confession; then, "because the concept of 'voluntariness' is one which concerns a mental state, there is the imaginative recreation, largely inferential, of internal 'psychological' fact"; finally, the application to this psychological fact of legal standards of judgment, the "rules of law" that involve also "induction from, and anticipation of, factual circumstances" (603). Thus he must determine the historical facts, recreate a psychological condition, and read these findings through the grid of the law. At an appellate level, the events of the story are part of the record passed on from the jury trial. They are unalterable. To use the analytic language of Russian Formalism, there is no fooling with the *fabula,* the story events, at this point in the process of adjudication. A moment's reflection on the analysis of narrative tells us, though, that the *fabula,* the way things happened "in reality," will inevitably be inflected by the *sjužet,* by the manner of its telling, by its presentation and interpretation, by the "point" given to it. And that *sjužet* itself, the presentational aspect of the narrative, is a complex interweaving of parts two and three of the process Frankfurter describes.

His analysis of the problem is quite remarkable. The second and third phases of the inquiry are "inextricably interwoven."

> This is so, in part, because the concepts by which language expresses an otherwise unrepresentable mental reality are themselves generalizations importing preconceptions about the reality to be expressed. It is so, also, because the apprehension of mental states is almost invariably a matter of induction, more or less imprecise, and the margin of error which is thus introduced into the finding of "fact" must be accounted for in the formulation and application of the "rule" designed to cope with such classes of facts. (604)

One can imagine Earl Warren throwing up his hands at this moment of his colleague's "treatise": go tell the New Britain police about the way language imports preconceptions about the unrepresentable mental realities it attempts to express! While never leaving the language of Enlightenment psychology, Frankfurter here performs a nearly Nietzschean or "deconstructive" gesture toward it, one that of course had been performed within classical psychology by Pascal, for instance, who argued that our linguistic instruments are too blunt ever to touch the truth.[4] Frankfurter's language of the will, freedom of choice, and the mind possibly twisted until it breaks, is shown in Frankfurter's own analysis to be a set of inadequate metaphors in approach to the unrepresentable.

Frankfurter now comes to heart of the matter:

> The notion of "voluntariness" is itself an amphibian. It purports at once to describe an internal psychic state and to characterize that state for legal purposes. Since the characterization is the very issue "to review which this Court sits" . . . , the matter of description, too, is necessarily open here. (605; citations omitted)

The notion of voluntariness lives on land and in the water, like the salamander, and perhaps with the same legendary capacity to survive. If voluntariness is a term of legal art, when used as a term of psychological analysis there is the possibility it will import some legal preconceptions about the reality to be expressed. The opposite importation is conceivable as well, as in cases where courts have struggled to deal with essentially psychological notions, such as "repression" and "recovered memory," in legal terms, as we shall have occasion to see in a later chapter. But most often the law would seem to be in the position of translating the psychological milieu of the amphibian into the legal one in order to reach a judgment, which is its purpose.

The law of course must deal with other "amphibian" concepts—such as "intent" or "consent"—that are half psychological and half legal, but the notion of voluntariness, as thoughtful commentators over the years have noticed, is a particularly troubling one. To cite a critic of *Miranda* who represents a fairly hard-line position on interrogation and confession, Joseph D. Grano in *Confessions, Truth, and the Law* notes that the "fairness limitations on police interrogation" must "stem from a conviction that while we want the police to succeed in ascertaining the truth, our morality places limits on the means that may be used to achieve this end. Respect for the individual, as an individual, as a member of humanity, yields limits on what will be permitted in the otherwise laudable search for truth."[5] Violent means of interrogation, for instance, infringe "broadly shared community beliefs concerning the inherent dignity and autonomy of human beings" (101). These statements strike me as generally accurate, and a fair brief summary of the motivations that led to the exclusion of compelled testimony and coerced confessions. It is not only that the coerced confession may be untrustworthy (a false confession) but also that the means of production of a confession—even of the truth—may violate our sense that individuals before the law, even as criminal suspects, must be conceived as autonomous human subjects.

The problem may be that the very act of confessing will so often be the product of a situation, a set of physical conditions, a psychological state that do not conduce to the fullest expression of human autonomy and dignity. It is indeed arguable that confession most often is produced from a state of dependency and abjection rather than from one of autonomy and dignity. This would seem to have been the reason ancient Talmudic law barred confessions in a criminal case. In the eloquent commentary of Maimonides:

> It is a scriptural decree that the court shall not put a man to death or flog him on his own admission [of guilt]. . . . For it is possible that he was confused in mind when he made the confession. Perhaps he was one of those who are in misery, bitter in soul, who long for death, thrust the sword into their bellies or cast themselves down from the roofs. Perhaps this was the reason that prompted him to confess to a crime he had not committed, in order that he be put to death. To sum up the matter, the principle that no man is to be declared guilty on his own admission is a divine decree.[6]

The Talmudic *Halakhah* in fact is cited in *Miranda,* and then again by Justice William O. Douglas in *Garrity v. New Jersey,* with the comment that "it discards confessions in toto, and this because of its psychological insight and its concern for saving man from his own destructive inclinations."[7] Confession in this view is contrary to the basic human will to self-preservation, and hence evidence of a sick soul, bent on self-destruction.

Certainly both the religious and literary traditions of confession would tend to confirm such a view of the motives of confessing. The Roman Catholic Church has taught, at least since the Council of

Trent (1551), that confession is necessary to the salvation of one's soul; it is a purgation through articulation and penitence, which of course implies that there is impurity to be purged, a state of soul-sickness needing cure. From Saint Augustine onwards, writers of personal confessions have claimed the need to expose their state of sin and error in order regain the path of righteousness. Often, as in the case of Jean-Jacques Rousseau, confession can appear an act of defiance and challenge to one's fellows, designed to implicate them as equally guilty of shameful acts, equally in need of the courage to confess. Rousseau's example, decisive for the modern confessional tradition, makes it explicit that the test of the "true confession" is not only the revelation of sin and crime—as in the episode of the "stolen ribbon" and the false accusation of the innocent Marion—but also, and even more, the confession of abject, unavowable, "unhealthy" behavior and inclinations, as in the exposure of his self-exposure in Turin. It is in connection with his avowal of his first experience of masochistic sexual pleasure that Rousseau comments, "I have made the first and most painful step in the dark and slimy maze of my confessions. It is not crimes that cost the most to speak, but what is ridiculous and shameful."[8]

Throughout the nineteenth and twentieth centuries, the confessional mode flourishes, and nearly always it promises revelation of the shameful, the abject, that which is normally covered over and repressed in polite or official social intercourse. The most telling examples may occur in the work of Dostoevsky. If Dimitri Karamazov's many-layered confession under interrogation (discussed in the last chapter) reveals a complex state of abjection combined with defiance, the master of the abject confession—confession from abjection, confession of abjection—is no doubt his father, Fyodor Pavlovich Karamazov, whose whole mode is one of both calculated and uncontrollable self-abasement:

> "Your reverence," he exclaimed with a sort of instant pathos, "you see before you a buffoon! Verily, a buffoon! Thus I introduce myself! It's an old habit, alas! And if I sometimes tell lies inappropriately, I do it even on purpose, on purpose to be pleasant and make people laugh. . . . I'm a natural-born buffoon, I am, reverend father, just like a holy fool; I won't deny that there's maybe an unclean spirit living in me, too, not a very high

caliber one, by the way, otherwise he would have chosen grander quarters, only not you, Pyotr Alexandrovich, your quarters are none too grand either. . . ."[9]

This sample from the first of many "scenes" created by old Karamazov (this one in the monastery) gives only a faint sense of the layers of self-exposure—often serving to the exposure of others as well—in the staging of a confessional mode that both is highly concerted and cannot be helped.

I mean in this too brief evocation of the Dostoevskian confessional mode—Meyerhold's tortured confession from a sense that punishment is his due offers another example—to suggest how the search for the true confession, the moment of baring of the soul, may uncover that moment as one of human abjection. Telling the shameful truth may reap all sorts of psycho-social benefits, including the implication of others in equal shame, but it does not necessarily promote an image of human autonomy and dignity. On the contrary, it reveals pathetic dependency and a kind of infantile groveling, which is entirely consonant with Theodor Reik's psychoanalytic study of confession, which sees in confession a call for punishment, a plea to a parental figure to punish the child in order that the child may be reintegrated into parental love.[10] Even the most indisputably "voluntary" confession may arise from a state of dependency, shame, and the need for punishment, a condition that casts some doubt on the law's language of autonomy and free choice. Thus the act of confessing may in its very nature undercut the notion of human agency that the law wishes to—and must—promote.

One view of the development of the privilege against self-incrimination is that it offers a protection against the Dostoevskian form of self-abasement in confession. The history and interpretation of the privilege are exceedingly complicated and contentious. A number of constitutional scholars have found it anomalous, contrary to everyday morality (which urges and often rewards full disclosure), and difficult to square with the history of trials in England and America, which until the late eighteenth century generally forbade defense counsel and thus made the accused's own testimony his only means of defense.[11] The privilege against self-incrimination extends beyond the simple exclusion of testimony that may be unreliable because coerced; it also includes testimony that is undoubtedly reliable but nonetheless cannot be coerced. There have indeed been calls to rescind the privilege. As I noted earlier, the privilege, famously summed up in the phrase *nemo tenetur seipsum prodere* and incorporated into the Constitution in the Fifth Amendment, seems to have developed, in its proto-modern form, in the context of state trials for treason and heresy in Elizabethan England, particularly by the Court of High Commission (the ecclesiastical counterpart of Star Chamber), and to apply exclusively to testimony compelled *under oath*. The oath is of crucial importance, since—to an age that invested more divine *tremendum* in the oath than we do today—it meant that the accused either had to speak (and thus call down human punishment upon himself) or else to lie and incur God's wrath and possibly eternal punishment.

Thus certainly one of the deep motives of the privilege was the protection of what R. H. Helmholz calls "something akin to the modern right of privacy. There was a sphere of life into which the public authorities, whether from church or state, were not entitled to enter."[12] When in the case of Thomas Edwards, in 1609, Lord High Justice Sir Edward Coke granted a "prohibition," removing the case from the ecclesiastical courts, he commented: "the Ecclesiastical Judge cannot examine any man upon his oath, upon the intention and thought of his heart, for *cogitationis poenam nemo emeret* [no man may be punished for his thought]." That is, interrogation under oath must not enter the private realm of belief and thought. Coke continues (I have cited this passage before, but it bears repetition): "And in cases where a man is to be examined upon his oath, he ought to be examined upon acts or words, and not of the intention or thought of his heart; and if any man should be examined upon any point of religion, he is not bound to answer the same; for in time of danger, *quis modus tutus erit* [how will he be safe] if everyone should be examined of his thoughts ... for it hath been said in the proverb, *thought is free.*"[13] To be forced under sacred oath to reveal the intentions or thoughts of the heart, to paraphrase Coke's eloquent words, appeared early in our legal and cultural history as a basic violation of human autonomy and dignity.

The privilege against self-incrimination—gradually extended from its original context to apply in all criminal procedure—thus stands opposed to the violation of the compelled confession, and may perhaps be conceived as a kind of redress of the human abjection associated with the scene of confession. It expresses a concern not only for the content of the confession (true or false) but also for its context of production (free or forced). Whether praised as a cornerstone of liberty by liberals, by Chief Justice Warren in *Miranda,* for instance, or condemned by conservatives as an anomaly needing correction, the privilege appears as a kind of joker in the legal deck.[14] The oddity that many commentators have found in the privilege—its seeming dissonance with the rest of legal procedure, its willful promotion of an obstruction of justice—may in part be explainable by its role as redress, as a kind of instinctual counterbalancing to the law's search for total disclosure. It's as if the law instinctively feared, found repugnant, the kind of abject confession practiced by old Karamazov.

The law wants and needs a model of human agents as free and rational decision-makers, even in the confession of guilt. So if we return to Frankfurter's language in *Culombe,* perhaps the slightly quaint notion of the "overborne will" makes sense. Not, to be sure, because it is susceptible to conclusive philosophical analysis: I recall that Milton's fallen angels were last seen debating such issues, which have been with us at least since Aristotle.[15] Judge Richard Posner has asserted in *United States v. Rutledge* that "the faculty of will approach . . . leads nowhere"; and Joseph Grano concludes his review of discussions of the issue as follows: "This analysis suggests that it probably would be best for the courts to drop the overborne will language not only in the law of confessions but in other legal contexts as well. Given the absence of an analytic construct of the will as an entity that can be coerced, the term arguably adds nothing, other than confusion, to our efforts to solve concrete problems."[16] Agreed, and yet the slightly fastidious and wholly Victorian image of the will and its overbearing may at least indicate the desirable ethical attitude to bring to the story of a suspect's interrogation and confession.

The question for Frankfurter, following his discussion of principles of analysis, then becomes: how do we know when a will has been overborne? What does this mean? If voluntariness is an "amphibian," its legal habitat must be derived from its mental habitat, and this can only be intuited externally. Frankfurter writes that "the mental state of involuntariness upon which the due process question turns can never be affirmatively established other than circumstantially—that is, by inference" (605). Establishing whether or not Culombe confessed voluntarily then means taking "the totality of the relevant circumstances" and drawing an inference from them. As Frankfurter now proceeds into the facts of the case, it is evident that the process of inference can only be a narrative one. It is the story of Culombe's interrogation that is the center of attention.

We have, then, a narrative unfolded in order to be able to stipulate at what moment Culombe's will could be said to be overborne: the nodal moment at which free will, free determination, passed over into compulsion—the narrative, one might say, of the mind twisted to that moment where it breaks. The narrative unfolds over fifteen pages of the U.S. Reports—a considerable length, when one considers that at the level of the Supreme Court "the facts of the case" often are disposed of very briefly, sometimes in a mere footnote (see *Miranda* for an example). But here the time covered in the narrative is of prime importance. Culombe was taken into custody at about 2:30 P.M. on Saturday, February 23, 1957 (he would never again be out of police control), and brought to State Police headquarters in Hartford. There then began a picaresque junket, always in police custody, to the scenes of various unsolved crimes, complete with meals at diners, visits to Culombe's home to look for guns, and with interrogation of the suspect pursued intermittently, both at headquarters and on the road. Culombe at one point asked to see a lawyer, whereupon Lieutenant Rome (in charge of the investigation) proposed a telephone directory, to call any lawyer he wanted, knowing that the illiterate Culombe could not use a phone book.[17] About 10 P.M. on Saturday night, Rome put Culombe under arrest. Since this warrantless arrest didn't yet have any demonstrable probable cause behind it, on Monday Culombe was taken to New Britain, and booked with the local police for breach of the peace. Interrogation continued, on and off, sometimes for considerable periods of time. On Tuesday, Culombe was brought to New Britain Police Court to be presented on the breach of the peace charge; he was penned with Taborsky in a wire defendant's cage; he was not allowed to plead, he was not brought before the bench; the court granted Lieutenant Rome's request for a week's continuance, and issued a writ of mittimus committing Culombe to the Hartford County Jail.

The breach of the peace charge, and the delay in presenting the suspect in court, were of course—as Rome admitted during trial—a dodge to gain more time for custodial interrogation of the suspect. Interrogation continued Tuesday afternoon. Then Rome visited Culombe's wife and brought her and the children back to headquarters where, at Rome's urging, she asked Culombe to tell the police the truth. Rome also tried to get Culombe's thirteen-year-old-daughter to talk about conversations between Culombe and Taborsky. This family scene left Culombe sobbing. Interrogation began again Wednesday morning at 10 A.M. By 3:30 in the afternoon, he agreed to show the police some guns hidden in his home, and during the drive there, under interrogation by Rome in the back seat of the car, made a partial confession: admitting to participation in Kurp's robbery, but blaming the shootings on Taborsky. Back at police headquarters, Major Remer and Commissioner Kelly were brought in to hear Culombe repeat what he had confessed to. Then, after dinner, there was another visit from Mrs. Culombe, accompanied by their five-year-old child, who was sick (and in fact had to be taken to the hospital that night with mumps). At 8 P.M., Rome returned with his associates to put Culombe's oral confessions into writing.

The process of making Culombe's rambling oral confessions into a coherent written narrative went as follows: "Rome questioned Culombe; Culombe answered; Rome transposed the answer into narrative form; Culombe agreed to it; Rome dictated the phrase or sentence to O'Brien. Each completed statement was read to and signed by Culombe" (616–17). This compositional process took four and a half hours. Frankfurter will underline that Culombe "agreed to the composition of a statement that was not even cast in his own words" (634). It must be said, though, that this is probably true, more or less, for most confessions of criminal suspects, who are not the first-hand authors of their confessional statements. Confessions of guilt are normally "as told to," indited by another hand and then presented to the suspect for signature. In *Escobedo v. Illinois,* we learn that the homicide squad employs an "experienced lawyer" who is summoned to "take statements" from suspects, and who "'took' petitioner's [Escobedo's] statement," making sure it fell into the correct legal form.[18] Warren in *Miranda* protests that police interrogation is designed to make the suspect confirm "the preconceived story the police seek to have him describe." Even though we may be fully persuaded of Culombe's guilt, the narrative written in his name—signed by him— is an alienated production. It is, in the manner of Freud's construction of the Wolf Man's infantile history or the construction of the story of Thomas Sutpen by Quentin Compson and Shreve McCannon in Faulkner's *Absalom, Absalom!* a plausible conjecture that will never be confirmed in the subject's own words.

In fact, it turns out that the signed "Wednesday-midnight" confession is false in a very important way. On Saturday, March 2, at 10 P.M., Culombe in his cell called to his guard and said he wanted to tell him something. He then proceeded to tell a new version of what happened at Kurp's, a version in which he, not Taborsky, shot Kurpiewski. So Sunday morning there was held a new compositional session, resulting in a new narrative signed by Culombe. Later that day, court-appointed counsel (Culombe had finally been formally charged in Superior Court on Thursday, provided counsel, and told of his right to remain silent) instructed Culombe not to sign any further statements, and told the police to cease interrogation. Nonetheless, Rome appeared the next day with still a new typescript (deleting references made in the Wednesday confession to a separate crime), and Culombe signed it.

"On all the circumstances of this record," Frankfurter concludes his narrative account, "we are compelled to conclude that these confessions were not voluntary" (621). I cannot determine whether Frankfurter's "compelled to conclude"—suggesting that he too is faced with a case of compelled rather than voluntary confession—is artful rhetoric or inadvertent tic, a contamination of his prose by the atmosphere of generalized compulsion (in the manner that all those who share the law office with Bartleby start using "prefer" in their speech, in Melville's novella).[19] Whether voluntary or involuntary, the use of "compelled to conclude" is effective, suggesting that the facts of the case admit of only one generic label: this is the story of compulsion, not free choice. The Court is constrained, like it or not, to reverse Culombe's conviction. The final pages of Frankfurter's opinion will rehearse the narrative again in the light of legal precedents, stressing all those elements that conduce toward the conclusion of compulsion. Near the conclusion he writes:

> It is clear that this man's will was broken Wednesday afternoon. It is no less clear that his will was broken Wednesday night when, after several hours in a car with four policemen, two interviews with his wife and his apparently ill child, further inquiries made of him in the presence of the Police Commissioner, and a four-and-a-half-hour session which left him (by police testimony) "tired," he agreed to the composition of a statement that was not even cast in his own words. . . . Neither the Wednesday-

afternoon nor the Wednesday-midnight statement may be proved against Culombe, and he convicted by their use, consistently with the Constitution. (634–35)

The result of Frankfurter's careful narrative, then, has been to locate the precise moment when Culombe's will was "overborne," was "broken." It was Wednesday afternoon, after more than four days of interrogation; the point in time is confirmed by the Wednesday midnight confession. By Wednesday afternoon, Culombe is no longer a rational decision-maker, no longer an autonomous human agent.

I admire Frankfurter's careful and humane reconstruction of the narrative of compulsion. It constitutes a high act of the imagination which, for all the judicial neutrality of the prose, conveys through inference and implication the overwhelming pressures on Culombe to confirm to the police a story they claim already to know. And I am fully ready to agree with Frankfurter that by Wednesday afternoon Culombe's will has been overborne. Yet it must be said that this determination is a bit like claiming to know at what moment Oedipus's fate, in Sophocles' play, becomes inevitable, or at what moment Macbeth becomes a villain. In retrospect—and narrative meanings are retrospective—can we imagine that Culombe's will was not fated to be overborne? A mentally retarded man linked to several shootings seems about as inevitably doomed as a Dostoevsky character: the police were bound to get him, sooner or later. And his confessions, however obtained, joined to the circumstantial evidence, suggest that he was indeed guilty of the crime committed at Kurp's. Should one then view his Wednesday confessions as does Justice John Marshall Harlan in dissent (joined by Clark and Whittaker), as "the product of a deliberate choice on his part to try to ameliorate his fate by making a clean breast of things, and not the consequence of improper police activity" (642)? Alternatively, should one accept the claim—made by Justice William Brennan concurring in the result, along with Warren and Black—that not merely the Wednesday statements but all the confessions made by Culombe were coerced and therefore inadmissible in evidence?

Between the "overborne will" and the "clean breast"—both punctually arriving on Wednesday—the choice must be made according to one's narrative judgment and ideological preconceptions. The situation of judgment concerning the voluntariness of Culombe's confession is not without analogies to the problem of consent in charges of rape. "Consent," too, is an "amphibian," in that the term characterizes a psychological condition or state and a legal threshold, and the latter can only be properly applied if you understand the former, for which external evidence may be only tenuous. What I think may be most peculiar about voluntariness in the confessional situation is the paradoxical conditions created for it by the law. On the one hand, the Court's insistence that the subject's will remain free, uncoerced; on the other hand all the efforts of police interrogators to break the will. The law itself, in its principles and its exercise, seems to be pulling in two different directions. The effort to produce the confessional truth would seem, in very many cases, to produce as the very condition of its production a state of abjection that undercuts the very claim of voluntariness on which the definition of truth reposes, and, beyond that, the very notion of human agency that the law must promote in order to do its judging.

The problem at least in part lies in confession, both the word and the action. The very model of confession is the slipperiest amphibian one can find. Consider Joseph Grano's discussion of why, among the arsenal of police interrogation tactics society should find permissible—and he wants to give very broad scope to these tactics— impersonation of the defense lawyer or the priest by the police falls beyond the pale: "Police impersonation of a defense lawyer or a member of the clergy would necessarily intrude on the special trust that individuals place in such professional people for the confidentiality of communications, a trust that our law broadly seeks to encourage."[20] Our law, and our society, see value in protecting the confidentiality of such relationships—and also, with some greater ambiguity, those with physicians and psychotherapists—because it is considered good for people to communicate fully and unreservedly with such professionals. In the case of the attorney-client privilege, the justification is one within legal process itself. In the case of the priest or the psychotherapist, the justification must be that baring one's soul to such people is good for the individual's spiritual or psychic well-being, and thus, as a result, for society as a whole.

The problem may be that police interrogation comes too close to these "benign" models of confessional communication. Consider such a case as *Miller v. Fenton,* where the police interrogator promised suspect Miller that he would get him psychiatric help if he talked, telling him that he was sick rather than a criminal.[21] This comes close—too close, for the Court—to impersonation. Consider the more difficult case of *Arizona v. Fulminante,* where an FBI informant in prison with Fulminante promised the suspect that he would protect him from other prisoners—out to get him because he's considered to have murdered his stepdaughter—but can do so only if Fulminante tells him the whole story of what really happened.[22] These cases merely point to what the police interrogation manuals make clear: that effective interrogation depends on creating a situation of dependency where "making a clean breast" of the matter is elicited by the situation itself. The suspect is in a locked interrogation room. His fate depends on propitiating the interrogator. He is told that things will go better for him if he tells everything, that of course he may remain silent but inevitably that will look suspicious. Above all, he is told in all sorts of ways that his release from the situation of constraint in which he finds himself can only come through full confession—as with the release from sin in religious confession, or the release from psychic anxiety in the psychotherapeutic dialogue.

To cite again David Simon in *Homicide:* "The fraud that claims it is somehow in a suspect's interest to talk with the police will forever be the catalyst in any criminal interrogation. It is a fiction propped up against the greater weight of logic itself, sustained for hours on end through nothing more or less than a detective's ability to control the interrogation room."[23] The "ability to control the interrogation room" is in some measure the ability to make it a confessional, a place where the revelation of secrets must take place. "The subject . . . may tell his story more readily if he feels that the investigator understands his helplessness," says Charles E. O'Hara in *Fundamentals of Criminal Investigation.*[24] To the extent that police interrogators can—and do—get suspects to break silence and begin talking, they have established the transferential situation in which confession takes place. They are able to exploit the range of meanings we assign to "confession," thus cashing in on that "fraud" that claims it is in the suspect's interest to confess.

The religious model of confession, which, I will argue in the next chapter, appears fundamental to other, later, versions, itself includes an element of "policing." An historian of religion has called confession a "system of discipline and consolation."[25] The disciplinary function has been discussed by Michel Foucault in his history of sexuality:

confession (*l'aveu*) is one of the large exercises of power on the individual by those seeking to order and control individuals within the social structure. "The individual was for ages authenticated by reference to others and by making manifest his ties to others (family, allegiance, protectors); then he began to be authenticated by the discourse of truth that he was able or obliged to proffer about himself. Power inscribes the confession of truth at the heart of its procedures of individualization."[26] When one recalls that the Fourth Lateran Council, in 1215, at once defines the elements of orthodox Christian belief and imposes, for the first time, the requirement of yearly confession, and also institutes an inquisition for the eradication of heresy, it becomes clear that the confession of sin and error has for centuries been used both to console and to discipline, and thus that criminal interrogation with the intent to produce confession further exploits a transferential situation already fraught with ambiguities. Yet in the religious context, the confessant's words are nonetheless placed under "the seal of confession," considered to be absolute, and thus cannot be divulged to do him harm; disciplining works through the direction of conscience. The situation in the "interview room"—the euphemism is not irrelevant—is in this regard entirely different, and the confessional analogue indeed fraudulent.

In his concurring opinion in *Culombe,* Justice Douglas charges that in order to evade the right against self-incrimination available in the courtroom, American police forces have set up a system of pretrial "administrative detention that has no constitutional justification" (639–40). He notes that "a son of a wealthy or prominent person" in Culombe's situation would have demanded and received legal counsel, to comment: "The system of police interrogation under secret detention falls heaviest on the weak and illiterate—the least articulate segments of our society" (641). Douglas's remedy is to insert legal counsel for the suspect into the interrogation process, thus providing another authority figure, this one actually working to protect the suspect rather than to promote the "fraud" that he should speak. Douglas thus looks forward to *Massiah v. United States,* which in 1964 will extend the Sixth Amendment right to counsel to pretrial custody after the suspect has been charged. Then *Miranda* will of course explicitly extend the Fifth Amendment privilege against self-incrimination to all custodial interrogation, and attempt, through the warnings that must be given before interrogation begins, to break the situation of abject dependency, to empower the suspect to maintain his will from being overborne.

There is persuasive evidence, I noted earlier, that *Miranda* has not stopped suspects from talking, that they often waive their right to counsel, and that they continue to sign confessions composed by their interrogators. As Albert W. Alschuler writes in a recent discussion of the privilege against self-incrimination, "92 percent of all felony convictions in the United States are by guilty plea," whether by confessions—made often on "waiver" of *Miranda* rights—or in plea bargains. "Few other nations are as dependent as ours on proving guilt from a defendant's own mouth."[27] One can have different reactions to this, the most common no doubt being: Well and good, we want the guilty to confess. Yet the problem of waivers simply makes the problem of the overborne will regress to another stage: how do we know that a suspect voluntarily waived his rights? And the high use of the plea bargain raises a host of disturbing issues: the plea bargain usually involves a confession of guilt of an admittedly fictional sort, a pleading to a lesser crime than one is held to be guilty of, on the assurance that if the case were to go to trial, more severe punishment would be in store. The context of the plea bargain is almost always one of clear constraint: if you don't own up to commission of the crime, we will prove you guilty and impose worse sanctions. Since most plea bargains receive only the most cursory inspection by a judge—who is supposed to assure himself that they have been "voluntarily" entered into—they constitute an area where police extortion of confession can proceed nearly unchecked.[28] Consider the statement of the defendant in *North Carolina v. Alford* (1970), who told the judge: "I pleaded guilty on second degree murder because they said there is too much evidence, but I ain't shot no man. . . . I just pleaded guilty because they said if I didn't they would gas me for it. . . . I'm not guilty but I plead guilty."[29] The Supreme Court found this plea bargain acceptable.

One can, I think, have some sympathy with the view expressed by Grano (among others) that the Supreme Court debates about voluntariness and how to know it have offered the wrong forum for addressing the true issues, which concern the rules of pretrial police interrogation. These procedures are part of a system largely elaborated by police forces themselves as they emerged into their modern form and responsibilities, a system entirely unknown to the Framers of the Constitution. "[I]t is quite arguable that the *Miranda* approach . . . has contributed to the failure to adopt more specific rules in the United States. As Professor Mark Berger has observed, '[t]he constitutional law focus of the American confession law debate has diverted attention from the substantive police interrogation issues that society should address.'"[30] That is, a thoughtful legislation of pretrial interrogation and its conditions and actors—including, perhaps, representatives of the law other than police officers—might offer a better approach. What this view leaves out, of course, is American society's failure to address these issues in an intelligent legislative way ("crime bills" tend to be "law and order" political messages) and thus the necessity of the Supreme Court's search for contexts and concepts to reach the pretrial interrogation.

What the failures to legislate rules of police conduct of interrogation suggest most to me is something akin to the point made by Robert Weisberg when he complains that "we have no coherent analysis of what it means to be autonomous in the face of the law, and we are left instead with shallow rationalizations about the psychology of volition. . . ." We have no analytic consensus on what we want the criminal suspect to be as human agent. It's not likely that we could reach such a consensus, given the profoundly divergent views of human nature and polity activated in criminal justice. There is indeed notably little public debate about the normative status we choose to confer on suspects before the law. That we continue to encourage the police to obtain confessions wherever possible implies a nearly Dostoevskian model of the criminal suspect: Frankfurter's language in *Culombe* to the contrary, we want his mind to break, we want him to break down and confess, we want and need his abjection since this is the best guarantee that he needs punishment, and that in punishing him our consciences are clear. That we on the contrary insist that the suspect's will must not be overborne, that he be a conscious agent of his undoing, of course implies the opposite, that we don't want Dostoevskian groveling in the interrogation room, but the voluntary (manly?) assumption of guilt. Hence the paradox of the confession that must be called voluntary while everything conduces to assure that it is not. Hence a kind of linguistic repression, in the conceptual language of the law, of what it otherwise may know to be true.

The conceptual language of the law thus appears to be curiously archaic though no doubt necessarily so. In order to adjudicate and to punish, the law must assume human moral agency, unless clearly disabled (the "insanity" plea) or subjected to forces beyond control. The "overborne will" and its cognates, however, appear excessively distant from the realities of what transpires in the interrogation room and from the existential experience of such as Arthur Culombe, IQ 64. Criminal procedure in the contemporary United States is largely exercised on the poor, the uneducated, the culturally unassimilated—"the least articulate members of our society," as Douglas says in his *Culombe* opinion—who don't match well to Enlightenment concepts of autonomous agency. In the context of the interrogations and confessions described in this case, and in the many described by Simon in *Homicide,* the language of the overborne will and unconstrained choice seems fastidious to the point of refusal of reality. The language of Dostoevsky and his successors (including Freud) would seem more apposite. But to ask the law to recognize the Dostoevskian nature of the situation might be to disable it entirely. Better, we may say, to live with a fiction in which the Supreme Court debates voluntariness in high-flown abstractions while the police continue to obtain confessions by almost any means, short of physical torture.

I am not able to provide an exit from the impasses of thinking I have evoked here—except to say that they tend to show that we don't really know what we think of confessions or what we want them to be and to do, which should sound an alarm concerning our system's dependence on them. Majorities of the Supreme Court have on the whole agreed that we don't want to eliminate the confession entirely, though Warren, Douglas, and Brennan on occasion sound as if they think this would be the only solution. Let the police find other ways of solving the crime than the "cruel, simple expedient of compelling it from his own mouth," as Warren writes in *Miranda* (384 U.S. at 460). Or at least, insist that confessions made be confirmed by other types of evidence. Greater skepticism about their reliability, and a reduced dependency on their role in crime detection, would in my view be a logical reaction to the uncertainties of confession we have uncovered.

For most of the Supreme Court justices, however, to give up the confession entirely would be to leave too many crimes unsolved and let too many criminals go free. After all, are we not reasonably convinced that most people who confess to crimes actually have committed them, even if the confession involves a certain amount of duress—the position urged with some cogency by, among others, Justice

Robert Jackson, dissenting in *Ashcraft,* and Harlan, dissenting in *Miranda*? Why abandon the avowal of guilt, especially in a society that has made avowal, the assumption of guilt, central to its morality? As Justice Byron White argues in his *Miranda* dissent, confessing may be good for the criminal suspect. "Is it so clear that release is the best thing for him in every case?" he asks. "Has it so unquestionably been resolved that in each and every case it would be better for him not to confess and to return to his environment with no attempt whatsoever to help him? I think not" (543). Even if "help" here really means imprisonment or execution, the purgative model of confession, the model of religious or psychotherapeutic confession, is in command.

The fact remains that our sense of what confession is and does hovers in a zone of uncertainty that has much to do with the multiform nature of confession and its uses for cleansing, amelioration, conversion, counseling, as well as conviction. To argue that "voluntariness" in the case of confessions by criminal suspects should be construed simply as a term of legal art, unconnected to other moral and psychological concepts of the voluntary, seems to me unacceptable. The legal concept reposes on profound social, historical, and ethical considerations of human agency and dignity. The notion of voluntariness, as Frankfurter observes, remains an "amphibian," and we cannot conjure away its ambiguities. If these ambiguities are a problem for the law, they also are useful, since they serve to shield the judges from a full confrontation with the administration of justice. They allow the cathartic uses of confession to pass imperceptibly into the judgmental. "What actually happens to [suspects] behind the closed door of the interrogation room is difficult if not impossible to ascertain," Frankfurter claims in *Culombe.* Despite Warren's effort to open that closed door in *Miranda,* despite his compelling reconstruction through the very manuals used by interrogators of what must be happening there, Frankfurter's remark remains largely true. In most cases of the ordinary dispensation of criminal justice, we don't know. One might simply add to Frankfurter's observation: it's not clear that we want to know. We seem, as a system of justice and perhaps as a society, to have concluded for now that we can live with the ambiguities of confession. They're too useful to give up.

4

CONFESSION, SELFHOOD,

AND THE RELIGIOUS TRADITION

Penance is the absolution of a penitent man, done by
certain words that are pronounced with proper intention
by a priest having jurisdiction, efficaciously signifying by
divine institution the absolution of the soul from sin.

Duns Scotus

When, in Joyce's *Portrait of the Artist as a Young Man,* the director of the Jesuit college where Stephen Dedalus is a student asks Stephen if he feels he has a vocation to the priesthood, the young man's first reaction is to evoke the mystery and power of the confessor:

> He listened in reverent silence now to the priest's appeal and through the words he heard even more distinctly a voice bidding him approach, offering him secret knowledge and secret power. He would know then what was the sin of Simon Magus and what the sin against the Holy Ghost for which there was no forgiveness. He would know obscure things, hidden from others, from those who were conceived and born children of wrath. He would know the sins, the sinful longings and sinful thoughts and sinful acts, of others, hearing them murmured into his ears in the confessional under the shame of a darkened chapel by the lips of women and of girls. . . . He would hold his secret knowledge and secret power, being as sinless as the innocent. . . .[1]

In Stephen Dedalus's temptation to the priesthood, it is above all the secret knowledge of secret sin that attracts him. Confession offers a

88

privileged insight, a knowledge of that which is normally hidden from us, concealed behind the exterior envelope that makes other people other, that creates their zone of privacy. In particular, it is the secret sins of women and girls—sexual secrets—that excite the adolescent Stephen, as the knowledge otherwise foreclosed to him. If knowledge is power, knowledge of secrets—of that which is consciously held back from knowledge—is the supreme and vertiginous power, offering the confessor a particular position of dominance in regard to the rest of humankind.

Stephen's heady sense of the power of the confession—of the secret transaction carried out in the closed space of the curtained and grilled confessional box—suggests the nearly magical effect of a space and a speech act that abolish the usual confines and censorships of everyday life. The act of confession must be considered private, protected, sacramental because it is so potent. It carries a potential use value which, in the Christian religious tradition, is carefully policed. Along with the power of the keys—the priest's power to absolve from sin—goes the seal of confession, the absolute imperative that the confession remain with the confessor alone. The seal, *sigillum,* images a letter sealed with wax, a communication that exists but is not to be opened. The confessional statement is what the law would call—in contexts other than the suspect's confession—a "privileged communication."

Stephen Dedalus's excitement by the secrets of the confessional sounds rather like that experienced a score of years earlier by the young Sigmund Freud when his mentor Josef Breuer whispered to him that the source of hysteria was to be looked for in hidden "*secrets d'alcôve.*" Freud reports further: "I asked him in astonishment what he meant, and he answered by explaining the word *alcôve* ('marriage-bed') to me, for he failed to realize how extraordinary the *matter* of his statement seemed to me."[2] Freud claims that Breuer later denied having thus designated the sexual origins of hysteria—as, said Freud, did the gynaecologist Chrobak and would have done the great Charcot, the other two mentors who offered him the secret clue to his knowledge of hysteria. So that the very secret of knowledge which stands at the basis of psychoanalysis was offered in the mode of a secret communication later denied public acknowledgment. The original secret concerning origins is conceived to itself require effacement in secrecy. And like the secret of the confessional, it issues from a closed and protected space, the *alcôve,* a recess in which the dark recesses of the soul are explored and revealed. The place of confession and the need for confession seem to touch on hidden secrets whose revelation, in the proper transferential relation of knowledge and power, takes place in a closed circuit of communication which, protected from divulgence to the outside, may have healing results.

The institution of confession by the Roman Church seems to me a key to understanding other uses of confession, and our cultural views of confession, not only because the practice is ancient and has been influential throughout Western culture—among those who opposed the practice as well as those who accepted it—but also because it appears to offer the quintessential form of confession, the form that is closely linked to our understanding of the self, its private sphere, its inwardness, and the needs both to express this self, and to maintain the privileged status of the expression. Other religious traditions, including the Judaic, have also emphasized the avowal of sin to the deity, but the Roman Church institutionalized and ritualized the practice in ways that had a momentous cultural impact. Some reflections on this tradition of confession, which make no claim to exhaustive treatment of a complex subject and its long and by no means self-evident history, may be useful here.

The Church: Confession and Lateran IV

The evolution of confession in the Roman Catholic Church demonstrates (to simplify a very complex question) a change from an emphasis on public penance, as a manifestation of one's sin and need for restoration to the Christian community, to an emphasis on the verbal act and fact of confession itself, and the corresponding speech act of absolution. To cite a historian of confession, Thomas N. Tentler:

> the institutions of forgiveness in Christian antiquity and the early middle ages relied principally on ascetic public acts to ensure obedience and offer consolation. Of course they demanded contrition and belief in divine mercy. Nevertheless, they were systems of shame and, above all, expiation. Private auricular confession, on the other hand, gradually turned the institutional energies of ecclesiastical penance inward. . . . by the thirteenth century it had become primarily a private act, protected by the

seal of the confessional, emphasizing the inner preparation and disposition of the penitent seeking help from a sacrament dispensed by a priest. . . . From a penance of shame and expiation, the church, through centuries of development, had turned to a penance of shame and remorse.[3]

In this movement from a penance of expiation, the performance of expiatory acts in order to demonstrate one's unworthiness and wish for reintegration with the sinless, to the verbal demonstration of one's sin and remorse for sin, one grasps the emergence of a key element in the modern sense of selfhood, of inwardness. As Tentler insists, auricular confession offers a "system of discipline and consolation" (xvi), one by which the individual seeks and receives absolution and at same time is subjected to a regimen of orthodoxy in behavior and belief. Under the guidance of the confessor, the confessant is personally responsible for his sins and their correction.

Practices of confession had been part of Christian communities since their origins. At first, these were apparently public and communal (as implied in the phrase, "a religious confession": *confiteor* can mean, for instance to Tertullian [c. 160–c. 230], to profess belief). While in some communities confession may have quite early begun to be made privately, originally to a bishop, the ensuing penance was a public act. For instance, near the beginning of the third century, this was the penance of Natalius, who had lapsed into heresy:

> he arose early in the morning, and put on sack-cloth, and sprinkled ashes (on his head), and with much earnestness and many tears prostrated himself before Zephyrinus the bishop, rolling himself under the feet not only of the clergy but also of the laity: and when he had moved with his tears the compassionate Church of the compassionate Lord, using much entreaty, and showing the weals of the stripes he had received, he was with difficulty admitted to communion.[4]

And there are many examples of the imposition of fasts and public humiliations as part of penance, conceived as public expiation. Later, the penitential pilgrimage became common. Since originally penance and absolution could be granted only once in a lifetime, there was a tendency to delay confession of sin until faced with death, a situation in which the performance of penance was of course difficult and one that increasingly came to seem unacceptable. Private confession and private penance would have the advantage of being repeatable as often as necessary. And they would come to be the precondition of admission to God's feast, to the communion, which stands at the very center of Church ritual.

Saint Augustine's *Confessions* (397–98) offer the example of an individual's accounting for his life, including his years of sin, in terms of his conversion to the faith. But there is no moment in the *Confessions* that records the practice of confession as we have come to know it—Augustine confesses directly to God—and indeed nowhere in his writings on Christian ethics and duties does Augustine address the task of the confessor.[5] The proto-modern practice of confession appears to have developed as part of monastic practice, in the monk's examination of conscience with his spiritual director. The origins of such self-examination may lie in the "Desert Fathers," who made confessions (though without absolution) to their elders. Private confession seems to have taken precedence over the ancient practice of public penance largely through the influence of the Irish clergy in the seventh century, though public penance certainly continued to be practiced, especially for grave public sins.[6] The Irish clergy—who kept learning alive at a time when much of the Continent suffered the aftermath of the barbarian invasions—provided the first "penitentials," guidebooks for confessors that taught them how to listen and what to listen for, detailing the sins they would encounter and suggesting appropriate means for their remission—a genre that would have a long future and provide society with its definitions of the acceptable Christian life over several centuries.

What is often referred to as the "Twelfth Century Renaissance" saw an increasing emphasis on the individual's self-examination, which we may view as evidence, and perhaps precondition, for the emergence of the "modern" sense of guilt and individual responsibility. Legal practice evolves in a similar manner—it would be difficult to determine precisely how law influences religious practice and religious practice the law; no doubt there is a reciprocal influence at work. If the admission of guilt is crucial in Imperial Roman law and could be obtained by torture from slaves, from the sixth to the twelfth centuries it is largely displaced by the Teutonic usage of "oaths of compurgation" sworn by the accused and his *cojurantes* (family or friends) and by "ordeals" (such as holding a hot iron in one's hand, walking on hot coals, or trial by combat) as a test of guilt: in these ordeals, proof of guilt or innocence was the work of God, the *judicia Dei*.[7]

The rediscovery of Justinian's Digest of Roman law in 1070 opened the way to a legal renaissance, led by the law schools of Bologna, and to the widespread influence of Roman-canon law throughout Europe. Roman-canon law institutes the model of the inquest, the *inquisitio,* in the place of the adversarial challenges of Teutonic models. It calls for a higher level of proof than was provided in the medieval ordeals, either from two reliable eyewitness accounts or else from confession of guilt by the suspect. Circumstantial evidence was in itself never enough to convict absent a confession, but it could provide the basis for torture in order to obtain a confession. Torture thus was viewed as a way to ensure a higher level of certain evidence, more "scientific" proof. The suspect's confession of guilt came to be regarded as the most probative form of evidence: in the phrase of the medieval glossators, *confessio est regina probationum.*

The Fourth Lateran Council, convoked by Pope Innocent III in 1215, stands as the key moment in creating the early modern religious practice of confession, and offers insights into how confession both reflects and creates the emergent sense of the individual we recognize as peculiarly "modern." Lateran IV, in canon 21, *Omnis utriusque sexus,* institutes confession to one's parish priest as an annual obligation on all the faithful once they have reached the age of discretion. The same Council offers an elaborate program of dogma in its very first canon, *Firmiter credimus,* which defines the orthodox teachings of the Church—what the professing Christian believes—and in canon 3, *Excommunicamus et anathemizamus,* the Council institutes an inquisition toward the extirpation of heresy, in which those suspected of heresy must take an oath to answer all questions fully, with the stipulation that refusal to take the oath will be *ipso facto* a sign of heretical belief.[8] With the declaration of an official inquisition into heresy, the disciplining of heterodoxy no longer is a matter for the judgment of local bishops but a papal concern—Innocent III immensely strengthens the power of the Papacy—and the result will be a number of thirteenth-century campaigns, including the extirpation of the Cathars in southern France. Lateran IV also decrees in canon 18, *Sententiam sanguinis,* that the clergy can no longer participate in "ordeals," which—since such participation was generally requisite to the ordeal—effectively put an end to this form of legal judgment.

Lateran IV is considered to be the most important Council before Trent, in 1551, responds to the Protestant dissidents. As Edward Peters states:

> The consequences of the first and twenty-first canons [those concerning the Christian dogma and the requirement of annual confession] were substantial. The publicizing of the content of belief was now readily possible and obligatory upon all those who had the care of souls; the mandating of personal confession incorporated a number of important twelfth-century ideas of conscience and its obligations; and confessions—the art of being a confessor—became a major part of the training of specialized clergy in the thirteenth century, a psychological transformation of a penitential system that had, for the most part, been mechanical and unreflective before.[9]

Lateran IV specifically requires confession to one's parish priest, that is, to the local shepherd of the flock who can, like a family doctor, keep tabs on one's spiritual condition, exercising both reprobation and healing. As canon 21 states: "The priest shall be discerning and prudent, so that like a skilled doctor he may pour wine and oil [Luke 10:34] over the wounds of the injured one. Let him carefully inquire about the circumstances of both the sinner and the sin, so that he may prudently discern what sort of advice he ought to give and what remedy to apply, using various means to heal the sick person."[10] A vast new mission, and power, opened before the clergy. Lateran IV recognized the need for training in pastoral care by calling for religious instruction in every diocese, initiating one of the great ages of preaching. Confession and preaching indeed move forward in tandem: the individual's self-examination and avowal of sin is accompanied by exhortation to live according to Christian example.

In the legislation of Lateran IV, the essential transaction of confession becomes verbal: the confessant's articulation of sin, which must be full and detailed, and the confessor's corresponding articulation of absolution. An earlier precatory formulation in the optative mood, "May God forgive you," came to be replaced by the sacramental words in the indicative: "I forgive you," where the priest uses his divine power to declare that the work of absolution has been accomplished. As Matthew Senior states:

Under a kind of speech act theory, it was held that the sacrament itself conferred forgiveness, and not the sinner's contrition alone. The actual words, "Ego te absolvo," were not declaratory on the part of the priest but judicial or performative, having operative power in themselves.[11]

In the performative quality of confession and absolution, we grasp the continuing power, and problematic, of confession: it depends entirely on the confessant's verbal act, what issues from his or her lips, in an interlocutionary situation in which a response is expected from the confessor, a response which acknowledges that the confession has taken place, and judges it to have been efficacious.

Confession as we know it originates in an oral culture, as a private verbal exchange that possesses mystery and power.[12] Saint Bonaventure claimed that confession must be oral because the shame is greater that way; and the verbalization of sin appears the terrible requirement still to Stephen Dedalus: "Shame covered him wholly like fine glowing ashes falling continually. To say it in words! His soul, stifling and helpless, would cease to be."[13] Confession implies a listener, however impersonal—an interlocutor to whom the confessional discourse is proffered. In this sense, it provides a particularly strong instance of language in the situation of discourse, as it has been described by the linguist Emile Benveniste: a situation in which the speaking *I* necessarily implies a listening *you* who can in turn become the *I* while the speaker becomes *you*.[14] Locution in this sense is at least implicitly interlocution, the expression of subjectivity takes place in a context of intersubjectivity. Saying *I* implies and calls to a responsive *you,* and in this dialogic, transferential relation consolation and self-definition are to be found. The form of address to a listener found in confession is similar to prayer, which addresses itself directly to God—the form of address that largely characterizes Augustine's *Confessions*—as another linguistic structure of appeal to a response. And indeed the modern written tradition of confessional autobiography—Rousseau and his progeny—operates on the same model, claiming, at least implicitly, that the act of confessing (rather than the facts referred to by the confession) is the primordially important gesture and that the addressee of the confession is called upon as witness and judge of its efficaciousness. The expression of inwardness cannot, it appears, proceed without a responsive interlocutor in the search for self-knowledge. Psychoanalysis of course will reiterate the model, and will make explicit a feature of interlocution that is certainly implicit in prayer and possibly in the penitent's confession: that the listener need not say much to be effective, that his simple presence brings to the speaker's discourse what Jacques Lacan calls "the dimension of dialogue": the shaping of one's inner thoughts to the ear of an external listener.[15]

To the extent that the law relies upon the model—the legal model of the *inquisitio,* which seeks the confession of guilt, emerges simultaneously with the religious model of confession—it, too, relies upon a bond between confessor and confessant that, in the situation of the criminal suspect before the law, leads to a somewhat perverse result: conviction rather than absolution. The religious and legal models of confession in fact intersect in the inquisition of heresy, where confession—obtained by exhortation or by torture—is considered to be both "medicinal" (necessary to the salvation of the heretic's soul) and judicial (the basis for punishment). And it appears that throughout the thirteenth and fourteenth centuries, criminal procedure will also assume that confession, for instance at the foot of the gibbet, is vital not only for the solution of crime but also for the purgation of sin on the part of the condemned about to face eternal judgment.[16]

One can see that the convergence, in the decrees of Lateran IV, of the promulgation of dogma, the obligation of confession, and the institution of an inquisition, provides a nexus of consolation and discipline that makes the individual, as psychic and social actor, a conscience subject both to self-examination and to external policing. In this sense, Lateran IV marks a recognition and institutionalization of the proto-modern sense of the self that many historians see as emergent in the twelfth century. Literature, especially in France, from the lyrics of the Provençal Troubadours to the romances of Chrétien de Troyes, begins to elaborate a "psychology" of the individual person. Poems of debate—*jeux partis*—begin to stage dialogues of self and soul. In moral philosophy, notably in the teaching of Pierre Abélard, issues of conscience, intention, and self-knowledge are intensely debated. "Self," Caroline Walker Bynum argues, is a more appropriate term than "individual" or "personality," since, she claims, medieval humanity had little sense of the individual as a well-demarcated person.[17] Introspection in the twelfth century led to the discovery of *homo interior* or *seipsum* as the self made in the image of God, an *imago dei* that is the same for all humans. If we are still far from the sense of uniqueness that resounds in Rousseau's *Confessions,* it seems clear that the notion of confession, along with the introspection and self-examination that it implies, both creates and is created by a new sense of selfhood. Without a sense of the self and its narrative, there could be no confession; and without the requirement of confession, internally or externally mandated, there would be no exploration of this selfhood.

In Dante's *Divina Commedia,* written early in the fourteenth century, sinners confess their sins and recount their lives in the first person, assuming a now eternally marked identity through a narrative of their own faults. When the pilgrim Dante inquires of his master Virgil about the identity of a figure in the flames of hell, Virgil replies: "da lui saprai di sè e de' suoi torti": "you will know from him of himself and his faults" (*Inferno* 19:36). The sinners must speak for themselves, in their own confessional discourses. The critic Francesco de Sanctis called Francesca da Rimini, a memorable figure in the *Inferno,* the first modern woman in literature.[18] Her modernity would seem to consist precisely in her act of confessional retrospection, in which her present misery is increased by the fond memory of the desire and passion that brought her to it, and yet that memory in its sweetness sustains and indeed defines her. To the pilgrim Dante's query how in the time of her *dolci sospiri* love made her know her "uncertain desires," she replies

> Nessun maggior dolore
> che ricordarsi del tempo felice
> ne la miseria; e ciò sa 'l tuo dottore.

As translated by Robert Pinsky:

> No sadness
> Is greater than in misery to rehearse
> Memories of joy, as your teacher well can witness.[19]

Francesca says she will recount her story as "one who weeps and tells," suggesting the nature and the need for a contritional narrative. The story of how she and Paolo fell in love and exchanged their first adulterous kiss while reading of the loves of Lancelot and Guinevere is proto-modern in its attention to private life, and especially to the life of desire within the subject.

Noi leggiavamo un giorno per diletto
  di Lancialotto come amor lo strinse;
  soli eravamo e sanza alcun sospetto.
Per più fïate li occhi ci sospinse
  quella lettura, e scolorocci il viso;
  ma solo un punto fu quello che ci vinse.
Quando leggemo il disïato riso
  esser basciato da cotanto amante,
  questi, che mai da me non fia diviso,
la bocca mi basciò tutto tremante.
  Galeotto fu il libro e chi lo scrisse:
  quel giorno più non vi leggemmo avante.
                              (V, 127–38)

[One day, for pleasure,
  We read of Lancelot, by love constrained:
  Alone, suspecting nothing, at our leisure.
Sometimes at what we read our glances joined,
  Looking from the book each to the other's eyes,
  And then the color in our faces drained.
But one particular moment alone it was
  Defeated us: *the longed-for smile,* it said,
  Was kissed by that most noble lover: at this,
This one, who now will never leave my side,
  Kissed my mouth, trembling. A Galeotto, that book!
  And so was he who wrote it; that day we read
No further.]

Lancelot "by love constrained" offers a powerful image of the force of desire within and how it can determine the destiny of the soul and of the person. That Paolo and Francesca's desires reach self-discovery and overt expression through the imitation of Lancelot's kiss to Guinevere suggests a role for the book and for reading that resonates as fully modern: the book as magic mirror for one's inner needs and identity; reading as a process of self-discovery, for better or worse. "That day we read no further"—because the romance of the book has passed into real life: we have here a theme that will resound from *Don Quixote* through *Madame Bovary* and beyond, in much of the literature that seems to us to represent the modern sensibility in its mediation of self-knowledge through the figuration of desire in the imagination. Francesca continues to be a truly fascinating figure for readers because her confessional discourse, in the fewer than twenty lines that she speaks, suggests all the depth and recess that we associate with modern subjectivity.

If we find in Lateran IV evidence of the emergence of the modern sense of the self, it is very much in the terms of Michel Foucault: a subject transversed by knowledge as power. For Foucault, "Western man became a confessing animal [*une bête d'aveu*]."[20] Foucault contends that the obligation to hide—he is speaking specifically of sexual secrets—is merely an aspect of the need to avow, to confess. And he sees the verbal act of confession as taking place in a context of obligation, in a relation of power:

> ... confession [*l'aveu*] is a ritual of discourse where the subject who speaks corresponds with the subject of the statement [*l'énoncé*]; it is also a ritual which unfolds in a relation of power, since one doesn't confess without the presence, at least the virtual presence, of a partner who is not simply an interlocutor but the agency that requires the confession, imposes it, weighs it, and intervenes to judge, punish, pardon, console, reconcile; a ritual where truth is authenticated by the obstacles and resistances that it has had to lift in order to be formulated; a ritual, finally, where articulation alone, independently of its external consequences, produces, in the person who articulates it, intrinsic modifications: it makes him innocent, it redeems him, purifies him, promises him salvation. (82–83)

Confession, in this view, offers a royal way into the individual's psyche, into his or her personal beliefs, aspirations, faults, but in the mode of social and ideological pressure, as the policing of individual belief.

"*Quis, quid, ubi, quibus auxiliis, cur, quomodo, quando*" ("Who, what, where, with what accomplices, why, in what manner, when"): this became the standard mnemonic formula for the confessor, indicating the necessary interrogation of the confessant in order to know in detail and to characterize the sin committed. As the Jesuit author of one of the most widely used confessor's manuals, Paolo Segneri, explains in 1685, the confessor should be above all a listener, since the word of the confessant is absolute (and his silence what condemns him), and the confessant is the one who knows what needs confessing. So rather than behaving like a hunter trying to take its prey in the nets of thousands of questions, the confessor ideally should wait patiently for the confessant to come to him, "like the Unicorn to the lap of the Virgin."[21] But alas, in practice the recalcitrance of the confessant requires the confessor to interrogate. Confessants are dumb and blind; they hide their sins through ignorance or malice. Hidden sin must be brought to light.

Stephen Dedalus's conflation of confession, secret, and sexuality is very much present in the work of preachers and moralists of the early modern period, such as the influential Jean Gerson whose writings, from early in the fifteenth century, urge the confessor especially to seek out the secret sexual sins of the confessant through detailed questioning, though always with precaution, so as not to create new temptations to sins unknown.[22] Excessive pleasure in sexual intercourse, even among the married, must be ferreted out; also "unnatural" positions in intercourse; "dishonest" touchings on the "shameful parts"; masturbation, especially, must be detected and reproved. The Church's seeming obsession with sexuality apparently responds not only to its fear of the flesh as the way of perdition, but also to its belief that what is most hidden, considered most private, secret, and possibly shameful, is precisely that which must be brought into the open and given articulation. The subject in this view is, like Dante's Francesca, defined in large part by the life of its desire, which must be uncovered and scrutinized.

The confessional subject thus is obliged to perform a scrupulous self-examination and to submit the results, in a verbal transaction, to an examiner who holds the power to absolve and, in absolution, to acknowledge and legitimate the individual as a valid part of the community. Much of Martin Luther's objection to auricular confession would arise from his belief that it promoted "scrupulosity," an overly refined and pernicious self-searching for violations of religious teachings, which interfered with the individual's true faith and allegiance to God. To Luther, the imposition of penances after absolution was a sign of the Church's corruption from an earlier, purer practice, in which penance before absolution gave evidence of the confessant's true contrition at his sin, which to Luther was the essential element. The sale of "indulgences," which were held to remit penances and years in Purgatory, was of course a blatant sign of corruption. Luther believed that private examination of conscience and "fraternal correction" in preparation for communion were more important than the sacrament of confession. To which the Council of Trent will reply that sacramental confession as practiced by the Church is ancient, of divine origin, and that those who believe otherwise are anathema.

The Counter-Reformation, particularly in the work of Saint Carlo Borromeo, the influential Archbishop of Milan and a major figure in the Council of Trent, enhanced the role of confession, and notably created the piece of furniture we know as the confessional, which Senior calls "the emblem par excellence of post-Tridentine spirituality."[23] The confessional, which appears to us today so much part of the interior of a Catholic church, makes its appearance only in the middle of the sixteenth century. It is of course designed to provide a private exchange of words through a grille, ensuring that vision has no place in the speech act of confession, protecting the identity of both confessor and confessant. Earlier, confessions were heard by the priest without veiling, though the confessor was taught to avert his eyes from the confessant. The confessional creates and envelops that private space in which Stephen Dedalus imagines women and girls avowing secret sins, and was indeed conceived in part to protect the privacy and chastity of women at confession. As Senior argues, using the psychoanalytic terminology of Lacan:

> Borromeo's grill institutes the "ghostly" conversation; it is characteristic of a spirituality that increasingly insists on the disposition of the soul and on language as the true means of mortification. Borromeo's grill puts a barrier between the Imaginary, face-to-face encounter between priest and penitent and reduces the encounter to the Symbolic. (85)

That is to say, the confessional makes the act of confession (and this is ideally true for the psychoanalytic encounter also) transindividual, impersonal in the sense that this most intimate and personal of discourses is now proffered to an ear without facial identity, and absolution is spoken by a voice without personality.

It seems fair to say that the requirement of confession declared by Lateran IV constitutes a revolution in the development of Western society and its members of the highest magnitude. What we are today—the entire conception of the self, its relation to its interiority and to others—is largely tributary of the confessional requirement. This is true, I think, even for those whose lives are untouched by the Catholic Church or by religion of any kind: the confessional model is by now deeply implicated in our everyday morality. We cannot think of the self, its education, its emergence into adulthood, without recourse to confession and what it implies about the inner life. If the law, in the United States—and a number of other countries—has seen wisdom in creating rules governing the production and use of confessions, and if these rules seem to many contrary to ethical common sense, no doubt both the creation and the critique of such rules derive from a sense of the deep importance of the confessional speech act and its close link to our very sense of the self.

The Emergent Self

I earlier mentioned Dante's Francesca as an emergent modern self, in her assumption of a confessional narrative of the self as the story of its desiring. Confessional discourse is clearly the prototype of that typically modern form of writing we call autobiography—it is a fragment of autobiography—and Rousseau's *Confessions* stand on the threshold of this modern genre. Rousseau's practice owes something to the tradition of auricular confession, and something to the Protestant tradition of examination of one's life, often in a written account—one thinks of the flourishing of Protestant autobiography in the seventeenth century, in such as John Bunyan. (Rousseau himself was born in Calvinist Geneva, later was converted to Catholicism as an adolescent in Turin, and still later returned to his own brand of Protestantism.) If the literature of Antiquity often gives the sense of taking place on a single plane (like a bas-relief) as Erich Auerbach famously argued, confessional literature gives the impression of depth and recess, delving into the subject's past and into the subject's deepest and most hidden thoughts and wishes, in order to account for the individual self.[24] The metaphor of "depth"—see, for instance, the phrase "depth psychology"—is a metaphor only, but highly indicative of the sense of something behind the surface, needing excavation (see Freud's frequent recourse to the archeological model), discovery, and opening up to the light of examination. That which is within is at the same time the most important and the most difficult to articulate.

One could tell the story of this opening of the depths to literary examination, at least from Dante to our own time; or, more modestly, the story of the autobiographical impulse in literature, and its rise to dominance. Either would be too vast an undertaking here. I propose to complete these remarks on the religious sense of confessional discourse and selfhood by way of the case of a sixteenth century impostor who assumed another's identity, then Montaigne's comments on the case, then the first page of Rousseau's *Confessions,* which will bring us up to the modern sensibility.

In *The Return of Martin Guerre,* Natalie Davis retells the celebrated tale of an impostor in southwest France in the sixteenth century—at the crucial intersection of the Renaissance and the Reformation, when the early modern sense of the self was emerging. Her main source is the account given by Jean de Coras, the chief judge in the case when it went to court on appeal before the Parlement de Toulouse. His *Arrest memorable* recounts the bafflements of justice faced with the clever peasant Armand du Tilh who, it appears, usurped the place of Martin Guerre—gone off to be a soldier for nearly eight years—in the village of Artigat, including the place of Martin Guerre in the marriage bed of his wife Bertrande de Rols. Justice would have underwritten the assumed identity, had not the true Martin Guerre—at least, someone more universally recognized as such—returned at the eleventh hour. Armand du Tilh confessed his imposture only at the foot of the scaffold, in the *amende honorable* he was forced to perform, dressed in a white shift and with the hangman's noose already around his neck—or so we are told in the second edition of the *Arrest memorable:* the first edition ends with the court's judgment and with du Tilh still insisting he is the rightful Martin Guerre, leaving some doubt in the mind of the reader, centuries later, that the mystery of this case ever was solved.[25]

How can someone usurp another's identity so thoroughly that he fools all the friends and neighbors of the rightful owner of that identity? And how, and up to what point, did he fool Bertrande? And what does this tell us about the sense of individual identity and its relation to memory and to personal narrative? Our own time has no doubt encountered examples of imposture—most famously, perhaps, the false Anastasia Romanoff—but it is difficult to conceive of a case so unresolved as Martin Guerre's in an age such as ours where individuals bear so many marks of personal identity: marks that were increasingly the preoccupation of the modern state as it emerged over the course of the nineteenth and twentieth century, from the classificatory measurements of Bertillon and criminal typologies of Lombroso, to photography, to fingerprinting, identity cards, and social security numbers, to DNA testing. In particular, it is hard to conceive of an impostor assuming the place of another in a small community and in a preexisting marriage.

To ask these questions is to reflect on the lack of marks of state-sponsored personal identity in early modern Europe. No identity cards, of course, and no photographs—and for the peasantry, no painted portraits and indeed no mirrors (those sources of knowledge of the self that were already for Renaissance poets the very trope of self-reflection, and the mechanism by which artists painted self-portraits). When the pseudo-Martin appeared in Artigat eight years after the disappearance of Martin Guerre, his claim to identity was based entirely on memory: the villagers' visual memory of what he looked like and his memory of who was who in Artigat and what they had done together in the past. The pseudo-Martin (assuming that he was an impostor) had somehow achieved the remarkable result of claiming another man's memories, without any recourse to written records, even without, so far as Davis can establish, ever having met the "real" Martin Guerre. He knew his relatives and neighbors, was able to furnish precise details of domestic life, including items of dress packed away in a household chest. We may presume, with Davis, that at some point on the road to Artigat he was mistaken for Martin Guerre, and then set about learning enough about the man that he gained the knowledge to impersonate him, and the desire to take his place as a peasant of substance with a wife and a child to adopt as his own.

The pseudo-Martin was able to get away with the imposture no doubt in large part because, as Davis notes, "he was wanted in Artigat" (43). The disappearance of Martin Guerre had created a kind of structural gap in the familial economies of the village, as well as in the life of Bertrande. By this logic, a plausible impostor had only to fill a missing box in the schematic diagram of village relationships. This is perhaps the most concrete definition of "identity": what one is as father, husband, nephew, landowner, heir, neighbor. Yet it is a sketchy sense of identity when it is not filled in with all the information that a novelist such as Balzac supplies about his characters in order to "compete with the Civil Registry," as he put it, or all the personal traits and quirks that Dickens provides to give his characters immediate recognizability. For the pseudo-Martin to have immediately assumed the place of Martin Guerre in Artigat suggests a certain fluidity of contour of the individual, especially the individual over time. It suggests "identity" defined in socio-structural terms without the recesses of interiority and subjectivity that are so much our own understanding of individual identity.

Eventually, some of the villagers came to doubt the authenticity of the new Martin. Trouble arose when he demanded that his uncle, Pierre Guerre, give an accounting of his use of Martin's land during the years of absence. Pierre Guerre, thus threatened, initiated the claim that the new Martin was an impostor, and the villagers began to choose sides. By the time the case came to trial, the village seemed to have three opinion groups of roughly equal size: those who thought the new Martin was an impostor, those who believed him authentic, and those who said they just couldn't tell. The only person with anything close to what we would call scientific evidence was the shoemaker, who claimed that the new Martin had smaller feet than the old one.

The testing of the new Martin was all by way of memory, by the villagers themselves and then at the first trial, in Rieux, and then the decisive trial on appeal, at Toulouse. And in this domain, no one seems to have been able to fault the new Martin: he could answer every question put to him, indeed he had a better memory of his pseudo-past, his self-created past, than the true Martin had of that same past when he appeared before the court. What is striking, though, is the extent to which—so far as one can tell from the written accounts—memory in this case meant recall of information and episodes from adult life. In a post-Rousseauist, and then a post-Freudian, age, we would expect memory to include the comprehensive narrative of the self from early childhood. Rousseau, for instance, repeatedly seeks the assurance that though he has been much changed by the vicissitudes of his life and his external image disfigured by the malevolence of his enemies, he is still the same person, still able to give a coherent if turbulent account of how the young Jean-Jacques evolved into the mature Rousseau. The very last pages written by Rousseau, shortly before his death—the opening of the tenth *Promenade* in the *Rêveries du promeneur solitaire*—evoke the moment fifty years earlier when, as an adolescent, he first met Mme. de Warens, the moment which, he tells us, "fixed" his character forever.[26] Rousseau is

constantly aware of his mutation, his fall and lapse from various para-
dises of his childhood and youth, yet always ready to assert that the
man is the product of the child, bound to what he was through a series
of transformations which enable him to say: I am different, yet the
same person. The case of Martin Guerre arises before what Philippe
Ariès calls "the invention of childhood," which makes identity so
closely predicated, psychologically and morally, on childhood experience and affect.[27] In this sense, too, it is legitimate to speak of the new
Martin's identity in Artigat as more nearly structural in nature: dependent on roles assumed as an adult member of a community more
than on the uninterrupted narrative of self-consciousness. Whereas
our modern sense of identity and personality, of those inner recesses
that appear to lodge the essence of the "self," would seem to be very
much tied to childhood formative experience, to affectivities reaching
deep into what we conceive of as a personal past.

A similar point about the new Martin is made by Stephen Greenblatt, in an essay where he argues that psychoanalytic understanding
often seems irrelevant to Renaissance texts because "psychoanalysis is
at once the fulfillment and effacement of specifically Renaissance insights": a distant production of the Renaissance that supersedes its understanding of the individual.[28] In our post-Freudian view,

> The testimony of the community is important—in the court of
> law, indispensable—but the roots of Martin's identity lie deeper
> than society; they reach down, as psychoanalysis would assure
> us, through the frail, outward memories of his sisters and
> friends to the psychic experience of his infancy—the infancy
> only he can possess and that even the most skillful impostor can-
> not appropriate—and beneath infancy to his biological individ-
> uality. (135)

Yet for those involved with the trial of Martin Guerre, including
Coras,

> what is at stake in this case is not psychic experience at all but
> rather a communal judgment that must, in extraordinary cases,
> be clarified and secured by legal authority.... At issue is not
> Martin Guerre as subject but Martin Guerre as object, the place-
> holder in a complex system of possessions, kinship bonds,
> contractual relationships, customary rights, and ethical obliga-

tions. . . . Martin's subjectivity—or, for that matter, Arnaud's or Bertrande's—does not any the less exist, but it seems peripheral, or rather, it seems to be the *product* of the relations, material objects, and judgments exposed in the case rather than the *producer* of those relations, objects, and judgments. (136–37)

What thus appears to be on trial in Rieux and Toulouse is a community-based structural definition of identity that has little recourse to what we today would consider the prime markers of individuality.

One of the structural roles unfilled in Artigat was of course that of husband to Bertrande, and here lies the most delectable mystery of the case. What did Bertrande know, and when? If she was at first taken in by the general acclamation that Martin her husband had returned, is it possible that she continued to believe him authentic? Coras believes so—perhaps he must, since he wants to find her innocent of consent to the imposture and thus find her children with the impostor legitimate.[29] Davis, on the other hand, believes she must soon have known that he was an impostor, and kept him in her bed because by that point it was too late to confess to having been fooled—and because she wanted him in her bed, where he may have been a more satisfactory husband than the original Martin, who after all was unable to consummate their marriage for a long stretch of time. She lived with the new Martin for over three years and bore him two children. And she would tell Coras intimate details of her life with Martin, including memories he recalled of "the places, dates, and times of the secret acts of marriage (much easier to understand than it is fitting to tell or write down) and the words they spoke before, after, and during the act," testimony tending to prove that she knew the new Martin was identical with the old.[30] This of course could have been merely the result of her concertation with the new Martin to tell consistent lies under examination. Yet a certain doubt persists. At least, one might say, if the new Martin was a good enough impostor to convince Bertrande, can one be sure he had not fully assumed the identity of the old Martin? Or should one simply say that "husband" is a structural category to be filled and that the new Martin filled it well, and that from Bertrande's point of view this was sufficient? The Church had after all for some centuries been seeking to regularize and control marriage, and if the union of the new Martin and Bertrande looked like the restoration of a marriage, here was another structural problem solved.[31]

The one advantage of the film *Le Retour de Martin Guerre* (written by Jean-Claude Carrière, directed by Daniel Vigne) over Natalie Davis's book—on the whole far superior—could be said to lie in the cinema's necessarily external approach to questions of identity. In particular, the role of Bertrande can be presented cinematically as an unresolved enigma. In this sense, the film as a medium may be faithful to the way issues of identity presented themselves to the villagers of Artigat: purely in terms of visual presence and recall of the past. The film puts before us the enigma of identity seen from the outside, whereas writing, for us moderns, inevitably entails an effort to open up interiority, depth: identity as experienced from within. When Bertrande identifies the new Martin as her husband by way of intimacies that Coras cannot repeat, we have an approach to inwardness that the text silences and which the film does not try to represent, as if to suggest that the question of identity is too tenuous, too fluid, too delicate to be produced in the public realm.

Davis suggests that the claims of the new Martin may have been more readily accepted by those who were inclined to the reformed religion. We are at a moment when Protestantism is making large inroads in France, perhaps especially among the educated classes, including the legal caste (for example Coras himself, who would later be hanged as a heretic). Davis also suggests that possibly the new Martin and Bertrande themselves sympathized with the reformers.[32] If this were the case, they would not have made confession to the priest of Artigat of what they knew to be a sin—the sin of adultery, at very least—but would rather have made their case of conscience directly to God. If this were indeed the case, it would make their confession an apologia for their choices set in the context of the justification of their whole lives, as in Rousseau's *Confessions,* as in the Protestant autobiographies of the following century. That is, their choice to continue to live a false identity and an adulterous marriage would be justified in terms of the benefits accrued by the arrangement, to themselves, to their children, to the community, and by their faith in the rightness of their course.

Montaigne, who is often taken to be the first writer with a fully developed sense of the self, whose *Essais* are a sustained meditation on his *moi,* an introspective inquiry, was apparently in Toulouse to hear the judgment pronounced on the pseudo-Martin—he was himself a judge in the Parlement de Bordeaux—and he uses the episode, in the essay

"Des Boiteux" ["On the Lame"], to discuss the limitations of human justice and to suggest that Coras and his fellow judges may have made a judicial error.[33] They didn't have the evidence necessary to pass judgment in this case; they should have concluded that on the facts as presented there could be no decision; they should have sent the parties away, says Montaigne, with orders to reappear before the court in a hundred years—in other words, human judgment should have admitted its radical insufficiency in establishing the identity of the true Martin. "To kill men, we should have sharp and luminous evidence," writes Montaigne. His reflection on the case of Martin then leads into a critique of witchcraft trials (Coras several times suggests that the pseudo-Martin achieved his imposture through "magic") and the admonition that even confessional truth is to be received with skepticism: "we should not always decide on the basis of the very confessions of these people, since one has seen them sometimes accuse themselves of having killed people who were found to be alive and well" (1157). In the realm of psychic pathology, not even confession produces evidence. Montaigne's evocation of witchcraft trials points to one of history's most notorious abuses of confession, to the repeated creation of situations of mass hysteria where confessions are extorted and used to the accusation of others. The "witch hunt" has become our very image of the aberrant extortion of confession and its destructive uses.

It is Montaigne who famously wrote: "Chaque homme porte la forme entière de l'humaine condition": each man bears the entire form, or imprint, of the human condition.[34] To Montaigne, this is assurance that in studying the one man he knows best—Michel de Montaigne—he produces knowledge of humanity in its entirety. It is an emblematic Renaissance statement of the microcosm, man, as representative of society and the world. The case of Martin Guerre is for him a representative example of the limits of human discernment and justice, the inability of human perception and analysis to reach through certain opacities in the knowledge of others' truth. What one can know is the self, which may be full of contradictions and contrary impulses, but which is ultimately unitary and capable of being seized in a process of introspective narrative cognition. Montaigne's confessional self is never expounded in a clear, linear movement, but rather through all sorts of detours and digressions, but it is always present to itself, as an entity that has developed from infancy to adulthood, and has the contours of an identity.

Rousseau is of course acutely aware of Montaigne as precedent and precursor, and the first page of his *Confessions* alludes directly to the famous phrase about each man's bearing the imprint of the whole human condition. "I am not made like any of those [other men] I have seen," he declares, to continue: "Whether nature did well or ill in breaking the mould in which she formed me is something one can only judge after having read me."[35] Here is the accent of something resolutely modern: the utter uniqueness and inimitability of the individual. No one else can have the same form, bear the same imprint: the mould has been destroyed. This claim stands with Rousseau's insistence that he can be judged only following the reading of his extended narrative of the formation of his individual personality, a self traced and explicated from infancy into adulthood. So that Rousseau—in a gesture unimaginable to Augustine, for instance—says that when the trumpet of the Last Judgment sounds, he will appear before his "sovereign judge" with "this book in my hand." The book of the individual's life, the confession of a whole life's deeds and, especially, its inner conditions, is now the justification of existence.

There is a preliminary note to the *Confessions,* discovered in the "Geneva Manuscript," which implores anyone finding the manuscript not to destroy it. "Here is the only portrait of man, painted exactly according to nature and in all its truth, that exists and which probably will ever exist" (3). Rousseau by the time he finished writing the *Confessions*—the time from which this note must date—was of course nearly clinically paranoid, subject to delusions of persecution on every hand—delusions which, it must be said, followed on very real persecutions, including the burning of his books and flight from imminent arrest and betrayal by friends. He is haunted by the notion that posterity will receive a disfigured portrait of him. Thus the crucial importance of the manuscript of his confessions, "the only sure monument to my character that hasn't been disfigured by my enemies." Rousseau makes the claim that only the individual's confessional discourse—the discourse of the self on the self—can be taken as perfectly authentic.

Upon reflection, can we say that we reject this claim? As Foucault suggests, the modern subject is held responsible for the discourse of his or her own identity and personality, and we tend to regard that discourse as privileged information. We may question it, we may find it self-glorifying or self-excusing, we may search for errors of fact in it, yet we regard it in its own terms—precisely, as a confession—as true to the self in ways that other discourses never can be. Courts, for instance, are almost always reluctant to throw out confessions—if deemed to be voluntarily made—even when they are later repudiated or disconfirmed by circumstantial evidence. We are held responsible for what we say about ourselves.

The religious tradition of confession, crucial to our conception of confession in law, literature, and everyday life even if we have not been raised in a church that practices it, promotes self-examination and the avowal of faults as necessary to spiritual well-being. This tradition, however modified in secular therapies, requires a certain degree of introspection and then articulation of what one has found "in oneself." It thus promotes the metaphors of innerness, depth, recesses within, where one can track the self in its life of desire, its ruses, untruths, failings—as well as in its aspirations to wholeness and betterment. It is a powerful tradition, in its conjoined claim to console and to discipline: to offer absolution for faults and omissions while simultaneously policing the contents of consciousness. And one might say, building on Foucault's insight that the Western subject became a "bête d'aveu," that the practice of confession creates the metaphors of innerness that it claims to explore: without the requirement of confession—one may overstate the issue—there might be nothing inward to examine. In other words, the very notion of inwardness is consubstantial with the requirement to explore and examine it. If we cannot imagine a requirement of confession absent a deep, recessed, secret self—to which psychoanalysis, following the clue of a number of writers in the Romantic tradition, will add the deepest level of the unconscious—it is equally true that we cannot imagine this self absent the imperative to scrutinize and attempt to articulate it. If in contemporary culture confession has become an everyday event in the media, this may in part be reassurance that each of us is still, in a world of massification, a unique individual, with a unique story to tell.

When this discourse of consolation and discipline is turned to the uses of the state seeking to hold individuals responsible for crimes, the self-exploratory and consolatory aspects clearly become problematic, despite the many declarations by Supreme Court justices and others that confessing is good for one. One cannot rule out the possibility that it is—there are certainly numerous incidents of felons coming forward years after committing an unsolved crime to confess because they have to get the crime off their conscience.[36] The notion that possible redemption depends on confession is deeply ingrained in our culture, and Raskolnikov's choice of confession and expiation surely still holds much power. The institutionalization of confession as a means of legal conviction nonetheless must always make us uncomfortable, since the state in search of a confession plays on the consolatory aspect of confession as a means to entrap for disciplinary purposes. Montaigne's warning that confession should not be used for burning witches still seems pertinent: the motives and modalities of the confession produced under the pressure to confess are complex enough that one doesn't necessarily want to trust it as the whole truth in a legal sense. Confession, one might say, belongs in the closed and protected space of the confessional.

I will close by coming back to Stephen Dedalus, at the moment he finally forces himself to enter the confessional and detail his "sins of impurity." The priest's words of admonition and absolution fall like "sweet rain upon his quaking parching heart" (145). His prayers ascend "to heaven from his purified heart like perfume streaming upwards from a heart of white rose." All of reality is profoundly altered by the experience of confession and absolution:

> The muddy streets were gay. He strode homeward, conscious of an invisible grace pervading and making light his limbs. In spite of all he had done it. He had confessed and God had pardoned him. His soul was made fair and holy once more, holy and happy. (145)

Joyce powerfully evokes the sense of purification and reintegration experienced by the confessant who believes in the power of the keys and in God's pardon. It is precisely the power of this paradigm that must make us suspicious of its use for other purposes: purposes that seek punishment rather than absolution, or, even, that claim that absolution and purification pass through punishment, rather than penance. One recalls Abe Fortas's eloquent words: "*Mea culpa* belongs to a man and his God. It is a plea that cannot be exacted from free men by human authority." Cannot, but often it is.

5

THE CULTURE OF CONFESSION,

THERAPY, AND THE LAW

In Confession the sinner tells what he knows; in analysis
the neurotic has to tell more.

Freud, "The Question of Lay Analysis"

In Alfred Hitchcock's film *I Confess,* a murderer confesses to a Montgomery Clift in holy orders so as—the spectator initially believes—to place his crime in safekeeping since the priest must put it under the seal of confession, which will prevent his giving testimony to the police. Yet, in a good Hitchcockian twist, things turn out to be more complex: the spectator gradually comes to realize that the confession to the priest was actually made in order to frame him: the murderer committed his crime disguised in a cassock, and with the priest prevented by the seal of confession from presenting any of the knowledge that would exculpate him, the priest becomes the criminal suspect. He is trapped in a nightmare situation, where he is unable to offer testimony of his innocence. Hitchcock effectively stages the logic of guilt and its secret confession and their profound incompatibility with the requirements of the law.

Father Michael Logan (Montgomery Clift) receives the confession of the killer, the church sacristan, Otto Keller (O. E. Hasse), which he cannot divulge because of the seal of confession and which therefore comes to implicate him. But Father Logan also has another guilty secret of his own—though not so much his own as that of the woman it involves. Before the war—and before taking his vows—he had been in love with Ruth Grandfort (Anne Baxter), who while he was overseas married the society figure Grandfort. Meeting Logan again when his troopship docks—before telling him she has married another man—she spends an idyllic day with him, a day which ends in a cloudburst, during which the two take refuge in a gazebo, where they in fact spend the night. (Since this is a Hollywood film of the 1950s, the viewer has no idea of what, if anything, transpires during the night.) In the morning, they are discovered by Villette, the man who later will be murdered (for pecuniary motives) by Keller. Logan becomes a priest, the film implies, because of his despair at the loss of Ruth, though he still loves her and she him. He cannot divulge the secret of his past relationship with Ruth—relevant, since he is with her at the time the murder is committed—not because of the seal of confession this time, but because of a manly code of honor. Ruth herself thus undertakes to tell it, implicating herself in what her husband takes to be a guilty relationship but exonerating Logan. Except that it doesn't work this way: telling the secret of their postwar rendezvous and discovery by Villette appears rather to provide a motive for Logan's killing of Villette (he has held Logan's guilty secret and might have been threatening to divulge it, blackmailing the priest in his most vulnerable point).

Father Logan is thus the repository of secret knowledge that he cannot tell and which appears more and more to implicate him as killer. Everything could be explained, if only Logan could unseal his lips. But he is reduced during the course of the film to silence, to a kind of grim twitching of the corners of his mouth that seems to indicate that he could tell all were he able to tell anything. As in traditional nineteenth-century melodrama, the role of the mute (in melodrama, often a literal mute) falsely accused of a crime of which he cannot exculpate himself—precisely because exculpation depends on articulation—becomes excruciating and starkly expressionistic, as the tortured face of the priest bears witness to all he cannot speak.[1] The situation reaches its excruciating climax as Logan undergoes his trial, and is let off by the jury since it finds the evidence doesn't prove the case beyond the shadow of a doubt—though it is clear that jury, judge, and public believe him to be guilty. Indeed, as he leaves the courtroom the crowd outside begins to jeer and jostle him. At this point, the wife of Keller (the true murderer), who holds the secret of the murder, can stand her guilty knowledge no longer and calls out Logan's innocence. Whereupon Keller shoots her and she dies before she can make a full confession of the truth.

This shooting precipitates a manhunt for Keller, which leads eventually into the auditorium of the Château Frontenac. In a lull in the shots exchanged between Keller and the police, the trapped Keller calls out an accusation: that Father Logan has broken the seal of the confession. Immediately, illumination spreads across the face of Inspector Larrue (Karl Malden): Logan's persistent silence is now explained; the secret hidden under his taciturnity is not his, but another's. Keller then is shot. Logan runs to him. As he holds the dying Keller in his arms, Keller attempts a final confession: "Father, forgive me." And the film ends as Logan makes the sign of the cross and speaks the sacramental words, "Ego te absolvo." The thriller ends where it had appeared to begin: in the speech-act of confession and, now, absolution. The legal problem of crime, guilt, and punishment is effaced in the ancient ritual of deathbed confession, absolution, and reconciliation of the sinner with the human community whose bonds he has so sundered.

I Confess suggests that there is no way to reconcile the religious tradition of confession, its use for the cure of souls and the reaffirmation of community, and the law's need for confession in a process of judgment and punishment. The two remain radically at odds, and only the chance occurrence of Inspector Larrue's overhearing Keller's accusation that Logan has violated the seal of confession unknots the dilemma of guilt misattributed and the innocent placed under suspicion. (In fact, in the play from which the scenario was derived—*Nos deux consciences,* by Paul Anthelme—the priest goes to prison, and the truth never is revealed.) If the law would no doubt suppress as evidence a confession made to a detective disguised as a priest, when the confession is made to a real priest, rather than a detective, the law reacts with confusion and panic. The "felicity conditions" of the confessional speech-act are wrong (to use J. L. Austin's language once again) and the results are devastating.

Hitchcock was apparently unhappy with the reception of *I Confess,* since he found that non-Catholic viewers simply did not understand the absolute nature of the seal of confession—upon which the whole film turns. As in melodrama, a vow of silence must be performed absolutely. And what may in fact be most impressive in the film is Father Logan's performance of taciturnity: the nightmare role of condemnation to muteness because of another's confession of a guilty secret where only articulation of that secret could save you. The murderer's name, Keller, is of course German for "cellar," and this may suggest the subterranean life of guilty secrets, producing a kind of contamination of apparent guilt in the wrong places. Yet the act of confession as practiced by the Church cannot be wholly separated from confession as required in the law—the two practices come of age together in Latin Europe and the dominance of Roman-canon law—even though its uses by church and by law are at odds with one another, the situation that Hitchcock exploits.

Confession, Psychoanalytic Truth, and the Law

Religious practices of confession must also stand as the distant origins of the modern, secular, and complex version of confession codified in psychoanalysis. The psychoanalytic model of confessional discourse no doubt offers our most sophisticated contemporary version of what it means to speak, against one's conscious intentions, a truth whose value is estimated by its difficulty. The analysand with the psychoanalyst of course resembles a secularized version of the penitent with the priest, the confessant with the confessor. With this difference that the analysand does not know the "sin" to be "confessed," but only the disorders, the stumbling-blocks, that have been produced by material that has been repressed. As Freud epigramatically states the difference, "In Confession the sinner tells what he knows; in analysis the neurotic has to tell more."[2] In fact, the work of Paolo Segneri, Jean Gerson, and others suggests that the confessor traditionally sought as well to make the confessant "say more." But to this "say more" (compare Rousseau's ambition to "say all"), psychoanalysis brings the concepts of repression and resistance, and a therapeutic and cognitive practice of working through in which the analysand's initial confessional discourse is superseded in favor of something seen to be more profoundly true.

The analyst must attempt to uncover what the analyst knows that the analysand knows, but knows only unconsciously. In working toward the knowledge of this blocked knowledge, the analyst—relying, like both priest and police interrogator, on a certain transferential bond with the analysand—must attempt to elicit a confessional mode of discourse. But it is a strange one, since the analysand's "confessions" of truth must always be regarded with suspicion, as serving some other motive—guilt, revenge, self-justification, self-abasement. The real truth of the psychoanalytic situation is marked by resistances, by the analysand's reluctance to articulate it, to come face to face with it. So that much of analysis usually is directed to resistances, precisely to the nonconfessional or the anticonfessional, on the assumption that this is where the truth is to be sought, the place that the unconscious has marked with its power of censorship.

Psychoanalysis in this manner recognizes that the speech-act of confession is a dubious guide to the truth, which must rather be sought in the resistance to such speech; the confession itself may simply fulfill other purposes, be an avowal of dependency on and propitiation of the analyst. The need to confess speaks *of* guilt, certainly, but it does not speak *the* guilt, does not locate that psychic configuration that needs discovery and healing. It is not the "voluntary" confession that interests the psychoanalyst, but the involuntary, that which, we can almost say, is coerced from the analysand. For psychoanalysis, the claim of confession is necessarily of limited value and the object of suspicion, not a sure guide to the truth, and the test of voluntariness an utterly misleading criterion. The true confession may lie most of all in the resistance to confession.

Psychoanalysis displays an awareness of the doubleness of the confessional act that we have seen in Rousseau and in Dostoevsky's fictional versions: the motivational discrepancy between the constative and performative aspects of confession, a suspicion that the referential matter of the confession—the sin or fault presented—is not necessarily the meaning or the truth of the confession, that which is intended by the speech act. In its understanding that speech, avowal, and, eventually, truth are transactional, transferential, dialogic, psychoanalysis warns us that the situations in which stories are told, that is, the relative positions and the affective relations of tellers and listeners, can make all the difference. In Freud's late essays, especially "Constructions in Analysis" (1937) and "Analysis Terminable and Interminable" (1938), the ability of the psychoanalytic transaction to reach any referential truth is radically put into question.

Recall that in "Constructions in Analysis," Freud concedes that the analysand's story may not be the product of his or her own recall. He notes that while "the path that starts from the analyst's construction ought to end in the patient's recollection," this is not always the case:

> Quite often we do not succeed in bringing the patient to recollect what has been repressed. Instead of that, if the analysis is carried out correctly, we produce in him an assured conviction [*sichere Überzeugung*] of the truth of the construction which achieves the same therapeutic result as a recaptured memory.[3]

It is the analysand's "conviction" that distinguishes this constructed history from mere "suggestion," a history that is purely the creation of the analyst. Yet there is clearly a fine and uncertain line between construction and suggestion, one which depends on the art and tact of the analyst for its correct demarcations. If Freud is confident that a false construction will be repudiated by the analysand because it has no power of explanation, this power does not necessarily depend on a correspondence to the fact of historical event. From the moment he rejected "seduction" as a necessary traumatic event in the lives of his patients—and thus discovered its status as a nearly universal fantasy, and in turn the structural omnipresence of the Oedipus complex—Freud was obliged to acknowledge that the truth status of psychoanalytic insight was rarely factually demonstrable, could rarely be verified by any family archival material, and would have to stand or fall on the basis of its explanatory and therapeutic power. Psychic truth—that truth of mind and emotion that offers a coherent and therapeutic life's narrative to the analysand—is not wholly dependent on referential truth or correspondence to a set of facts. The psychoanalytic transaction uses what the confessional discourse it induces can produce, without any further verification other than its results in understanding and psychic repair.

Now: if Hitchcock's *I Confess* gives a version of the catastrophic intersection of the religious discipline of confession with the law, what happens when the psychoanalytic model of confessional truth intersects with the law? What risks may be created about the confusion of different kinds of truth-seeking, different realms of "conviction"? A striking and troubling instance of a broadly psychotherapeutic instance of confessional discourse entering the precincts of the law is provided by recent cases concerning so-called "repressed memories" and the legal system's attempts to deal with them. In most of these cases, we are faced with a confessional kind of "truth": someone comes forward with a dark secret from long in the past, a secret whose status has been so encrypted that it has been unavailable to the subject himself (or, more often, herself), but has now been retrieved by memory and must be spoken—spoken, in most cases, in the mode of accusation, since most often these memories involve the abusive deeds of another. Confessions, we have already seen, can be aggressive. Ideally, the accused abuser should be brought to confess as well, in order that retribution, healing, or both may take place. Sometimes the result of confession as accusation can be a proliferation of further confessions, as in the case of Paul R. Ingram, accused by his daughters of rape and ritual satanic abuse, who showed an extraordinary compliance in confessing to even the most outlandish acts: rape of his daughters and sons; orgies involving his poker partners and his children; satanic rituals, including the mutilation of his children and the murder of babies; forced abortions; and bestiality.

Paul Ingram's confessions were elicited in the context of interrogations that combined in a confused manner elements of standard police interrogation, psychotherapy, and religious penitential confession. Ingram was a deputy in the Thurston County Sheriff's Office in Olympia, Washington, and his interrogators were colleagues and long-standing friends. They were joined for most of the interrogations by a local psychologist. And Ingram was a Pentecostal Christian, who had surrendered his life to Jesus: when accused by his daughters, he seems to have decided that they must be telling the truth and it was up to him to find in himself the sins they attributed to him. His confessing, which went on over days and weeks, generally took a strange form: at first he would deny any recall of the alleged events. Then, under pressure from his interrogators, he would slowly—with long silences devoted to prayer—begin to uncover scenes recounted in hypothetical form which he at first claimed he could not visualize. Under further pressure, he would end by moving from the conditional to the indicative, subscribing to the truth of the scenes. Lawrence Wright, who in *Remembering Satan* provides a thorough report of the Ingram case, cites extensively from the recorded interrogations.[4] Here is one brief excerpt from the interrogation concerning Ericka Ingram's accusations of rape:

Q: Let's try to talk about the most recent time, Paul. Ericka tells me that it was toward the end of September, just before she moved out. Do you remember that?

A: Well, I keep trying to, to recollect it, and I'm still kind of looking at it as a third party, but, uh, the evidence, and I am trying to put this in the first person, it's not comin' very well, but, uh, I would've gotten out of bed, put on a bathrobe, gone into her room, taken the robe off and at least partially disrobing her and then fondling, uh, her breasts and her vagina and, uh, telling her that if she ever told anybody that, that I would, uh, kill her. . . .

Q: Now you've talked about this in the third party. I'm going to ask you directly, is this what happened?

A: Whew, I'm still having trouble gettin' a clear picture of what happened. I—I know in my own mind that these things had to have happened. (194–95)

If Freud in "Constructions in Analysis" finds that patient and therapist often have to content themselves with: "It must have happened in this way," here Ingram is pushed to turn the "it must have" into "it did"—and repeatedly complies, creating memories where there were none to begin with. When, late in the case, psychologist Richard Ofshe interviewed Ingram, he made the experiment of giving him an accusation that his daughters had not made—that he forced his children to have sex with one another while he watched—and found that a day or so later Ingram had written a full confession to that "event" as well.[5] Ingram later tried to repudiate all his confessions. But courts will rarely go behind a signed confession, and his appeals have been fruitless. He is still in prison, serving a twenty-year sentence, which he apparently accepts as divine punishment.

It is hard to know what to conclude from the Ingram case, since the man convicted is such an extraordinarily compliant confessant that his behavior appears to fall outside the boundaries of normality. Yet the case does suggest the possibly toxic results from the admixture of different models of interrogation and confession, where the suspect/confessant apparently feels the need to accept and ratify any and all charges laid to him. Ingram stands as a kind of parody of Rousseau as viewed by Paul de Man: an example of the confessing machinery gone berserk. It is almost impossible to believe in the content of

Ingram's confessions, and no confirmation for any of them has been discovered: for instance, the allegations of scores of infant sacrifices entailed the burial of scores of infant corpses on the Ingram property, but intensive digging found no remains of any sort. Yet the law as a system has accepted and continues to accept Ingram's confessions as formally valid and thus as truth, and has acted in accordance. At the very least, the Ingram case shows the troubling results of admitting such confessional evidence into the discourse of the law.

Ingram confessed to all accusations, however bizarre. More often, of course, similar accusations, presented in the form of a confessional discourse on the part of the person claiming abuse, and turned into an accusation of the abuser, will be met with denial, setting the stage for the law to adjudicate the claims. And whereas the "memories" brought forth by Ingram's daughters were of recent as well as older provenance, many of the most-discussed cases involve memories from deep in the past, presented with the claim that they were for years totally blocked from memory and suddenly retrieved. What interests me here is not so much the claims of "recovered memory therapy" per se, but the strange results produced when the law is called upon to respond to these claims. There are scores of such cases, with varied outcomes, and much has been written about the most sensational of them. I want to consider two instances where appeals have produced appellate opinions that contain interesting reflections on the issues raised by these kinds of confessional accusation.

One such case is *Franklin v. Duncan,* where the United States District Court for the Northern District of California, on a *habeas corpus* appeal, overturned the conviction of George Franklin, who was found guilty by the trial court of the September 22, 1969, murder of eight-year-old Susan Nason on the accusation of his daughter (and Susan Nason's schoolmate), Eileen Franklin-Lipsker, brought twenty years later in November 1989.[6] Eileen Franklin-Lipsker testified that the memory of the murder suddenly returned to her in January 1989, as she watched her daughter playing on the floor. Other evidence, not presented at the trial, suggests that the claimed memory did not return so suddenly and spontaneously, but was gradually elicited over the course of therapy with a psychologist.[7] In the appeals court, Franklin's conviction was overturned for a number of violations of procedure during the trial, most of all for the trial judge's refusal to allow the defense to introduce "public domain" testimony, consisting mainly of newspaper articles describing the murder scene, that tended to show that all the vivid details of the murder "remembered" by Franklin-Lipsker could in fact have been derived from contemporary press accounts. Since the prosecution had successfully argued that only an eyewitness could have possessed these details, and that their vividness proved the validity of her claim of a recovered memory, exclusion of this evidence compromised the trial in a serious way.

In its preliminary considerations, the appeals court declares that "reliance by a jury on 'recovered memory' testimony does not, in and of itself, violate the Constitution." The court develops this line of thought by noting, "By definition, trials are based on memories of the past." The issue is the credibility of those memories, which the jury must decide. "This case, then, may be described as a 'recovered memory' case, but in reality it is a 'memory' case like all others. After direct and cross examination, after consideration of extrinsic evidence that tends to corroborate or to contradict the memory, the focus must be on the credibility, the believability, the truth of the asserted memory." So that Franklin-Lipsker's testimony—really the sole matter of the trial, since no other kind of evidence was available—simply needs to be tested "by the time-honored procedures of the adversary system" (1438).

These declarations, at once bold and reassuring, may nonetheless be put under the shadow of a certain doubt by the court's own logic. Consider the following:

> Admissibility of the memory is but the first step; it does not establish that the memory is worthy of belief. In this regard mental health experts will undoubtedly, as they must, continue their debate on whether or not the "recovered memory" phenomenon exists, but they can never establish whether or not the asserted memory is true. That must be a function of the trial process. (1438)

The court seems to be saying that a memory, as a kind of empty form, can be admitted as evidence in court, and then the credibility of its content tested at trial. First one judges the admissibility of the concept of the recovered memory, then one judges its specific credibility. At the same time, it concedes that there is disagreement among "mental health experts" as to whether this kind of memory—memory wholly blocked from recall for twenty years, then wholly recovered—really exists. Simultaneously the court asserts that these experts can never determine whether these memories, if they exist, are true, while the trial process can and must make this determination. One may admire this profession of faith in the adversarial trial process and jury deliberation as guarantors of "truth." But one may also question whether any such process can determine the "truth" of something that may not exist. That is, if the memory itself is false—not a memory at all in our usual understanding of that term, but rather a mental image concocted, whether consciously or not, from other material (newspaper reports, for instance) and, through psychotherapy, given the status of memory—it is not clear how the process of judging its credibility can proceed at all.

The problem I detect here is the court's bland assertion that memory, as a concept, can be separated from its content, and that judgment of that content—its credibility—can go forward without establishment of the validity of the memory as recall. There appears to be here a collision of psychotherapeutic and legal understandings of memory. When Freud asserts in the famous case of the "Wolf-Man" that whether the notorious "primal scene"—the infant witnessing his parents' copulation—really took place or was rather a "primal phantasy" doesn't essentially matter because the psychopathological results were the same, we can assent to that proposition.[8] The Wolf Man's confessional discourse is in fact initiated through a dream, the dream of the white wolves in a tree, and the incidents of early childhood subsequently established in analysis all derive from this kind of recollection. In an earlier case-history, that of "Dora," Freud presents a long piece of construction and interpretation to his analysand that concludes:

> "So you see that your love for Herr K. did not come to an end with the scene [by the lake], but that (as I maintained) it has persisted down to the present day—though it is true that you are unconscious of it."—And Dora disputed the fact no longer.

We may instead feel that here the therapist's version of events has taken over from the analysand's and that this unconscious love is his own invention. Many readers of Freud have gone into revolt at this moment of *Dora*.[9] Were Freud's constructions and interpretations in these two case-histories to be submitted to testing in a court of law, one wonders what the results might be.

The point is, of course, that Freud never intended them to be subjected to legal determinations of truth. If in the earlier case, in *Dora,* he still seems to believe that the psychoanalyst has access to the truth of an individual's factual biography, in the later example, the *Wolf-Man,* and in much of his subsequent writing, he makes it clear that the status of truth in psychoanalysis is different. It is a truth constructed in a transactional, transferential interaction of analyst and analysand, a truth whose verifiability finally is not at issue, since what counts is its explanatory force and its therapeutic value. It is worth noting that Freud ends his discussion of the question of primal scenes *versus* primal phantasies with the legal term, *non liquet:* it cannot be decided, whereas the court in the trial of Franklin precisely must decide.

The Franklin trial turned largely on Franklin-Lipsker's vivid narrative of Susan Nason's murder and on the testimony of the expert witness Lenore Terr, author of *Unchained Memories,* who argued that repressed memories are real and their reality provable from later psychic and behavioral symptoms displayed by the victim. Frederick Crews refers to "the mesmerizing quality of Terr's self-depiction as a Freudian Sherlock Holmes," a role that was, according to later reports of jurors, decisive in obtaining Franklin's conviction.[10] If there can be a Sherlock Holmesian drama to psychoanalysis—as Freud was himself aware—as it retrieves a putative past history, the kind of facts and the kind of narrative coherence it seeks result in a "conviction" that is psychic rather than legal. The "Recovery Movement" tends to claim that its opponents reject the existence of "repression" as a mental phenomenon, and in many cases this is true—true, for instance, of Crews, but not of Elizabeth Loftus. The point, I think, is that one may well accept the postulate of repression—however difficult it may be to establish scientifically, it may correspond with clinical and indeed everyday experience—but then one must understand that the operations of repression place us in a realm comparable to dreams and similar forms of psychic process. For Freud, repression and the unconscious are correlate concepts; the unconscious is the product of repressions, and to deny the existence of repression is to deny the possibility of unconscious process. But the unconscious is inherently unknowable, except through its derivatives; it is the domain of "primary process," comparable to the dream work, which represents censored and repressed wishes in distorted, condensed and displaced form.[11] Thus believers in repression must accept that the products of repression, including the "return of the repressed," will be marked by condensation, displacement, hysterical conversion, compromise-formations. The return of the repressed no doubt speaks of something psychically real and powerful, but to judge it an accurate representation of the factual past misconstrues the whole notion of psychic process.

There is considerable evidence that George Franklin was an abusive father and a consumer of pedophile pornography, and for many reasons someone his daughter might have come to loathe. That Eileen Franklin-Lipsker came to believe in her recovered memory of her father's rape and murder of Susan Nason need not be doubted: the crime and the villain seem well-matched, and together they offer a powerful explanatory narrative for her troubled life. It is certainly conceivable that George Franklin did murder Susan Nason. Yet Eileen Franklin-Lipsker's testimony is shot through with contradictions, and she altered significant details of the story several times in its retellings—including indications of time of day and scene of the crime—and twice declared that her memory had been recalled under hypnosis, later to reject this version when she learned that memories induced by hypnosis are not admissible as legal evidence. In her testimony at trial, she insisted that the memory returned suddenly, involuntarily, while watching her own daughter at play, and the trial did not sufficiently explore how the memory may, on the contrary, have emerged in the psychotherapeutic dialogue, as a hypothetical explanation of present symptoms. For if the patient in psychotherapy may feel her present to be hostage to an unmastered past, within the psychotherapeutic session the past is a product of the present discourse.

One further moment in the case of George Franklin deserves mention (and was a further ground for reversal of his conviction on appeal). Following her father's arrest, Eileen Franklin-Lipsker arranged through Deputy District Attorney Martin Murray to pay her father a visit in detention, to see if she could get him to confess. In the jail's visiting room, Franklin-Lipsker told her father that "he should tell the truth." To which George Franklin said nothing, but pointed to a sign in the visiting room that read: "Conversations May Be Monitored" (1445). Franklin's silence became an issue at the trial; indeed, the prosecutor referred to it four times during her closing argument, claiming that the silence was as good as a confession of guilt, "worth its weight in gold." The admission of Franklin's silence as evidence against him was construed by the appeals court as a violation of due process since silence following *Miranda* warnings cannot be taken as indicative of guilt. In his silent gesture to the sign indicating that confessional statements in the jail visiting room would not necessarily be under any seal of secrecy, Franklin was refusing confessional discourse, in a gesture that the trial court read as in and of itself confessional, but which on appeal was judged to be—the court here cites the words of *Doyle v. Ohio* (1976)—"insolubly ambiguous" and therefore no evidence at all. In a case where the truth of the accuser has the quality of the confession of dark past secrets, and calls for a matching confession on the part of the accused, Franklin's silent pointing to a sign warning of the infelicitous conditions of confessional discourse may be the symbolically appropriate response. Unlike Paul Ingram, he refused the confessional mode (and never took the stand during the trial).[12]

The kind of truth purveyed in recovered memories and their status before the law receives a very different treatment in *Tyson v. Tyson,* a case decided by the Supreme Court of the State of Washington in 1986.[13] Nancy Tyson had brought an intentional tort action against her father, Dwight Robert Tyson, in 1983, alleging that he had committed multiple acts of sexual assault on her from 1960 to 1969, when she was between the ages of three and eleven. Nancy Tyson "further alleged that the sexual assaults caused her to suppress any memory of the acts and that she did not remember the alleged acts until she entered psychological therapy during 1983. Plaintiff filed the complaint within 1 year of her recollection of the alleged acts" (227). The precise question to be decided by the Supreme Court of Washington (which took the case on certiorari from the U.S. District Court for the Western District of Washington) concerns the "discovery rule" and the statute of limitations. Normally, in Washington law, an action for personal injury must be brought within three years of the time the cause of action has occurred, but the statute of limitations is "tolled"—i.e., the clock is stopped—until the plaintiff is eighteen years old or until such time as the plaintiff, using reasonable diligence, would have discovered the cause of action. The statute of limitations began to run, then, with the plaintiff's eighteenth birthday and expired on April 20, 1978; or, by Nancy Tyson's account, began to run when she recovered the repressed memory, in

1983. Can the statute of limitations be tolled when the plaintiff claims to have blocked the incident that is the cause of action from her conscious memory during the entire course of the statute of limitations?

The dissenting opinion in *Tyson v. Tyson* makes much the same claims about the role of memories in a trial as will the court in *Franklin v. Duncan:* it is the business of trials to determine the credibility of evidence in the form of memory. "The trier of fact frequently is asked to determine the outcome of a lawsuit by deciding which party is telling the truth. . . . It is illogical to foreclose a cause of action alleging sexual abuse just because the parties' credibility will be determinative, when such 'swearing contests' are common to other contexts" (231–32). Thus Nancy Tyson should be allowed to submit her case to the normal testing procedures of the courtroom. To impose the statute of limitations on such a case is unfair, since sometimes a "triggering event" is necessary "to arouse a plaintiff's suspicions regarding a defendant's potential liability." The "triggering event" in this case is psychotherapy itself. The precedent cited by the dissent concerned a man who discovered that the insurance policy on his fishing gear had been canceled some years earlier without notification—a cancellation he detected only when he applied to cover a loss and found that he was no longer insured. The equation of this insurance event and the recovery of a memory through psychotherapy gives one pause: is memory in the nature of an event? The dissent here seems to have absorbed much of the literature on abuse, memory, and healing: "Once the victim begins to confront her experiences and link her damages with her father's incestuous conduct, she has taken a step as a *survivor* of childhood incestuous abuse" (235). One might ask if it is not precisely the matter of that "link" that is at issue. The dissent believes that Nancy Tyson must be allowed to make a showing "that she has suffered injury, that such injury was the result of childhood sexual abuse, and that the defendant was her abuser" (237), and it objects to the majority's "denigration of mental health professionals' contribution to our justice system" (232).

What prompts this reaction from the dissent in *Tyson* is the majority's decision that Nancy Tyson's case against her father cannot go forward, that her story of childhood sexual abuse cannot be told in a court of law. The majority rules against Nancy Tyson's claim that discovery should proceed with the argument that the statute of limitations protects the pursuit of truth by barring "stale evidence." As time passes, key witnesses may be unavailable. The evidence that is available becomes less trustworthy as memories fade or are colored by more recent events. Citing a number of medical malpractice suits as precedents, the court notes that in these cases there was "empirical, verifiable evidence"—a sponge found twenty-two years after surgery in someone's abdomen, evidence of the misuse of oxygen in an incubator—whereas Nancy Tyson's claim rests only on "a subjective assertion" (228–29).

The court then focuses on what the dissent calls the "triggering event," Nancy Tyson's "discovery" of her abuse through psychotherapy, to ask whether this may properly be considered an event in our usual understanding of that term. Citing an article by Marianne Wesson, "Historical Truth, Narrative Truth, and Expert Testimony," the court asserts that studies show that "the psychoanalytic process can even lead to a distortion of the truth of events in the subject's past life," that memories can be influenced by the analyst's interpretations, that there can be a large gap between psychoanalytic truth and historical occurrence.[14] "The purpose of emotional therapy is not the determination of historical facts, but the contemporary treatment and cure of the patient. We cannot expect these professions to answer questions which they are not intended to address" (229).

The *Tyson* court here trenchantly adjudicates the vexed question of psychoanalytic truth—or "narrative truth," as it is sometimes called—*versus* historical truth (or what Freud at times calls "material truth").[15] It does so by adopting the prudent and probably the dominant contemporary model, which disclaims the ability of psychoanalysis to reconstruct a true life-history in the sense of a history verifiably consonant with "the facts." Even Rousseau in his *Confessions,* for all his insistence on his desire for utter accuracy, admits that the truth of memory may not be that of strict historical truth. For Rousseau, as for psychoanalysis, this does not so much matter, since it is less event that counts than emotional reaction to event, less—to take the best-publicized issue in the development of Freud's theory—the fact of "seduction" than the emotional experience or fantasy of seduction. In arguing that the arena of psychoanalytic treatment and cure is not the patient's past but rather his or her present, the court aligns itself with a view of confessional truth as an intersubjective, transactional, transferential kind of truth, where the care of souls—

to speak the language of the Church—is really, whatever the claims to historical accuracy, a matter of the present speech-act.

"We, therefore, hold that the discovery rule does not apply to an intentional tort claim where the plaintiff has blocked the incident from her conscious memory during the period of the statute of limitations," the court concludes its ruling (230). In disallowing Nancy Tyson's claim to discovery, the court implicitly says that there are some stories of a private and confessional nature that are too uncontrollable, in an evidentiary sense, to be permitted telling in a court of law: some narrative discourses so inherently unaccountable to, so fundamentally untestable against, events in the real world that they must be legally silenced. This is a radical judgment. To the dissent's commonsensical view that all stories should be given the chance to test themselves in adversarial proceedings, it replies that some stories are inherently untestable, and thus that convincing a jury of their truthfulness would result in an unjust conviction. One could say that the unverifiability of stories such as Nancy Tyson's is matched by their unrebuttability. As with "Victim Impact Statements," there is simply no counter-story that can stand up to them.

Franklin v. Duncan and *Tyson v. Tyson* suggest in their different ways the difficulties of passing confessional discourse of the psychotherapeutic sort through the eye of the legal needle. The confident assumption of the court in *Franklin* (and the dissent in *Tyson*) that a trial can adjudicate the evidentiary value of the confession of a dark secret from the past, put forward in the mode of accusation, seems unwarranted when there is no way of knowing to what extent the secret, however deeply believed in by the confessant, is the creation of the psychotherapeutic process itself. Psychotherapeutic "truth" might be labeled "for internal use only." When its claims are used to implicate others in a putative crime, the legal system might more prudently resort to the position of the court in *Tyson:* that a trial has no way of sorting out such claims. Interesting in this regard is the *Ramona* case, in which a father accused of sexual assault by his daughter successfully sued his daughter's psychotherapist for malpractice in the creation of the memory of abuse.[16] It is probably in the logic of psychotherapeutic discourse taken up by legal discourse that eventually psychotherapy itself should be put on the bench of the accused. This offers, I think, further evidence that the use of psychotherapeutic truth as putatively legal truth represents a dangerous category error, a confusion of realms. The law is perhaps overeager to hear confessional discourse. Let it at least stay with that elicited by police interrogators, and eschew that garnered by psychotherapists—as it does eschew that garnered by priests.

Victims and Their Statements

Since the decision in *Tyson v. Tyson,* Washington and some thirty other states have extended the statute of limitations in cases of alleged childhood abuse, thus effectively overruling the *Tyson* court. There is at least an indirect connection between the desire of some courts— and many state legislatures—to allow allegations of abuse from the distant past to make their claim in a trial, and the movement known as "Victims' Rights."

The Victim's Rights movement seeks to correct a perceived imbalance in the criminal justice system by giving voice to the emotional hurt of the victims of crime. If centuries ago criminal prosecutions were brought directly by the victim, that has long since ceased to be case: now it is the state that prosecutes criminal charges, and the victim is at most a witness for the prosecution, often marginalized, left with the sense that his or her particularized set of wrongs don't make much difference in the way the prosecution pursues its case. The Warren Court was seen by many as excessively concerned with the rights of criminal defendants, leading to the accusation that victims of crime were "invisible" or "forgotten" by justice. The "Victims Rights Movement," dating from the late 1960s, marked a reaction, seeking for victims financial compensation and a greater role in determining the sentence of perpetrators.[17] The desire to enhance the place of the victim or the victim's surrogates in the legal process became focussed, most visibly and most controversially, in the issue of the "Victim Impact Statement": a testimonial to the victim's suffering introduced into the trial, either as oral evidence or as a written statement read in court, designed to lay before the sentencer (judge or jury) a personal and particularized account of the victim's wrongs. Paradoxically, the Victim Impact Statement may appear most needed—as well as most controversial—in the case of homicide, when the victim is dead and therefore wholly silenced in the context of the courtroom.

The major legal controversy has come to focus on the introduction of VIS testimony at the sentencing phase of a murder trial, where the issue is whether the perpetrator of the crime should receive the death sentence or not. As Martha Minow notes:

> the victims' rights movement directly assaulted liberal reforms and recast the death penalty. The introduction of the victim impact statement specifically seeks to render vivid and palpable the effects of the crime on the specific victim and that person's family and friends. . . . The movement features respect for the subjective experiences and feelings of the victims and for their need to tell their own stories. There is also a calculated judgment that the sentencer who hears from the victim or the victim's family will find the victim's suffering more reason to hold the defendant responsible and thus will sentence more stringently.[18]

The issue, then, concerns the place of a personal narrative of extreme suffering—often an aggressive confessional narrative—introduced at the point the trial is deciding the fate of the convicted defendant. The Supreme Court addressed the issue in two bitterly contested cases: *Booth v. Maryland,* in 1987, which excluded the VIS during the sentencing phase of capital cases, and then, in a stunning reversal— the personnel of the Court having changed in the interim—*Payne v. Tennessee,* in 1991, which readmitted the VIS in the same circumstances.[19]

The kind of Victim Impact Statement at issue in *Booth* and *Payne* aims to present for the jury's consideration at the sentencing phase of the trial information about the full consequences of the criminal act, including economic loss and physical injury suffered by the victim, change in personal welfare or familial relationships, need for psychological services, and other information "related to the impact of the offense upon the victim or the victim's family that the trial court requires" (*Booth,* 499). As Justice Antonin Scalia writes in his dissent in *Booth:*

> Recent years have seen an outpouring of popular concern for what has come to be known as "victims' rights." . . . Many citizens have found one-sided and hence unjust the criminal trial in which a parade of witnesses comes forth to testify to the pressures beyond normal human experience that drove the defendant to commit his crime, with no one to lay before the sentencing authority the full reality of human suffering the de-

fendant has produced—which (and *not* moral guilt alone) is one of the reasons society deems his act worthy of the prescribed penalty. (520)

Scalia thus summarizes the political force behind the mandate for VIS, and the argument that since the defense is allowed to introduce mitigating evidence, the prosecution should be able to counter with this kind of aggravating evidence—the argument that triumphed in *Payne*.

In the case of homicide, the victim has suffered ultimate harm. Does it make sense to go beyond this ultimate harm, to include the grim, retributive narratives of collateral harms inflicted upon others, essentially the surviving members of the victim's family? Or is there here a confused multiplication of victim stories? In particular, what is the effect of bringing these stories into a capital sentencing deliberation where, as Justice Lewis Powell writes in the majority opinion, "the jury is required to focus on the defendant as a 'uniquely individual human bein[g]'" (504, citing *Woodson v. North Carolina* [1976]). Capital sentencing must, by the Court's own prior holdings, consider any mitigating circumstances that may make the criminal less liable to execution. Should it also consider these victim stories that appear to aggravate his culpability? Is there such a thing as aggravated murder, or is murder in the first degree itself an ultimate case? Is the kind of information supplied by the VIS relevant to a determination of culpability, or is it, by its nature, unduly inflammatory, thus likely to produce violations of the Eighth Amendment's prohibition of "cruel and unusual punishment"?

In *Booth,* the majority argues essentially that in "the unique circumstance of a capital sentencing hearing," the VIS is irrelevant, since it does not focus on the character of the defendant, but rather on the character and reputation of the victim and the effect on his family, which "may be wholly unrelated to the blameworthiness of a particular defendant" (504). The VIS, a story on behalf of the victims rather than the criminal, in effect introduces the wrong story, in the wrong place. It extends the narrative beyond its pertinent courtroom boundaries. The decision on capital sentencing ought not to turn on perceptions that the "victim was a sterling member of the community rather than someone of questionable character" (506): a life taken is a life taken, and it should not matter, morally, whether the victim was a bank president or one of the homeless. As Justice John Paul Stevens argues in his dissenting opinion in *Payne,* "if a defendant who had murdered a convenience store clerk in cold blood in the course of an armed robbery, offered evidence unknown to him at the time of the crime about the immoral character of his victim, all would recognize immediately that the evidence was irrelevant and inadmissible" (501 U.S. 808, 856–57). Evidence of this kind "can only be intended to identify some victims as more worthy of protection than others. Such proof risks decisions based on the same invidious motives as a prosecutor's decision to seek the death penalty if a victim is white but to accept a plea bargain if the victim is black" (866).

The rhetoric of the victim reaches some sort of nadir in *South Carolina v. Gathers,*[20] a case that comes two years after *Booth* and two years before *Payne,* in which the Court, again by a 5–4 margin, excludes testimony offered by the prosecutor at the sentencing phase of Demetrius Gathers's trial for the killing of Richard Haynes, a homeless person living on a park bench, who apparently considered himself a preacher and apostle and referred to himself as "Reverend Minister." Near Haynes's corpse were found two Bibles, rosary beads, plastic angels, a voter registration card, and a tract entitled "The Game Guy's Prayer." The prosecutor, developing his own informal VIS, used Haynes's religiosity as the basis for a maudlin homily:

> "He had a plastic angel. Of course, he is now with the angels now, but this defendant Demetrius Gathers could care little about the fact that he is a religious person. Cared little of the pain and agony he inflicted upon a person who is trying to enjoy one of our public parks.
>
> "But look at Reverend Minister Haynes' prayer. It's called the Game Guy's Prayer. 'Dear God, help me to be a sport in this little game of life. I don't ask for any easy place in this lineup. Play me anywhere you need me. . . . When in the falling dusk I get the final bell, I ask for no lying, complimentary tombstones. I'd only like to know that you feel that I have been a good guy, a good game guy, a saint in the game of life.'
>
> "Reverend Haynes, we know, was a very small person. . . ."
> (808–10)

The prosecutor makes maximal use of Haynes's minimal legacies to focus sentimental attention on the victim and on victimhood, providing an example of what Minow sees as a characteristic of "victim talk" in general, "the emphasis on subjective accounts of feelings and experiences to validate victim status and to secure the listeners' sympathies."[21] The Supreme Court of South Carolina was not sympathetic; it reversed Gathers's death sentence and remanded the case for a new sentencing proceeding, with the comment that the prosecutor's speech "conveyed the suggestion appellant deserved a death sentence because the victim was a religious man and a registered voter"—a judgment that the majority of the U.S. Supreme Court then upheld.

In *Booth,* the Court further argues that capital sentencing should not depend on the degree to which the victim's family has been articulate in its expression of grief and harm—as it very much was in that case. There is a variability in the narratives provided by Victim Impact Statements—in the effectiveness, indeed, of their impact—that must make their influence on sentencing open to suspicion. *Gathers* offers a kind of limit case not mentioned in either *Booth* or *Payne:* the situation of a murder victim who had no surviving relatives or friends. Such a victim might be bereft of any VIS—the problem evidently faced by the prosecutor in *Gathers,* which he rather too vigorously attempted to rectify. Such a victim might be essentially unnarratable, a zero-degree victim. Without a story, he would, in relative terms, be less a victim, though equally dead.

The Court in *Booth* notes also how difficult it would be for the defendant to attempt to rebut the evidence presented in Victim Impact Statements. What kind of counter-story could be introduced to contest these narratives of grief and rage? As Justice Thurgood Marshall concludes in his dissent in *Payne*—effectively summarizing Powell's majority opinion in *Booth*—"the probative value of such evidence is always outweighed by its prejudicial effect because of its inherent capacity to draw the jury's attention away from the character of the defendant and the circumstances of the crime to such illicit considerations as the eloquence with which family members express their grief and the status of the victim in the community" (846). The VIS gives the wrong story, defined as a story in the wrong place, diverting attention from the relevant narrative to illicit questions.

In *Payne,* Chief Justice William Rehnquist himself provides an utterly grisly narrative of the crime scene—the eighty-four knife wounds inflicted by Pervis Tyrone Payne in killing Charisse Christopher and her daughter Lacie, and the bare survival and continuing distress of her son Nicholas—as if to supplement the actual VIS presented orally by Charisse's mother during the sentencing phase of the trial. In *Booth,* the VIS was a written statement, prepared by the State Division of Parole and Probation, read to the jury. The appendix to the Court's decision gives us the text, detailing the reactions of son, daughter, and granddaughter to the discovery of the bodies of Irvin and Rose Bronstein, stabbed to death in the course of a robbery for money to buy drugs. The VIS is mainly concerned with the mental states induced in the survivors by the murder: the consequent depression, fright, sleeplessness, the feeling that their lives have been permanently changed by this tragedy. Much of the VIS unfolds in *style indirect libre,* indirect discourse summary of emotional affect. For instance, concerning the daughter:

> They didn't have to kill because there was no one to stop them from looting. Her father would have given them anything. The murders show the viciousness of the killers' anger. She doesn't feel that the people who did this could ever be rehabilitated and she doesn't want them to be able to do this again or put another family through this. She feels that the lives of her family members will never be the same again. (513)

The effectiveness of such a passage—as novelists since Flaubert, at least, have understood—results from its effacement of the mediating narrator, its claim to render impersonally, without mediation, the thoughts and feelings of the individual subject. The anonymous author of the VIS comes forward only at the end, in a peroration all the more telling in that she has let the story "tell itself" up to that point:

> It became increasingly apparent to the writer as she talked to the family members that the murder of Mr. and Mrs. Bronstein is still such a shocking, painful, and devastating memory to them that it permeates every aspect of their daily lives. It is doubtful that they will ever be able to fully recover from this tragedy and not be haunted by the memory of the brutal manner in which their loved ones were murdered and taken from them. (515)

"It is doubtful that . . . ": at this phrase, one wants to ask—as Roland Barthes does of some narrative statements in Balzac—"who is speaking?"[22] In the absence of a clear answer, the phrase appears to be proffered on behalf of the reader, as the reader's judgment. The conclusion reached by this anonymous employee of the Department of Parole and Probation appeals to an impersonal, and therefore irrefutable, construction, one devoid of specific human agency, endowed with all the power of the *doxa,* the truth invested with general societal authority.

One can imagine the effect of this dire story of irreparable harm at the moment of its enunciation, when the jury weighed whether or not Booth was to be executed. Consider, in this context, Justice Byron White's dissent on the matter of "[t]he supposed problems arising from a defendant's rebuttal of victim impact statements" (518). There is nothing in the Maryland statute that prevented the defendant from attempting to rebut the VIS, writes White. He adds: "Petitioner introduced no such rebuttal evidence, probably because he considered, wisely, that it was not in his best interest to do so." The remark appears either disingenuous or obtuse. How would one go about rebutting a narrative of inconsolable grief? Perhaps, on the model of the Marquis de Sade, by the argument that murder merely furthers the destructive work of nature herself, and thus cannot be considered contrary to a natural morality? But the point is really that certain narratives—narratives of victimhood, of the irreparable, of what cannot be undone—are not susceptible of rebuttal. To speak of the possibility of rebuttal of what is recounted in the VIS appears as a misunderstanding of the nature of narrative and the ways one listens to it, receives it, the way it makes an effect. No more than those listeners on board the ship "Nellie," anchored in the Thames estuary, who have listened Marlow's tale in *Heart of Darkness,* can the members of the jury neutralize the VIS with a counter-story. Once told, certain darknesses do not dissipate.

Booth and *Payne* demonstrate the Supreme Court's difficulties in dealing with the relevance and the effect of victim narratives and the rules concerning their presentation to listeners. As in the case of confessions, the problem is one of narrative rules governing the telling of and the listening to particularly crucial and problematic kinds of personal stories. In *Miranda,* the Court had to decide when the story of a suspect's inculpation began—thus when his Fifth Amendment right to silence could be invoked—whereas in *Booth* and *Payne* it must decide when the story of the crime ends, the limits of its retelling. More specifically, *Booth* and *Payne* consider, with contradictory results, rules about how, when, and by whom narratives can legitimately be heard. In my view, the issue is most succinctly disposed of by Justice Stevens, in his *Payne* dissent, when he writes: "Evidence that serves no purpose other than to appeal to the sympathies or emotions of the jurors has never been considered admissible" (856–57).

Yet "sympathy" is itself by no means an unproblematic concept, as another Supreme Court case, *California v. Brown* (1987) makes clear.[23] In that case, the Court debates whether or not an "anti-sympathy" clause in a jury instruction precluded the convicted criminal's receiving fair treatment during the sentencing phase of his trial. Brown was found guilty of rape and murder; the judge instructed the jury that in determining Brown's sentence it should consider and weigh the aggravating and mitigating circumstances, but that: "You must not be swayed by mere sentiment, conjecture, sympathy, passion, prejudice, public opinion or public feeling" (548). Brown was sentenced to death. The California Supreme Court reversed the sentence on the grounds that federal constitutional law "forbids an instruction which denies a capital defendant the right to have the jury consider any 'sympathy factor' raised by the evidence when determining the appropriate penalty" (540). In a 5–4 decision, the U.S. Supreme Court reversed and remanded, upholding the jury instruction.

The debate between the majority opinion, written by Chief Justice Rehnquist, and the dissenting opinions written by Justices Brennan and Blackmun, turns on the word "sympathy" in the jury instruction. Since in the sentencing phase of a capital case a jury must consider all mitigating evidence intended to induce consideration of "compassionate or mitigating factors stemming from the diverse frailties of mankind," as the Court held in *Woodson,* is the instruction not to be swayed by sympathy a violation of the defendant's rights?[24] Does it ask the jury to listen to his story in the wrong way? For the dissenters in *California v. Brown,* the interpretation of the uses of sympathy is crucial because so much is at stake. As Brennan states: "it is highly likely that the instruction eliminated [Brown's] only hope of gaining mercy from the sentencer" (561). Majority and dissent both understand that listening sympathetically or unsympathetically makes all the difference in the meaning and the result of the story told.

Sympathy has long been recognized to be at once a powerful and an unstable emotion. Like compassion (it is the Greek equivalent of

that Latin derivation), it implies the capacity to participate in the suffering of another (*sym-pathos*) and, more generally, to feel a like emotion, to experience "fellow feeling," to put yourself in another's place.
It became a key concept in the Enlightenment's concern with the
foundations of a secular humanist ethics: both the cornerstone of
ethics (for Rousseau, for instance) and something more problematic
and worrisome because of the potential for theatrical enactment and
deception implicated in the concept. As one critic writes in explica-
tion of Adam Smith's discussion of sympathy in his *Theory of Moral
Sentiments:* "For Smith, acts of sympathy are structured by theatrical
dynamics that (because of the impossibility of really knowing or entering into someone else's sentiments) depend on people's ability to
represent themselves as tableaux, spectacles, or texts before others."[25]
Smith himself puts it this way:

> Though our brother is upon the rack, as long as we ourselves are
> at our ease, our senses will never inform us of what he suf-
> fers. . . . By the imagination we place ourselves in his situation,
> we conceive ourselves enduring all the same torments, we enter
> as it were into his body, and become in some measure the same
> person with him, and thence form some idea of his sensations,
> and even feel something which, though weaker in degree, is not
> altogether unlike them. His agonies, when they are thus
> brought home to ourselves, when we have thus adopted and
> made them our own, begin at last to affect us, and we then trem-
> ble and shudder at the thought of what he feels.[26]

If the recreation of what another feels depends to this extent on the
imagination and on representation of another's feelings, resulting in a
powerful reaction based on "the thought of what he feels," it is evident that the capacity of sympathy to bridge the boundaries between
separate subjectivities is matched by its capacity for manipulation and
its susceptibility to a theatrical staging.

It is in large part this capacity for inculcating compassion that has
repeatedly, over the ages, led to the multifarious attempts to ban or
suppress imaginative literature, on the premise that it is morally
destabilizing. In particular, the theatre, as the most public enactment
of the passions, was for centuries under attack in Europe, and indeed
banned for long periods of time. Even Rousseau, the theoretician of
compassion, undertook to preserve the moral purity of his native

Geneva by attempting to repulse the proposal of the French *philosophes* that Geneva's ban on the theatre—in place since the days of John Calvin—be lifted. Theatre, Rousseau says in his *Letter to d'Alembert on the Theatre,* inculcates make-believe passions; it arouses false emotions, and thus it makes people discontented with their lives; it displaces the spectators, making them lose their moral bearings. Entering into the feigned passions of others depends on an act of spectatorship based on compassion, or sympathy, which is inherently dangerous. It leads to vicarious participation rather than honest emotion. The imaginative sympathy inculcated by theatre is a school for vices. In another twist on the argument, Diderot's *Paradox on the Actor* suggests that the most accomplished actor is the one who is most distanced from the emotion to be simulated because his detachment allows him to create that emotion from the point of view of the spectator, who alone matters. Sympathy may in this conception be the most artificial of emotions—the creation of a pure fiction.[27]

California v. Brown does not enter into a detailed analysis of sympathy, but one nonetheless senses that the Court has trouble dealing with the place and consequences of sympathy in the jury instruction because it understands that sympathy is, almost epistemologically, a slippery concept. To what extent do we want a jury to change places, imaginatively, with the criminal defendant? To what extent do we want jurors to use their imagination to represent the suffering of the defendant and, through representing to themselves what it would be like to be in his place, to "tremble and shudder" at what he must feel? Conversely, should the cries of the victims, however transmitted to the courtroom, be allowed a similar hearing, so that the narrative of mitigation be counterbalanced by the narrative of aggravation? What is the right story, what is its correct place, and how should it be listened to?

We have diverged quite far from the specific narrative of confession. But I have hoped to show that there are similarities in the narratives of "repressed memory" and of "victim impact": these both come forward, originally, with the claim that they are painful hidden stories—replete with an element of shame that has kept them hidden—that need to be told, listened to, acknowledged. They demand a sympathetic, transferential listening. Yet in the context of the law, where their confessional status is also aggressive and accusatory, they may be dangerously problematic, eliciting a sympathy on the part of listeners that can override a lack of evidence (as in *Franklin v. Duncan*), or create an emotional impact that may be devastating to the person whose fate is under adjudication (as with the VIS). The legal system has reacted in various and contradictory ways, from enthusiastic acceptance of such stories to suspicion of their pertinence.

In a contemporary American culture characterized by confessional discourse and multifarious therapeutic practice, a high value has come to be placed on speaking confessionally, and along with this a belief that confession is therapeutic, or at least the precondition of therapy. Such disasters as school shootings are immediately followed by the appearance of therapists—"grief counselors"—to talk through the reactions of the survivors. Talk shows—Oprah Winfrey, Geraldo Rivera, Sally Jessie Raphael, and others—put on television ordinary people speaking confessionally about their own lives in ways unthinkable to earlier generations. What the inaugural patient of psychoanalysis, Anna O., called "the talking cure" has evolved into a generalized belief in the catharsis of confession, of the value of telling all, in public.[28] It is as if the definition of modern selfhood which began to emerge hand-in-hand with the early modern practices of confession defined by the Church in Lateran IV, and reached their full modern expression in Rousseau's *Confessions,* had now come to the point where many feel their very definition as persons, as selves, depends on their having matter to confess. Without confessional talk, one might say, you simply don't exist.

The result is surely a trivialization of confession, one that may already be implicit in Rousseau's evident enjoyment of the staginess of the scene of confessing. Another result may be a cultural overvaluing of victims' stories, so that the law, for instance, is caught off its guard in allowing such stories into its arena. On the other hand, our very conception of selfhood would collapse without the confessional discourse which, whether trivial or profound, indicates the uniqueness of the individual subject, and its claim to a hearing.

Psychoanalysis, as that curious and impossible profession devised for the cure of individual subjects, works toward making the individual assume his or her confessional discourse, accepting and justifying the peculiarities of the individual's story as told by that person, while offering something of a set pattern into which to fit that story—since, for instance, most life stories will include such inevitable patternings as the Oedipal. If psychoanalysis diverges from religious confession in its suspicion that confessional discourse may be a cover-up of more deeply repressed material—though the religious confessor, and the inquisition into heresy, can take the same stance—it offers its own model of reintegration of the patient: not so much in this case with a sense of community as with the self, though this restored self can then presumably rejoin community in more effective ways. Both models of the confessional act claim to work toward the healing of the individual subject in terms of a normative standard of psychic health which is at least partially measured against community norms. And both depend on a transindividual search for truth, one where the affective, transferential bond of confessant and confessor is itself productive of the articulation of truth. The Church's carefully crafted confessional and the psychoanalyst's couch are both places designed for the telling of intimate, dark secrets, in an atmosphere that is supposed to be free from the prying ears of the outside world, sealed in a special place and an atmosphere of consolation and healing.

When the law intervenes, or perhaps more accurately, when the law opens itself to admission of such confessional discourse, be it in the interrogation of the individual criminal suspect, in the presentation of recovered memories of abuse as evidence, in the stories of victimhood, there is at least a risk that the kind of truth produced by confession will be misconstrued, or given a factual existence whereas its true nature may be more accurately described as emotional. If confessional discourse might at first glance seem to be the most personal and honest an individual is capable of, its honesty, its intimacy, its truth to the self don't necessarily always conform to the truth of the external world, the truth of fact. Certainly the confessional talk of psychoanalysis suggests that confession can be less a definition of the truth than a search for it, a posing of the question: who am I? The emergence of the modern sense of the self and the identity of the individual is closely tied to a valuing of the confessional act, suggesting that the discipline of confession is in part a search to define the self, morally and psychologically. Both psychoanalysis and the religious tradition would indicate that this self-definition takes place in the context of a certain law. The subject emerges as determined by certain "thou shalt nots," be they seen as divine commandments or as laws of structural or developmental process: the dissolution of the Oedipus complex installs the law of the father within, as the superego. Jacques

Lacan likes to speak of the "Nom-du-Père," the name of the father, as the primal structuring, rule-giving symbolic force, a term which suggests the consonance of this kind of law with the religious. But human law—the legal system—may not so much mimic as parody divine or psychic law when it deals with the individual's self-expression in confessional discourse. For the law takes literally what the other two domains express symbolically.

I want to end by evoking a tale by Jorge Luis Borges which—like so many of his brief meta-fictions—appears to emblematize something in our response to confessional discourse of the deepest and blackest sort. In "The Shape of the Sword," the narrator encounters in the Argentine countryside a man the locals call "the Englishman from La Colorada," whose face is marked by a semi-circular scar. In fact, he is Irish. When the narrator asks him to recount the origins of the scar, he agrees "under one condition: that of not mitigating one bit of the opprobrium, of the infamous circumstances."[29] This sounds like preparation for a confessional discourse in the mode of Rousseau, a display of a scene of guilt and humiliation. Yet as the story unfolds, the narrator appears to be merely a witness to treachery. He tells of an incident in the Irish rebellion against the "Black and Tans" in which the rebels are betrayed by one of their number and go to execution at the hands of the British. The traitor, Vincent Moon, is referred to throughout in the third person by the Irish narrator who speaks as one of the band of rebels. When Moon's treachery becomes apparent, the narrator recounts that he seized a cutlass and "with that half moon I carved into his face forever a half moon of blood."

At this point, the Irishman addresses his interlocutor: "Borges, to you, a stranger, I have made this confession. Your contempt does not grieve me so much." Borges the narrator at first reacts with incomprehension.

> "And Moon?" I asked him.
>
> "He collected his Judas money and fled to Brazil. That afternoon in the square, he saw a dummy shot up by some drunken men."
>
> I waited in vain for the rest of the story. Finally I told him to go on.
>
> Then a sob went through his body; and with a weak gentleness he pointed to the whitish curved scar.

"You don't believe me?" he stammered. "Don't you see that I carry written on my face the mark of my infamy? I have told you the story thus so that you would hear me to the end. I denounced the man who protected me: I am Vincent Moon. Now despise me." (71)

The confession concerns so black a betrayal—it is so unspeakable—that only the narrative ruse of making it appear another's story allows it to be told at all. The traitor presented in the third person turns out in fact to coincide with the first-person narrator.

We think of confessions as preeminently first-person narratives—even though we know they may be the product of collaboration between confessant and confessor, analysand and analyst, suspect and interrogator. Here the ruse of the third person assigned to the confessant allows an apparent objectification of his treacherous act that in itself constitutes a judgment on it, staging shame and guilt perhaps more effectively than Rousseau's first person at odds with his own incoherent identity. When at the very end of the tale the third person collapses back into the first person, and the treachery is assumed by Moon the narrator, Borges and his readers are left with the problem of what to do with such a confession. "Now despise me." To be sure, this is the appropriate moral response. But there is still the problem of the motives of the confession, the search for opprobrium, the desire to have one's interlocutor despise one. What is going on here? What strange set of psychic and moral needs are being accomplished in such a confession? And if the response of the law to such a confession would be evident and unambiguous—Moon brought to justice at last—would it really get to the heart of the matter?

6

THE CONFESSIONAL IMAGINATION

It is difficult to tell with certainty what makes a suspect speak.

Justice O'Connor, in *Oregon v. Elstad*

You'd be surprised what they can make you do.

Peter Reilly

Where do we stand, today, on confessional speech, its intentions, its "voluntariness," its truth value, its therapeutic uses? How, as a society, do we think about confession? What is its place in our cultural imagination? If we live in a culture that seems today to be characterized by a generalized demand for transparency, including the demand that public figures—not least, the President of United States—offer full public avowals of private behavior, aren't there also signs that the proliferation of pleas of guilt and requests for exculpation makes us uneasy? Self-exposure, in books and on television and in public discourse, attracts a ready audience, yet the reaction of the audience is more difficult to gauge. I want here to consider the current status of confessions in the law, our imaginative fascination with confessions, including those inquisitorially extorted, and to make some assessment of the place of confession as a cultural ritual.

After *Miranda*: Two Cases

The afterlife of *Miranda v. Arizona* in the Supreme Court has not been easy. The more conservative majorities that followed the Warren

Court have declared a general allegiance to its holdings but continued to chip away at its edges, arguing in particular that a violation of
Miranda warnings does not necessarily constitute an infringement of
the Fifth Amendment itself, but only of those "prophylactic rules"
designed to protect a suspect's Fifth Amendment rights; that these
rules don't constitute a "constitutional straitjacket"; that an "unwarned" statement by a suspect, though barred from use by a prosecutor in his case in chief, can nonetheless be used to impeach
testimony if it can be made to pass muster on the old "due process
voluntariness test," and can be used to discover derivative evidence
admissible at trial.[1] Thus the Court has managed to keep from total
exclusion from the prosecutor's arsenal certain statements made by
suspects before they are given the *Miranda* warnings, and indeed,
some would argue, has provided the police a convenient tool for
obtaining confessions which, if themselves barred from evidence,
nonetheless lead to other usable evidence and indeed to later confessions produced according to the rules.[2] While *Dickerson v. United
States* reaffirmed the constitutional rule of *Miranda* in 2000, it did
nothing to resolve a number of ambiguities about the extent and application of the rule, and provided no further protections for suspects.

    Oregon v. Elstad (1985) presents the case of eighteen-year-old
Michael Elstad, suspected in the burglary of a neighbor's house.[3] Police arrived at the home where Elstad lived with his parents and
found him lying on the bed in undershorts, listening to the stereo.
The police told him to get dressed and go into the living room. While
Officer McAllister took Mrs. Elstad into the kitchen, where he explained that they had a warrant for her son's arrest, Officer Burke began to question Michael Elstad and obtained an admission that he
was at the burglary scene. Transported to the sheriff's headquarters
an hour later, Elstad was given his *Miranda* warnings and made a full
statement of his involvement in the burglary. At trial, Elstad's attorney moved to suppress both his initial admission and his signed confession, on the grounds that the original unwarned admission "let the
cat out of the bag" and tainted the subsequent confession as "fruit of
the poisonous tree." The judge excluded the earlier unwarned statement, but allowed the subsequent confession since any "taint" had
been dissipated prior to the written confession (302). Elstad was convicted. The Oregon Court of Appeals reversed, arguing that the ini-

tial unwarned statement had "coercive impact" because "in a defendant's mind it has sealed his fate" and that the "cat was sufficiently out of the bag to exert a coercive impact on [respondent's] later admissions." The Supreme Court, in a 6–3 decision, reversed again, and reinstated Elstad's conviction, with a majority opinion written by Justice O'Connor, and dissents by Justice Brennan (joined by Justice Marshall) and Justice Stevens.

"The arguments advanced in favor of suppression of respondent's written confession," says O'Connor, "rely heavily on metaphor" (303). The "tainted fruit of the poisonous tree" metaphor comes from *Wong Sun v. United States,* a Fourth Amendment case, and has had a long life in debates about whether illegally seized evidence can ever be used at trial, or must rather be excluded because the method by which it was obtained permanently taints it as evidence.[4] O'Connor argues that when there is a sufficient break between an illegally obtained confession and a legally obtained one, the second confession is judged "sufficiently an act of free will to purge the primary taint" (306).[5] O'Connor's response to the "taint" metaphor hence is to find language in which the taint is judged to be purged by an act of free will (which may simply compound the metaphorical problem).

The "cat is out of the bag" metaphor comes from *United States v. Bayer,* a case from long before *Miranda,* where Justice Jackson stated:

[After] an accused has once let the cat out of the bag by confessing, no matter what the inducement, he is never thereafter free of the psychological and practical disadvantages of having confessed. He can never get the cat back in the bag. The secret is out for good. In such a sense, a later confession always may be looked upon as a fruit of the first.[6]

Here, O'Connor finds the Oregon Court of Appeals has "identified a subtle form of lingering compulsion" (like a lingering poison?) in the "psychological impact of the suspect's conviction that he has let the cat out of the bag and, in so doing, has sealed his own fate" (the open bag equals the sealed fate). She objects that "endowing the psychological effects of voluntary unwarned admissions with constitutional implications would, practically speaking, disable the police from obtaining the suspect's informed cooperation even when the official coercion proscribed by the Fifth Amendment played no part in either his warned or unwarned confessions" (311). She continues: "This Court has never held that the psychological impact of voluntary disclosure of a guilty secret qualifies as state compulsion or compromises the voluntariness of a subsequent informed waiver" (312). This, of course, assumes that Elstad's original unwarned admission was voluntary—though *Miranda* doctrine would presume it was not—and then makes the connection between that admission and the later confession a matter of psychology, a guilty secret that will out—a matter in which Court won't deal. "[T]he causal connection between any psychological disadvantage created by his admission and his ultimate decision to cooperate is speculative and attenuated at best. It is difficult to tell with certainty what motivates a suspect to speak." Having so disposed of the darker reaches of psychological motivation, she at the end of her opinion implicitly reestablishes the language of the will: "We hold today that a suspect who has once responded to unwarned yet uncoercive questioning is not thereby disabled from waiving his rights and confessing after he has been given the requisite Miranda warnings." In other words, the suspect's volition is still intact, his will is not overborne—he can choose to put the cat back in the bag—his choice to waive his rights to counsel and to silence and to make a confession is free and knowing.

"Taken out of context, each of these metaphors can be misleading," O'Connor writes of the "tainted fruit" and "cat out of the bag." Yet the metaphors of *Elstad,* as my quotations should suggest, keep proliferating. Replying in a footnote to Brennan's fierce dissent in the case, O'Connor rebuts the relevance of the many cases he cites against her conclusion: "Finally, many of the decisions Justice Brennan claims require that the 'taint' be 'dissipated' simply recite the stock 'cat' and 'tree' metaphors but go on to find the second confession voluntary without identifying any break in the stream of events beyond the simple administration of a careful and thorough warning." Unpacking the metaphors of this sentence, from dissipating taints through stock cats and trees (where "stock" is perhaps a metaphor of metaphor, or of metaphor reduced to cliché) to streams broken by the administration of warnings, would be an ungrateful enterprise. The metaphors of *Elstad* proliferate no doubt precisely because it *is* difficult to tell exactly what motivates a suspect to speak. And the Court's admixture of legal doctrine and "common-sense" psychology applied to motivation seems to produce an imagistic texture of dubious clarity.

Brennan in dissent accuses the Court of "marble-palace psycho-analysis" that "demonstrates a startling unawareness of the realities of police interrogation" (324). Turning to the question of motivation, he cites Justice Cardozo: "The springs of conduct are subtle and varied. . . . One who meddles with them must not insist upon too nice a measure of proof that the spring which he released was effective to the exclusion of all others." This sounds to me like a clock spring (or the spring of some wind-up object, such as an automaton), but a moment later Brennan cites a standard interrogation manual on the importance of securing the initial admission from a suspect: "For some psychological reason which does not have to concern us at this point 'the dam finally breaks as a result of the first leak' with regards to the tough subject. . . . Any structure is only as strong as its weakest component, and total collapse can be anticipated when the weakest part begins to sag."[7] Here we are in a watery world (were those springs really wellsprings?) that is again evoked in the next paragraph, which quotes another interrogation manual to the effect that the first admission is the "breakthrough" and the "beachhead."[8] Later, Brennan will object that O'Connor's approach is "completely at odds with established dissipation analysis" (which sounds vaguely like a chemical procedure) and claims that "today's opinion marks an evisceration of the established fruit of the poisonous tree doctrine"—where the process of evisceration of the doctrine seems, by taint, to take place on established fruit and the poisonous tree on which it hangs in a curiously vivid image.

I stress the metaphors of *Elstad* not in an attempt to ridicule the Court's language—though the importance of the issue joined in this case does not appear to have produced a correspondingly authoritative rhetoric—but rather to suggest how the problem of what prompts a confession almost of necessity elicits a confused, imagistic language in which an everyday psychology traversed by legal dogma yields unconvincing and dubiously analytic pronouncements. It is indeed difficult to tell what motivates anyone to confess, and the Court's split on the case of Michael Elstad's confession has very little to do with legal interpretation and much more to do with ideology, psychology, and differing senses of how we want those accused of crime to behave. The key metaphors of the case point to our uncertainties about how we describe the strange production of confessional discourse. And it is worth thinking further how people in general let the cat out of the bag and how the dam bursts from its first leak.

Rousseau, in book 4 of the *Confessions,* describes how he for a time became secretary and interpreter to a Greek Orthodox monk who was traveling in Switzerland to collect money for the renovation of the Holy Sepulchre in Jerusalem. It's never clear whether the collection is bona fide or a scam. The French Ambassador, in Soleurre (near Berne), who had earlier been in the embassy at Constantinople, is evidently not persuaded of the monk's good faith, since after he meets with him he takes Rousseau aside for an interview, exhorting him to tell the truth (Rousseau has been passing himself off as a Parisian and part of the monk's official mission). Once alone with the ambassador, Rousseau throws himself at his feet to tell all—"for a continual need of outpouring [*épanchement*] always puts my heart on my lips"—and recounts his "little story," his *petite histoire.*[9] This *petite histoire* returns on other occasions in the *Confessions,* at other moments when his disguises, pretenses, or his sense of not being recognized as what he takes himself to be, leads to the need to define himself through the narrative of his young life. His heart is always near his lips, his little story ready for someone who asks for it in a situation of confidence.

Rousseau's confession, here as so often elsewhere, combines both an admission of guilt (imposture, dissembling, lies) and an affirmation of essential innocence. Michael Elstad's first confession to Officer Burke is not dissimilar, in that he admits to have been at the scene of the burglary, but only that. In his second confession, he claims that he was paid to lead acquaintances to a defective sliding door that would give them access to the house. His admission was enough to bring him a five-year prison sentence and an $18,000 fine in restitution of stolen goods. But it seems evident that the admission was designed to minimize his guilt, to claim that he took no actual part in the burglary, and to proclaim his essential innocence despite appearances. It is entirely conceivable that he believed that he was not a housebreaker and thief at the same time he admitted to a degree of complicity in the burglary, and indeed made the confession he did both to admit guilt and to deny that it should be defined as serious guilt.

Once he said to Officer Burke, in his first, unwarned admission, "Yes, I was there," the cat was very much out of the bag, and it is not clear that any further statement could have exculpated him. An experienced criminal, once warned, might have refused to answer any further questions; but an experienced criminal would no doubt have avoided the first admission as well. The first leak, in Elstad's case, surely meant that the dam could not hold, since he was obliged to explain the circumstances of his "yes, I was there." The interrogation manuals are surely right that the first admission constitutes a "breakthrough" and a "beachhead." And that breakthrough, as in Rousseau's case, almost appears a normal psychological component of everyday life: concealment, imposture, lies are uncomfortable to maintain (hence the efficacy, however limited, of polygraph testing). The compulsion to confess, as Reik argued, is a common part of psychic process, an act of propitiation to those who have caught you out.

A striking instance of the suspect's desire to appease and conciliate his interrogators can be found in the case of Peter A. Reilly, which became a *cause célèbre* in the Connecticut town of Canaan from 1973 to 1976 and received national publicity in large part because of the intervention of playwright Arthur Miller on behalf of the eighteen-year-old Reilly, convicted of murdering his mother on the basis of a dubious confession. Reilly arrived at the cottage he lived in with his mother—alcoholic, often abusive but also fun-loving, and the only parent he had ever known—the night of September 28, 1973, to find her brutally knifed to death on the floor. He called for an ambulance and called the hospital, which in turn called the state police—who took Reilly into custody, read him the Miranda warnings, and began to question him.

Reilly waived the right to counsel—as he later stated to Mike Wallace of 60 Minutes, "Because I hadn't done anything wrong and this is America and that's the way I thought it was."[10] The interrogation, over the next twenty-four hours—most of it recorded—involves a polygraph test which the police claim shows he is lying in his affirmation of innocence. The police create a version of events in which Reilly has "a lapse of memory" about the moment of the murder. The interrogators suggest that he needs psychiatric help. "Pete, I think you've got a problem," says Sergeant Kelly. "These charts [from the polygraph] say you hurt your mother last night" (65). Reilly begins to consider, in a string of hypothetical statements, how he might have done it—how perhaps on arriving home he found his mother not dead but in bed, how they might have had an argument, how he might have slashed her with a razor. After some hours of this kind of dialogue, Lieutenant Shay, who has taken over the interrogation, asks Reilly to trust him, and then states—in an outright lie—"We have, right now ... without any word out of your mouth, proof positive that you did it." To which Reilly replies: "So okay, then I may as well say I did it" (73). By the end of the interrogation, Reilly signs a statement, written by Trooper Mulhern, in which he confesses to having slashed his mother's throat.

The picture of abjection and dependency that emerges from a reading of the Reilly interrogation is truly pathetic: a young man whose only close relative has just died a violent death, who is wholly disoriented, deprived of sleep, unable to eat, without human contact other than his tormentors (friends who tried to make contact with him were told he could not be seen), who is promised that admission of guilt will mean only "three months" in a mental institution. His interrogators prey on his natural distress and guilt at his mother's murder to make him assume the burden of guilt. The most pathetic moment of the interrogation may come following a violent verbal outburst by Lieutenant Shay: "Now you're trying to treat us like muck. . . . If you want to play this way we'll take you and we'll lock you up and treat you like an animal. . . . Now somebody is dead. You are responsible; we know. We can prove it with extrinsic evidence. Now, we're telling you that we are offering you our hand. Take it" (75–76). Reilly's response, moments later, is to ask Shay: "I was wondering . . . if some way . . . I could possibly live with your family if you had the room? . . . I wouldn't want to impose and I know my godmother would pay my way" (77). To turn to one's abusive interrogator and ask to become his ward: this Dostoevskian moment surely is revelatory of the strange transvaluation of values that can occur in custodial interrogation, where the need for propitiation of the authority figure, and the need for punishment for the guilt of being in the situation of interrogation, leads to the utter abjection of asking one's tormentor to become one's protector. As Miller, who of course effectively dramatized the psychology of false confession in *The Crucible,* summarized the situation: "The confession? There's Peter and authority—the absent father—and Peter saying, 'I'm on your side,' and the cops saying, 'These are our terms. This is what you must say,' and so Peter confesses" (277).

Once the cat was out of the bag in Peter Reilly's case, it took three years to put it back in. Convicted of manslaughter at trial despite the taped evidence of how the confession was obtained, it took the publicity campaign mounted by Miller, plus the effective investigation led by Attorney T. Gilroy Daly and the work of private investigator

James Conway, to find other exculpatory evidence—some of it known to the prosecution but not released to the defense—to win a hearing for a new trial, at which psychiatric evidence concerning the coerced character of the confession could finally be presented. The retrial was granted; the State eventually abandoned the prosecution. The case of Peter Reilly—no doubt repeated in various forms from time to time throughout the United States—stands as a haunting example of criminal procedure as usual that borders on the inquisitorial, and on the police's conviction that the best way to solve a crime—even in the post-*Miranda* universe—is to make a breach in the dam, to produce an admission of some sort—even if it be through lying polygraph tests and the postulation of a memory blank—that will then lead to a full confessional narrative, however implausible.

Psychologists Richard J. Ofshe and Richard A. Leo have studied and classified false confessions. What they say about "persuaded confessions" applies to Reilly's case: "Persuaded confessions depend upon a successful attack on a suspect's confidence in his memory—specifically his lack of memory of having committed the crime."[11] Ofshe and Leo cite a similar case, that of Edgar Garrett, whom the police persuade to confess having murdered his sixteen-year-old daughter despite (or because of) the fact he has no memory of any interaction with his daughter on the morning she disappeared. His interrogators postulate a "blackout" that they gradually fill with details of the crime, which Garrett then gradually accepts as his own actions. Garrett eventually recanted his confession, and at trial the jury, impressed by discrepancies between his statements and the physical evidence, acquitted him. Thereafter, the Goshen, Indiana police ceased to record its interrogations.[12]

Making reference to the experts in interrogation whose work I have cited (see chapter 2), Ofshe and Leo remark:

> The promoters of psychological interrogation methods give no significant thought to how they will affect the innocent, but instead merely assume that the methods they advocate will not cause an innocent person to confess (see Inbau et al. 1986; Jayne and Buckley 1992). The unanticipated and unappreciated fact about psychological methods of interrogation is that they are so influential that if allowed to go forward without restraint or if directed at the exceptionally vulnerable they will have devastat-

THE CONFESSIONAL IMAGINATION

ing consequences. These methods produce false confessions because they convince innocent suspects that their situations are
hopeless just as surely as they convince the guilty that they are
caught. (195)

The hopelessness or abjection of the suspect's situation makes confession, even false, the only solution—the only act that the will can perform—in the given circumstances.

To Ofshe and Leo, the courts' emphasis on a "voluntariness" test
does not really address the issue of false confessions induced by psychological stress, since such stress does not always meet classical tests
of "coercion." They argue that "current constitutional safeguards do
not provide an adequate bar to the admission of involuntary and often unreliable confessions" (213). In conclusion, they propose that to
current safeguards (essentially *Miranda,* in somewhat diluted form)
the following need to be added: (1) the requirement of tape recording
interrogations; (2) making the admission of a confession contingent
on corroboration by independent evidence, to assure that the confession is not merely the story fed a suggestible suspect by his interrogators; (3) a reasonable reliability standard for confessions, that is, a
confession should not merely meet the voluntariness test, but also
should be judged against the known facts of the crime to see if the
confession actually fits with those facts (238–39).

These recommendations make persuasive sense, and the failure
of courts and legislatures to have enacted something like them argues
once again society's ambivalence about confessions and its general reluctance to inquire too closely into the circumstances of their production. Tape recording of interrogations, for instance, is now more
widespread than it once was, but by no means universal. And of
course it is subject to manipulation: interrogators may turn on the
recording device only when the suspect has agreed to make a confession. A reasonable reliability test should of course always govern evidence, but the example of plea bargains gives some sense of how
superficial review of an evidentiary basis may be when overworked
courts have a confessional statement disposing of the case on the
docket. Perhaps the only truly probative way to detect and exclude
the false confession would be insistence that the alleged crime be con-
vincingly substantiated by other means (apparently the procedure in
German courts).[13] But taken to its logical conclusion, this would be

tantamount to saying that we do not need to use confessions in criminal procedure. And so many centuries of usage have accustomed us to them, have led those who enforce the law to get the cat out of the bag, to make the dam break.

Inquisition and Imagination

In thinking about how the dam breaks, leading to the outflow of confession, one might turn back to the image of "the Inquisition," which for centuries held a kind of dark fascination for the literary imagination. (The image is of course in part mythic, derived mainly from the Spanish Inquisition at its most powerful.) In M. G. Lewis's *The Monk*—the greatest, most authentically dark and haunted of the Gothic novels—the sinning monk Ambrosio, guilty of rape, incest, matricide, as well as unchastity, is summoned before the Spanish Inquisition:

> In these trials neither the accusation is mentioned, or the name of the accuser. The prisoners are only asked, whether they will confess: If they reply that having no crime they can make no confession, they are put to the torture without delay. This is repeated at intervals, either till the suspected avow themselves culpable, or the perseverance of the examinants is worn out and exhausted: But without a direct acknowledgment of their guilt, the Inquisition never pronounces the final doom of its prisoners.[14]

As a description of Inquisitorial proceedings in their generality, this may be a bit too categorical. But it captures some essential elements that were widely used: the absence of a specific charge and the name of the accuser; the request for a general confession to crimes, including crimes of belief (to be made under oath); the use of torture, of course; and the need for an explicit avowal of one's faults.

When inquisitors visited a town, they began by issuing an Edict of Grace and Faith, usually proclaiming a period of two weeks to several months "for private confessions and identifications to be made and cases prepared."[15] When a suspect was arrested, usually he was not at first specifically charged, but urged to examine his conscience, to himself find his guilt, and confess it. Capital cases, I noted earlier, demanded full proof—the testimony of two eyewitnesses to a crime, or confession by the accused; since heretical beliefs do not generally involve eyewitnesses, most cases of heresy could detect only partial proofs, *indicia*. Thus a confession was needed. Provided there were indicia, torture now came into play to obtain a confession. The famous *Directorium Inquisitorium* of Nicolau Eymerich gives detailed rules for the use of torture and the status of resulting confessions.[16] For example:

> the value of confessions is absolute if they have been obtained by the threat of torture or by the presentation of the torture instruments: in this case, it will be considered that the accused has freely confessed since he has not been tortured. The same is true if confessions are obtained when the accused is already stripped naked and bound in order to undergo torture. If the accused confesses in the course of torture, he should afterwards ratify his confessions, since they will have been obtained by pain or terror. (162)

The rules thus held that a confession made under torture must be repeated the next day without torture, "voluntarily," but of course the retraction of the tortured confession could simply lead to a repeat of torture. And the "presentation of the torture instruments" was often quite enough to loose the suspect's tongue.

Confession—here the Inquisition had a somewhat different task than other courts—was necessary not only to provide full proof in order to condemn but also to save the soul of the accused and to preserve the unity of the Church. One cannot overemphasize the Inquisition's insistence on the need for the detailed articulation of guilt—an articulation meticulously recorded, which has made Inquisition archives so valuable to scholars.[17] Full avowal was thought necessary if the Inquisition were to succeed in its task of purging heresy and maintaining purity of Christian dogma. "Heresy" itself was considered an erroneous word, a *sententia* contrary to Sacred text.[18] Only when the culpable avow themselves culpable, verbally assume their guilt, can there be purgation. The confessed can then be given penance and punishment which, even when it consists of burning at the stake, is conceived to be salvational of the penitent's soul. Those condemned by the Spanish Inquisition went to the stake clothed in *sanbenitos,* penitential garments signifying their sacrificial status.

If the Inquisition exercises a gothic imaginative appeal, it may be in part because of the image of a nightmare situation in which one is summoned to confess guilt and sin without specific charge, and one is tortured until the confession comes, and the confession then is used both to absolve and condemn one. In this nexus lies something of profound psychological significance. If there is always more than enough guilt to go around within any person's psyche or soul, then the generalized external compulsion to confess will very often elicit some kind of avowal (Ambrosio will eventually admit crimes for which he is not even suspected, and others for which he is not guilty). That the avowal leads simultaneously to absolution and punishment is within the psychic logic of confession, as a plea for punishment in order to be readmitted to love and community (Peter Reilly comes to mind). That the punishment in this case is death merely takes that logic to its ironic and grim conclusion: that the guilt is so fearful absolution can come only through extinction. Propitiation of the interrogators makes one finally into a sacrificial animal.

Along with the nightmare image of the Inquisition comes that of the Grand Inquisitor, an aged man (regularly imagined as ninety years old), a veritable "Name of the Father" who must enslave and burn in order to save mankind. The Romantic fascination with the figure of the Grand Inquisitor reaches back to Friedrich Schiller's *Don Carlos* (1787), behind which stands a long line of literary explorations of the Inquisition, including the influential *A Discovery and Plaine Declaration of Sundry Subtill Practices of the Holy Inquisition of Spain* (1567), by Reginaldus Gonsalvius Montanus (probably the work of Casiodoro de Reina and Antonio del Corro, Spanish Protestant exiles), written in Latin and quickly translated into English, French, Dutch, and German; and César Vichard de Saint-Réal's novel *Dom Carlos* (1672); and includes also a long line of Gothic novels, from Ann Radcliffe to Charles Robert Maturin and the mid-nineteenth century thriller *Les Mystères de l'Inquisition* (1846), by V. de Féréal (Madame de Suberwick).[19] Schiller's play offered the libretto, concocted by two journeymen of melodrama, Joseph Méry and Camille du Locle, for Giuseppe Verdi's opera—perhaps his greatest—*Don Carlo,* which offers an impressive blind Grand Inquisitor who reigns over King Philip II, and a spectacular auto-da-fé scene. Less well known but almost equally spectacular—could so long and unwieldy a drama ever be staged—is Victor Hugo's *Torquemada* (largely written in 1869; completed and published in 1882).

Torquemada is the revery of a liberal imagination on the repressive imagination. Hugo's Inquisitor is a monster of the intellect whose broodings on the sins of humanity are taken to their hyper-logical conclusion. The play is set in the Seville of Ferdinand and Isabella, and its central action turns on the monarchs' indecision as to whether or not to expel the Jews from Spain. Torquemada's victory over their self-interested clemency (for the Jews have produced 30,000 gold marks as ransom) comes when he goes to stage rear and "violently" pulls aside a curtain to uncover a scene of auto-da-fé, the plaza covered with flaming pyres. It is against the backdrop of this spectacle of flame and torture that Torquemada launches into an eighty-line meditation on the need to punish in order to purify—the use of the pyre on earth to extinguish the fires of hell.

To "the damned" in flames, Torquemada offers absolution: "Damnés, soyez absous!" The auto-da-fé becomes "pardon, goodness, light, fire, / Life! dazzling of the face of God! / Oh! what a splendid exit and how many souls saved!" ("Autodafé! pardon, bonté, lumière, feu, / Vie! éblouissement de la face de Dieu! / Oh! quel départ splendide et que d'âmes sauvées!"). As the flames rise, he waxes more and more enthusiastic at their beauty, like rubies and other precious stones, and he calls on the flaming martyrs to burn ever brighter: "Sparkle! shine out, pyre! prodigious tiara / Of sparks that will become stars" ("Pétille! luis, bûcher! prodigieux écrin / D'étincelles qui vont devenir des étoiles!"). To those dying in the flames he addresses the supremely self-confident benediction of the Inquisitor: "Ah! without me, you were lost, my dearly beloved! / The pool of fire purges you in flames. / . . . Now you are delivered! go! Flee far above! / Enter into paradise!" ("Ah! sans moi, vous étiez perdus, mes bien aimés! / La piscine de feu vous épure enflammés. / . . . Vous voilà délivrés! partez! Fuyez là-haut! / Entrez au paradis!")[20] Hugo, like Verdi, gives a visual and lyric representation of the ultimate logic of inquisition as consolation and discipline.

The Inquisitor, in his most famous avatar, saves mankind from freedom. Such is the mission of Dostoevsky's "Grand Inquisitor" in *The Brothers Karamazov,* who in the "poem" Ivan creates for his brother Alyosha makes the point: "Oh, we shall convince them that they will only become free when they resign their freedom to us, and submit to us."[21] Ivan's Grand Inquisitor—who of course is imagined as speaking to Jesus returned to earth in Seville—explicitly understands that confession is the royal way to the abandonment of free choice to authority: "The most tormenting secrets of their conscience—all, all they will bring to us, and we will decide all things, and they will joyfully believe our decision, because it will deliver them from their great care and their present terrible torments of personal and free decision" (259). His notorious conclusion is that the return of Jesus after fifteen centuries during which the Church has asserted its discipline on humanity constitutes an unacceptable scandal: "For if anyone has ever deserved our stake, it is you. Tomorrow I shall burn you. *Dixi*" (260).

All these Grand Inquisitors, and surely Dostoevsky's in particular, lie behind those figures of banal, bureaucratic inquisitors in the literature of our century, made perhaps most chillingly familiar by Arthur Koestler's representation of the Stalinist purges in *Darkness at Noon*. In that novel, Rubashov, imprisoned for deviance from the Party line, is interrogated in the first instance by his old associate Ivanov:

> Rubashov was silent. Quite a long time passed. Ivanov's head bent even closer over the writing desk.
>
> "I don't understand you," he said. "Half an hour ago you made me a speech full of the most impassioned attacks against our policy, any fraction of which would be enough to finish you off. And now you deny such a simple logical deduction as that you belonged to an oppositional group, for which, in any case, we hold all the proofs."
>
> "Really?" said Rubashov. "If you have all the proofs, why do you need my confession?"[22]

As the dialogue continues, Ivanov outlines the confession that Rubashov must make—and that he will in fact make eventually, at the hand of the more brutal interrogator Gletkin (Ivanov himself having in the meantime been liquidated), and that will be presented at his "show trial," which will pronounce the inevitable death sentence. The final chapter of *Darkness at Noon* is entitled "The Grammatical Fiction," which we may take to refer to Rubashov's confession and guilty plea: their fictionality could be said to lie in their very linguistic form, in their claim to be a first-person confession and admission of guilt—whereas they are in fact the work of the interrogators and judges, and forced into the mouth of the accused.

Like the Inquisition, the Party needs avowal of guilt not only to legitimate its sentences but also to affirm publicly, from the lips of the accused, that what it considers guilt, or heresy, is recognized as such by the guilty person. If the heretic recognizes his belief as heretical, as mistaken, as wrong, then his punishment becomes merely a purgation, a reaffirmation of true belief. Without confession, we are dealing in prosecution and a finding of guilt. With confession, however extorted, it is rather a matter of exposure and sacrifice, to the greater glory of God, or the Party.

The inquisitorial requirement of confession before trial, sentencing, and execution is different from, yet related to, the long tradition of confession at the foot of the gallows by mundane criminals. Late medieval criminal procedure, I noted earlier, appears to regard confession as serving both to the detection of crime and the purgation of the criminal's soul. For many centuries the condemned were required to perform some version of the *amende honorable* that we noted in the case of Martin Guerre—to proclaim their crimes and to beg forgiveness of the community they had offended. As Michel Foucault describes it, there was a "ritual" of execution designed to show the triumph of the law. This ritual generally included: parading the condemned person through the streets, often with a placard on his chest or back proclaiming his crime; having him stop at crossroads and before churches for a public reading of his sentence; his kneeling repeatedly to declare his repentance for his horrible crime. When the place of execution was reached, the criminal was given a moment's respite to confess his crimes anew and to reveal any accomplices hitherto concealed.[23] In England in the late seventeenth and early eighteenth centuries there came to be a published genre of the "Newgate biography," purporting to convey the last confessional statement of the condemned at the "hanging tree" of Tyburn. The "official" texts were the work of the Ordinary, or chaplain, of Newgate Prison, who maintained a kind of monopoly of these "Accounts."[24] These "true confessions" to often lurid crimes sold well, and brought the Ordinary a supplementary income. They have the same function as the *amende honorable* in reassuring society that justice is being done, and in demonstrating the power of the law over would-be malefactors. Yet since these confessions are in fact written by the Ordinary and are very much the product of a confessor pressing a confessant for a declaration through the combined power of the state—the system of justice, which has already pronounced sentence—and the church—with its offer of the hope of redemption for penitent sinners—one must take the genre as perhaps no more authentic than Rubashov's. They indeed became a source for a considerable body of fiction of the outlaw, notably in the novels of Daniel Defoe and Henry Fielding.

Here is the title one of these brief "accounts," this from 1680 and fairly typical of those I have seen: *The True Confession of Margaret Clark, Who Consented to the Burning of her Master's Mr Peter Delanoy's House in Southwark. Delivered in Prison to many Witnesses a little before her Death. And confirmed by her self at the Place of Execution, by answering all the Questions then put to her by the Reverend and Worthy Divine, Dr Martin, now Minister of St. Saviour's Southwark.* Her confession then begins:

> I Margaret Clark being shortly to suffer Death for that which I have deserved, and am much humbled for, and desire to lye low before God under the sense of my own Guilt, do give the World an Account of the truth of my Case, for I would not be guilty of a lye now I am to appear before my judge within a few minutes. Therefore I do say, and shall declare the Truth of the matter, as I shall answer it before my Lord and Judge.[25]

One senses that this pathetic declaration, and others in the same vein, belong to the religious as well as the legal tradition of confession, and in this case specifically to a Protestant tradition of accounting for one's life: in the Protestant view, a true form of confession as opposed to Jesuitical murmurings in the confessional. It looks forward to Rousseau's claim that he will come to his Sovereign Judge at the last trumpet with "this book in my hand." But Margaret Clark at Tyburn Tree is under duress to confess, a duress that makes her declaration disquieting to the modern reader. Is this a true confession? Is it anything more than the placard around the condemned criminal's neck? Is it so different from those confessions signed Rubashov, or Peter Reilly?

Transparency and Confession

In the demand for a final confession by the convicted criminal—who will be executed with or without it—we may recognize society's need to confirm its assignments of guilt and punishment, and, beyond that, perhaps a generalized desire for transparency. The notion of transparency is vital to Rousseau, whose desire to abolish all veils between himself and his readers is a repeated motif in the *Confessions*. One of the most explicit statements of this ambition comes at the end of book 4 of the *Confessions,* where he offers an apology for the long detail of his childhood. He needs, he says, to give the reader a full account of everything he has done, thought, and felt in order for the reader to assemble the details in a full portrait of Jean-Jacques, and to judge him. "I would like to be able in some manner to make my soul transparent to the eyes of the reader," he writes (175). This means that he has to fear, not saying too much or even saying untruths, but not "saying everything." Thus the desire for total transparency is linked to the ambition to confess entirely, to provide a seamless narrative of the inwardness as well as the exterior life story of a person. As Rousseau states in book 2, "In the enterprise I have undertaken to show myself in my entirety to the public, nothing of myself must be obscured or hidden from the reader; I must hold myself ceaselessly under his eyes, so he can follow me in all the extravagances of my heart, in all the recesses of my life" (59).

Transparency for Rousseau suggests the very abolition of language as the mediator of communication among people—since language harbors the possibility of mendacity, the possibility of truth deviated or covered over. There is a moment in Rousseau's novel, *La Nouvelle Héloïse,* when the "beautiful souls" gathered around Julie at Clarens become transparent to one another, during a "matinée à l'anglaise" when they sit together and communicate without words. "How many things are said without opening the mouth! How many ardent feelings are communicated without the cold go-between of the word!"[26] The wordless ecstasy of Clarens has its political counterpart as well, in Rousseau's notion of the public festival that would take the place of the iniquitous relation of spectator and spectacle in the theatre. In his *Lettre à M. d'Alembert sur les spectacles,* I noted, Rousseau opposes the notion of establishing theatre in Geneva (where theatre was banned by the Calvinist government) and proposes in its place a kind of civic public festival uniting the whole population in the open air in celebration of its happiness. "What would be the objects of these spectacles? Nothing, if you will."[27] Nothing, because the distinction between spectator and actor, and the whole notion of representation, should be abolished. "Better still: make the spectators the spectacle;

make them actors themselves; make it so that each sees himself and loves himself in others, so that all become better united." Citizens thus united in an objectless public celebration will be transparent to one another.

Rousseau's imagined popular festival would become literalized in the festivals of the French Revolution, including those staged by the Jacobins—such as the "Fête de l'Unité" and the "Fête de l'Etre Suprême"—vast pageants elaborated, some under the artistic direction of the painter Jacques-Louis David, to impose the values of the "Republic of Virtue." And in the Revolutionary Festivals, the darker side of the notion of perfect transparency begins to become apparent: transparency here becomes forcing the idea of a republic in which there is nothing to hide. The rhetoric of the Jacobins, especially Robespierre and Saint-Just, is full of exhortations to pierce the veil of the enemies of the republic, to penetrate their dissimulation, to bring everything to light. The Reign of Terror works by denunciation, accusing its enemies of hidden conspiracies and unpatriotic thoughts. It prescribes purgation of those who resist total transparency and who are not able to give a full account of their patriotic sentiments and actions. For the Republic of Virtue is absolute, founded on the elimination of everything and everyone who does not participate fully and publicly in its values. As Saint-Just puts it in a famous lapidary formulation: "A republican government has as its principle virtue; if not, terror. What do they want who want neither virtue nor terror?"[28] Transparency is allied both to virtue and to terror. The requirement to bear witness to one's conduct in the confessional mode is an absolute imperative; those who are opaque are sent to the guillotine. Saint-Just's most famous speech before the Convention, his "Rapport sur les Suspects incarcérés" (26 February 1794), ends with a decree that the Comité de Sûreté Générale will be given the power to judge whether or not imprisoned suspects may be freed. "Any person claiming the right to be freed will account for his conduct since 1 May 1789" (204). This is a demand for total transparency in one's life history—over five tumultuous years—with a vengeance, a demand where the failure to be totally transparent will result in execution.

I cite this more sinister side to the Rousseauist demand for total transparency because it represents, in the political sphere, an aspect of confession that cannot be ignored. If transparency seems generally a beneficent ideal, one in which the dissimulations that mark social life are abolished in favor of complete openness to one another, posing it in the form of an imperative to confess creates a tyranny of transparency, a generalized requirement of openness that can quickly become the imposition of orthodoxy, the elimination of dissent, the forced confession of deviance—as in Rubashov's case. The tyranny of transparency takes the imperative to confess to a chilling logical conclusion: the abolition of all zones of privacy around the individual, the claim that the individual's conscience must be legible to all, that there can be no zones of obscurity. The Inquisition, the Reign of Terror, and the Stalinist show trials constitute a partial list of what the uncontrolled demand for generalized confession can mean.

One further instance of the invasive confession needs consideration, since it is presented as a powerful parable for the modern sense of guilt and its creation of complicity. This is Albert Camus' *La Chute*— *The Fall*—first published in 1956, which has only slowly won recognition as possibly the greatest of his novels. *The Fall* presents a narrator-confessant who accosts the person he makes into his narratee-confessor in an Amsterdam bar. Over the course of their subsequent encounters, the narrator, Jean-Baptiste Clamence, makes his listener into the accomplice of his confessional discourse. While this listener never speaks in the text, Clamence's discourse contains many signs of interlocution, suggesting his listener's questions and attitudes, the place he takes up as interlocutor, making Clamence's monologue dialogic in the manner of many a Dostoevskian confession: the reactions of the listener are factored into the speaker's speech; indeed the listener's response is in a deep sense what that speech is all about. Clamence describes himself as a "judge-penitent," in a kind of oxymoron that characterizes his entire narrative manner and his moral position.

Clamence's confession circles around the moment when, one November night in Paris, he hears a woman throw herself into the Seine and does nothing to save her. This failure of moral courage saps from within the egotistical competence with which he has led his life—as a lawyer, often an advocate of the unpopular and disfavored—and in particular puts an end to any possible plea of innocence for his life. His response is not an attempt to regain innocence through penance—like Raskolnikov, for instance—but rather the claim that innocence does not exist, that guilt is general. After evoking the medieval cell known as the "little ease," he argues that it is unthinkable that one should be reduced to living bent over in such a cell and still be innocent. The idea is radically offensive to moral reason. "Moreover," says Clamence, "we cannot affirm the innocence of anyone, whereas we can surely affirm the guilt of all. Every man testifies to the guilt of all the others, there is my faith and my hope."[29]

Once one has eliminated the very possibility of innocence—eliminated the idea that there might be unjust punishment in the world—one can go about the business of judging with a certain relish. The problem with being a judge is that the sentences you pronounce on others may return to strike you, may bring a reversal in which you become penitent. The solution: heap crimes on one's own head, become first a penitent in order then better to become a judge. Judgment then arises not from innocence but from the assumption of guilt, which allows one to perceive guilt as pervasive. The work of the judge-penitent proceeds through the practice of public confession, finding interlocutors—such as the narratee—to whom he can accuse himself. But—as the dual role of judge and penitent implies—self-accusation functions also as an invitation to his listener to do the same, indeed "to go one better" (145; 139). In this manner, Clamence creates a portrait that is simultaneously of everyone and of no one in particular. And if this portrait shows Clamence as he is, it also acts as a "mirror" that he holds out to his contemporaries.

Here we come to a key description of how confession and penitence, figured in traditional terms of ostentatious public penance, lead to judgment:

> Covered with ashes, tearing out my hair, my face scoured by my fingernails, but with a piercing glance, I stand before all humanity, recapitulating my shames, without losing sight of the effect that I am producing, while stating: "I was the lowest of the low." Then imperceptibly I pass, in my speech, from "I" to "we." When I reach, "this is the way we are," the trick is turned, I can tell them off. I am like them, of course, we're in the soup together. I nonetheless possess a superiority, that of knowing it, which gives me the right to speak. You see the advantage, I'm sure. The more I accuse myself, the more I have the right to judge you. Even better, I provoke you to judge yourself, which in that measure eases me. Ah! my friend, we are strange, miser-

able creatures and to the extent that we look back on our lives, they are not lacking in subjects of astonishment and scandal to ourselves. Do try. Be assured that I will listen to your own confession with a great feeling of fraternity. (146; 140)

Confession on this account turns into a subtle act of aggression, a demand for self-judgment and counter-confession on the part of the interlocutor, a demand for a kind of common transparency in the assumption of generalized guilt.

Clamence's version of confession is clearly a perversion of the traditional intent of confession, yet no doubt a perversion latent in the tradition from its origins. To the extent that confession, and the demand for confession, begins in the affirmation of common guilt rather than the quest for innocence, it enables Inquisition on the one hand, and on the other hand may simply produce a proliferation of confession and guilt leading to bathos, passivity, and delectation in confession itself, since confession, rather than a now impossible absolution, appears as the end of the road. Clamence notes that the practice of confession allows him a double pleasure, combining a complacent egotism with the charm of repentance. Confessional discourse takes the place of what would be truly redemptive: a second chance. "'O young woman,'" he says, ventriloquizing words for his interlocutor, "'throw yourself again in the water so that I may have a second chance to save us both.'" He turns back on his plea, to conclude: "A second chance, hum, what a risky idea! Suppose, dear sir, that we were taken literally? We'd have to perform. Brr . . . ! the water's so cold. But we can be reassured. It's too late now, it will always be too late. Fortunately!" (153; 147).

Jean-Baptiste Clamence: the name evokes Saint John the Baptist, *clamans in deserto*. Clamence indeed describes himself as a vile prophet for shabby times, and the outcome of his confession appears to be a generalized abjection that has no value for spiritual renewal. At the same time, the confession contaminates: the narratee is tainted by it, the reader is made complicit by his very reading, and the final invitation to join the confessional game can be rejected only with a sense of discomfort. That Clamence's monologue occurs in an Amsterdam likened to Dante's hell, and that there are passing evocations of the slave trade that built some of the rich houses of the city and to the former Jewish ghetto emptied by the Nazi holocaust, suggest some of the parabolic dimensions Camus wishes to confer on his tale. *The Fall* is a fable for contemporaries, a demonstration and a showing-up of how the confessional impulse, considered to be redemptive, can in fact produce a sterile, passive, self-satisfied complicity in the negation of the possibility of redemption. Confession on this model is the natural tool of those who want to affirm the fallen condition of mankind and therefore the necessity to keep it enslaved. If Dostoevsky's Grand Inquisitor invites humanity to surrender its freedom, Camus' prophet represents a world where it has already done so. And to the extent that contemporary societies have allowed their law enforcement agencies to infringe the freedom and individual autonomy from which the state supposedly derives its authority and its sovereignty, Camus' image is just.

"It is difficult to tell with certainty what makes a suspect speak": Justice O'Connor's phrase in *Oregon v. Elstad* stands as something of an understatement. The motives of confessional speech are multiple and difficult of precise analysis. Surely one of them, Camus suggests, is the desire to find some version of one's own guilt in others, to generalize the taint, to suggest the omnipresence of sin. To confess may in this manner be the search for a generalized absolution for the human condition or, on the model of Clamence, to seek consolation rather in the sense that the world is past redemption, that there are only choices of various circles in hell. To the extent that contemporary culture, especially in the United States, has established a high popular cultural value on confession, it is difficult to know whether the results of confessing are supposed to be redemptive or rather an acceptance of the banality of guilt. How, for instance, are readers supposed to react to Kathryn Harrison's memoir of sex with her father, *The Kiss*? If the book is a sincere and needed act of exorcism on the part of the writer, what gain in knowledge or insight does it afford the reader? Similarly, are all those participants in talk shows who uncover the secrets of their intimate lives seeking absolution from the public before which they display themselves, or are they rather somehow attempting to pass on a taint, to produce a general contamination, one that includes their listeners as well as themselves? If, in the proverbial phrase, "misery seeks company," so does guilt, and the "unburdening" of one individual's sense of guilt may be produced simply by speaking it to listeners. The situation of interlocution itself is in this manner therapeutic—an insight provided by the first patient of the nascent therapy of psychoanalysis, Anna O., when she referred to her sessions with Josef Breuer as a "talking cure." To be sure, psychoanalysis came to be established as a practice because Freud and his successors understood that this situation of interlocution demanded a special discipline of the listener/confessor, whose interventions—interpretations, constructions, skepticisms, calls for self-inspection—structure the progress of therapy. Nonetheless, as Jacques Lacan has noted, the simple presence of the analyst, prior to any interpretative intervention he or she may make, creates in the analysand's discourse "the dimension of dialogue."[30] In the real or imagined dimension of dialogue—Clamence with his blank narratee, the criminal suspect with the detective—the speaker has the impression, or the illusion, that his confessional discourse produces a response, an acknowledgment.

What, then, to say of a situation in which much of the American media was in 1998 demanding further confession and the expression of contrition from President Bill Clinton in the matter of Monica Lewinsky, while the public in general gave the impression that it had heard enough and wanted no more? The media, including the normally sober *New York Times,* attacked Clinton's recourse to "legalisms" and demanded that he admit publicly to perjury and that he apologize at greater length for his guilt. The public, on the other hand, appeared to believe that lying about sexual matters was not only normal but possibly justified, an accepted part of the rules of the sexual game. Clinton himself combined legal evasion with the repentant fervor of the sinner—he assembled a variety of clergy to help guide him in the path of righteousness—while displaying signs that he wished to be treated as a recovering addict. Had he not been under the shadow of the perjury charge, one suspects he would happily have appeared on a talk show to tell all, to seek consolation in the community of fellow-sinners. A grotesque situation would have then reached the bathos of full self-exposure.

It is not easy to analyze what was at stake in the demands that Clinton say more: something along the lines of wishing him to display a more dramatic moral consciousness of his wrongful actions, perhaps, or maybe a desire to have him grovel more fully in public? The situation was one of public humiliation, indeed abjection. And it was my sense that much of the public felt it did not want its President, however guilty, to be an abject object; it considered that the public display of humiliation had gone far enough. Whereas the professionals of public talk, of television and public commentary, felt that the rituals of display and abjection had not yet been fulfilled. I found myself thinking that some of the traditional forms of public penance—sackcloth and ashes, the *amende honorable*—might have been useful: had these still held currency, they would have provided properly ritualized ways to resolve the matter. In the absence of such rituals, we are suspended in a strange confessional medium, somewhere between the guilty plea at the law—entailing punishment—and the psychotherapeutic expression of guilt, entailing working through and maybe cure. What is lacking is a socially defined Sacred in terms of which to plead for true absolution. If, on the Camusian model, we are all guilty, there is no possibility of absolution.

Contemporary society's apparent demand for transparency—a demand that the media, at least, seems to consider total, absolute—has created a situation in which there is no evident end to the confessional process, no ritual of closure. Sociologist Richard Sennett has argued that some of the asperities of contemporary urban civilization derive from the loss of ritual privacy that characterized earlier centuries: no longer do we have the proprieties, or hypocrisies, that allowed people to interact in crowded spaces without the demand for intimacy, without the requirement of transparency.[31] What we may be lacking is a code of manners that would dictate when opacity is preferable to transparency in public situations.

The demand for transparency, the implied situation of interlocution in the meeting of relative strangers, the valuation of confessional discourse: these all need to be seen as elements weighing on any situation in which someone is suspected of guilt and put in a situation where his confession is called for. And assuming there is guilt to be confessed, once an initial admission is made, the cat is indeed out of the bag—there is no reason for the confessional discourse to cease. *Miranda* warnings caution the suspect that anything he says may be used against him and that he has the right to remain silent. But silence in the situation requires a radical effort of the will: everything in the culture presses toward speech. The will is in this sense often easily "overborne," to recall Justice Frankfurter's term in *Culombe v. Connecticut.* I sense that as a culture we are uncertain about our feelings on the matter. And hence perhaps we are content to have the scene of confession largely veiled from us, content that it take place in the closed precincts of the "interview room."

It is not my intention here to formulate policy recommendations in the field of criminal justice. But in closing it is worth citing key moments from a strange 1986 Supreme Court case, *Colorado v. Connelly.*[32] In August 1983, Francis Connelly withdrew money from his bank, bought a plane ticket, and flew from Boston to Denver, where he approached a policeman on the street and stated that he had murdered someone and wanted to talk about it. Given his *Miranda* warnings, he confessed to the killing some months earlier of a young girl, and took the officers to what he claimed was the scene of the crime. Police records revealed that there had been an unidentified female body found in Denver in April. As Connelly was interviewed by the public defender's office the next day, he became disoriented and confused, he began to claim that voices had told him to come to Denver and then had urged him either to kill himself or to confess. Psychiatric examination led to the conclusion that he was psychotic, experiencing "command hallucinations," and damaged in his "volitional abilities" (161). The trial court suppressed Connelly's confession as involuntary, as well as his waiver of counsel and of the privilege against self-incrimination, citing Justice Frankfurter's language of the will in *Culombe v. Connecticut;* and the Colorado Supreme Court affirmed the suppression, stating that confessions must be "the product of a rational intellect and a free will."

But the U.S. Supreme Court reversed, accepting Connelly's confession as voluntary and remanding the case for trial. Writing for the Court, Chief Justice Rehnquist states: "Only if we were to establish a brand new constitutional right—the right of a criminal defendant to confess to his crime only when totally rational and properly motivated—could respondent's present claim be sustained" (166). Since there was no coercive interrogation by the police, the question of free will is not involved. In dissent, Justice Stevens finds the notion that a waiver of rights can be voluntary even if it is not the product of an exercise of "free will" to be "incomprehensible."[33] And in another dissent, Justice Brennan returns to the classic Court decisions on voluntariness, including *Brown v. Mississippi, Blackburn v. Alabama,* and *Culombe v. Connecticut,* to argue: "We have never confined our focus to police coercion, because the value of freedom of will has demanded a broader inquiry. . . . Until today, we have never upheld the admission of a confession that does not reflect the exercise of free will" (177–78). Since the Court "redefines voluntary confessions to include confessions by mentally ill individuals," writes Brennan, one must ask about the reliability of such confessions. And there is nothing to substantiate the reliability of Connelly's confession:

> . . . the record is barren of any corroboration of the mentally ill defendant's confession. No physical evidence links the defendant to the alleged crime. Police did not identify the alleged victim's body as the woman named by the defendant. Mr. Connelly identified the alleged scene of the crime, but it has not been verified that the unidentified body was found there or that a crime actually occurred there. There is not a shred of competent evidence in this record linking the defendant to the charged homicide. There is only Mr. Connelly's confession. (183)

This case involves no police interrogation, no coerced confession—which is why the Supreme Court majority finds no violation of "voluntariness." But it makes one wonder what has happened to the language of "free and unconstrained choice" *versus* the "overborne will" deployed by Frankfurter in *Culombe,* and the "free and rational will" test articulated, just a year before *Connelly,* in *Miller v. Fenton.* Connelly appeared to the trial court such an abject defendant it refused to try him, whereas the Supreme Court remands the case for trial. While granting that a psychotic confessant presents a special case, one may have the uncomfortable sense that the Court here abandons its historic concern that criminal suspects at least appear to be rational agents who are free to choose the words that can be used against them. If we accept Connelly's confession as voluntary, we must be prepared to say that almost any confessional statement will pass muster, absent police coercion, and that the standards for rational self-awareness on the part of the confessant-defendant are low indeed.

Colorado v. Connelly may, because of its special facts, be something of an aberration in Supreme Court rulings on confessions. But it once again points to, and creates, an unease about confessional speech and the wisdom of holding it to a standard of "voluntariness" that seems better designed for almost any other kind of speech. Is the psychotic's discourse voluntary? Is that of any criminal suspect? Do we care? Have we become so easy with the notion of confession—and the need for confession—that we don't want to bother with the kind of painstaking analysis Frankfurter undertook in *Culombe*? Confession, I have argued, is deeply intricated with our sense of the self, its interiority, its capacity for introspection, self-knowledge, self-evaluation. If we, as a culture, are going to attach such importance to it, see it as so definitional of the person, we need to continue to scrutinize the conditions of its production and the source of its articulation. And if criminal justice is going to continue to rely on confession to the extent that it does, it should return to the disquieting inquiries of Frankfurter, Warren, and Brennan, at the time when the Court was attempting to open up the "interview room" to scrutiny, to ask more closely about the conditions and the sources of confessional speech. If the day comes when the interrogation of criminal suspects is, for instance, broadcast live on Court TV, we may feel simultaneously a fascination and a revulsion. We might not be able to keep from watching; we might be deeply disturbed by what we saw.

NOTES

Chapter One

1. These essentials of the narrative are presented on the title page of the most recent recounting of the case, by John Spargo, *The Return of Russell Colvin* (Bennington, Vt.: Bennington Historical Museum and Art Gallery, 1945). See also Leonard Sargent, *The Trial, Confessions and Conviction of Jesse and Stephen Boorn, for the Murder of Russell Colvin, and the Return of the Man Supposed to have been murdered* (Manchester, Vt.: Journal Book and Job Office, 1873). Sargent, later Lieutenant Governor of Vermont, was one of counsel for the defense at the trial.

2. *Miranda v. Arizona,* 384 U.S. 436 (1966).

3. On the "prophylactic standards," see *Michigan v. Tucker,* 417 U.S. 433 (1974).

4. *Culombe v. Connecticut,* 367 U.S. 568 (1961). Frankfurter's plurality opinion in *Culombe* is characterized as a "treatise" by Chief Justice Earl Warren, concurring, who points out that the opinion is going to offer very little helpful guidance to police officers (thus necessitating the *Miranda* decision). 367 U.S. at 636. See my discussion of *Culombe* in chapter 3.

5. *Massiah v. United States,* 377 U.S. 201 (1964); *Escobedo v. Illinois,* 378 U.S. 478 (1964).

6. The Court has limited and reduced some of the protections implied by *Miranda* in subsequent cases. E.g., *Harris v. New York,* 401 U.S. 222 (1971); *Michigan v. Tucker,* 417 U.S. 433 (1974); *Rhode Island v. Innis,* 446 U.S. 291 (1980); *New York v. Quarles,* 467 U.S. 649 (1984); *Oregon v. Elstad,* 470 U.S. 298 (1985); *Colorado v. Connelly,* 479 U.S. 157 (1986); see also my discussion in chapter 6. But the substance of *Miranda* can nonetheless be said to have remained in place. It was reaffirmed—against its most direct challenge to date—in *Dickerson v. United States* in 2000. See my discussion of *Dickerson* at the end of this chapter.

For a thoughtful discussion of the issues raised by *Miranda,* see Louis Michael Seidman, "*Brown* and *Miranda,*" *California Law Review* 80 (1992): 673. Seidman considers whether *Miranda* should be considered a "rejection of liberal individualism" or a "victory of liberal individualism," effectively bringing out the contradictions that inhabit the decision.

See also the penetrating comments of Robert Weisberg, in "Criminal Law, Criminology, and the Small World of Legal Scholars," *University of Colorado Law Review* 63 (1992): 521.

For a wealth of additional detail about the *Miranda* case, see Liva Baker, *Miranda: Crime, Law and Politics* (New York: Atheneum, 1983). (Ernesto Miranda himself, incidentally, was convicted at his retrial.) On the continuing ability of the police to obtain confessions despite *Miranda,* see in particular the two-part series by Jan Hoffman, "Questioning Miranda," *New York Times,* 29 and 30 March 1998. See also Brooke A. Masters and Tom Jackman, "Justice System Worries about 'Miranda,'" *Washington Post,* 16 February 1999; they report the finding of criminology professor Richard A. Leo that 78 percent of suspects waive their *Miranda* rights (B-5).

7. See *Ashcraft v. Tennessee,* 322 U.S. 143, 161 (1944).

8. See *Blackburn v. Alabama,* 361 U.S. 199, 206 (1960).

9. See Wolfgang Iser, *The Implied Reader [Der Implizite Leser]* (Baltimore: Johns Hopkins University Press, 1984).

Note that Justice Harlan in dissent objects to Warren's extrapolation of the story of the closed room from police interrogation manuals, which he characterizes as "merely writings in this field by professors and some police officers" (499).

10. In *Escobedo v. Illinois,* we learn that the police summon "an experienced lawyer who was assigned to the Homicide Division to take 'statements from some defendants and some prisoners that they had in custody' [who] 'took' petitioner's statement by asking carefully framed questions apparently designed to assure the admissibility into evidence of the resulting answers." 378 U.S. at 483.

11. Henry J. Friendly, in "The Fifth Amendment Tomorrow: The Case for Constitutional Change," *University of Cincinnati Law Review* 37 (1968): 671, writes:

> [W]hile the other privileges accord with notions of decent conduct generally accepted in life outside the court room, the privilege against self-incrimination defies them. No parent would teach such a doctrine to his children; the lesson parents preach is that while a misdeed, even a serious one, will generally be forgiven, a failure to make a clean breast of it will not be. Every hour of the day people are being asked to explain their conduct to parents, employers and teachers. Those who are questioned consider themselves to be morally bound to respond, and the questioners believe it proper to take action if they do not. (680)

Friendly's comment elides the difference between confessing to benevolent authorities and confession to the police, who are not about to forgive a misdeed, as he partially acknowledges in a footnote. But he makes the important point that the Fifth Amendment privilege is counterintuitive to everyday morality.

12. I follow here largely the work of Edward Peters, *Inquisition* (New York: The Free Press, 1988), 65, and John H. Langbein, *Torture and the Law of Proof* (Chicago: University of Chicago Press, 1977), 3–17. See also Nicolau Eymerich and Francisco Peña, *Le Manuel des Inquisiteurs,* trans. and ed. Louis Sala-Molins (Paris: Mouton, 1973). Eymerich, a Dominican from Catalonia,

composed the *Directorium Inquistorium* in Avignon in 1376; it was printed in 1503. Peña's recompilation and updating of the *Directorium* was published in Rome in 1585.

13. The classic study of the history of the right against self-incrimination is Leonard W. Levy, *Origins of the Fifth Amendment,* 2d ed. (1968; New York: Macmillan, 1986). Some of Levy's historical arguments have been challenged: see in particular, R. H. Helmholz et al., *The Privilege against Self-Incrimination* (Chicago: University of Chicago Press, 1997). The *nemo tenetur* phrase is attributed to Saint John Chrysostom, and its use by defendants may be part of the ancient European common law derived from Roman law, the *ius commune.*

14. Coke's Rep. 9, at 10, 77 Eng. Rep. 1421, 1422 (1609), cited in Levy, *Origins,* 246.

15. See Levy, *Origins,* 328. Justice Frankfurter makes the same point in his opinion in *Culombe,* discussed in chapter 3.

16. For a probing analysis of this issue, see Louis Michael Seidman, "Rubashov's Question: Self-Incrimination and the Problem of Coerced Preferences," *Yale Journal of Law and the Humanities* 2 (1990): 149. Partly in reference to the permissible compulsion of *United States v. Doe,* 465 U.S. 605 (1984), in which the defendant was forced to sign a "consent decree," Seidman argues: "The point is not that the government *ought not* to coerce such statements [regarding internal mental states]. Rather, the government *cannot* coerce such statements because the application of coercive pressure makes them something other than statements regarding internal mental states" (158). I will argue later that this may be correct, but the statements may in that case hold another kind of confessional truth. I am not convinced that a "preference coercion theory of the [Fifth Amendment] privilege" can wholly respond to the root objections to compelled confessions, which seem to me to be ethical. In this context, see the appropriately skeptical remarks of Robert Weisberg:

> The jurisprudence of the Fifth Amendment directly raises the question raised indirectly by searches and seizures: What image of the autonomous human being do we believe in? ... We have no coherent analysis of what it means to be autonomous in the face of the law, and we are left instead with shallow rationalizations about the psychology of volition, abetted in the Sixth Amendment area by hilarious rationalizations about the effects of the invisible formalities of state prosecution on the volition of a poor wretch of a subject. Weisberg, "Criminal Law," 538–39.

See my further discussions of these points in chapter 3.

17. Abe Fortas, "The Fifth Amendment: *Nemo Tenetur Seipsum Prodere,*" *The Journal* 25 (Cleveland Bar Association, 1954): 91, 98–100. Cited in Levy, *Origins,* 431.

18. Jean-Jacques Rousseau, *Confessions, Autres textes autobiographiques,* ed. Bernard Gagnebin and Marcel Raymond (Paris: Bibliothèque de la Pléiade, 1962), 5. Translations from Rousseau are my own.

19. Paul de Man, "Excuses (*Confessions*)," *Allegories of Reading* (New Haven: Yale University Press, 1979), 285.

20. See J. L. Austin, *How to Do Things with Words* (Cambridge: Harvard University Press, 1962); see also Austin, "A Plea for Excuses," *Philosophical Papers* (Oxford: Clarendon, 1961). One could discuss at some length whether Rousseau's argument here is really an "excuse" or a "justification" (to use one of Austin's distinctions). For my purposes, it is perhaps enough to note that the speech act of confessing always carries a certain, if variable, illocutionary force: it is doing something as well as stating something.

21. See the Talmudic rule that in a criminal case, a person can be condemned only on the testimony of two witnesses, and that his or her own confession, even if voluntarily given, cannot be admitted as evidence. See the commentary by Maimonides cited in chapter 3. As Levy pertinently comments, in this view "confession was a form of suicide, which was sinful and violative of the instinct of self-preservation." *Origins,* 438. For Freud's view, see Sigmund Freud, "Some Character-Types Met with in Psychoanalytic Work," chap. 3: "Criminals from a Sense of Guilt" (1916), in *The Standard Edition of the Complete Psychological Works of Sigmund Freud,* ed. James Strachey (London: Hogarth Press, 1953–1974), 14:332–33.

22. *Escobedo v. Illinois,* 378 U.S. 478, 483 (1964).

23. See David Simon, *Homicide. A Year on the Killing Streets* (1991; New York: Ivy Books, 1993), 204ff. It has also been noted that the *Miranda* warnings have not significantly reduced the number of confessions: "Nonetheless, suspects agree to talk without the need for pressure or deception (often because they think they can talk their way out of trouble)." Stephen J. Schulhofer, "Reconsidering *Miranda,*" *University of Chicago Law Review* 54 (1987): 456–57. The attempt to "talk their way out of trouble" often involves unwitting confessions to incriminating knowledge.

24. Schulhofer quotes the pre-*Miranda* edition of Inbau and Reid's *Criminal Interrogation and Confession,* in which the interrogator is instructed to say to the suspect: "Joe, you have the right to remain silent. That's your privilege. . . . But let me ask you this. Suppose you were in my shoes and I were in yours . . . and I told you, 'I don't want to answer any of your questions.' You'd think I had something to hide" (Schulhofer, "Reconsidering *Miranda,*" 447 n. 25). "Most commonly, detectives tell suspects that there are two sides to every story and that they will only be able to hear the suspect's side of the story if he waives his rights and chooses to speak to them." Richard A. Leo, "The Impact of *Miranda* Revisited (1996)," in *The Miranda Debate,* ed. Richard A. Leo and George C. Thomas III (Boston: Northeastern University Press, 1998), 216.

25. *Brewer v. Williams,* 430 U.S. 387, 434 (1977).

26. Burger refers his reader here to Theodor Reik, *The Compulsion to Confess: On the Psychoanalysis of Crime and Punishment* (New York: Farrar, Straus & Cudahy, 1959). He does so, I think, without understanding the full implications of Reik's argument, which suggests that the need to confess may have little to do

with the crime committed. (See my comments on Reik in chapter 2.) Indeed, in his "Postscript" on "Freud's View on Capital Punishment" (a contribution to a 1926 symposium to which Reik gave a statement based on his conversation with Freud), Reik argues, along the lines of "Criminals from a Sense of Guilt," that crime may be the result of guilt, rather than vice versa:

> Freud has shown that, in the criminals at whom criminal legislation is re-ally directed, a powerful unconscious feeling of guilt exists even before the deed. . . . It is hence not the consequence of the deed, but its motive. . . . As a result, punishment, according to accepted views, the most effective de-terrent against crime, becomes, under certain psychological extremely common conditions in our culture, the most dangerous unconscious stim-ulus for crime because it serves the gratification of the unconscious feeling of guilt, which presses toward a forbidden act. (473–74)

This understanding of the relation of guilt, crime, and punishment is fully con-sonant with what we have seen in Rousseau.

27. 3 J. Wigmore, *Evidence* § 824 (3d ed. 1940).

28. Technically, *Brewer v. Williams* is not a "voluntariness" case since it was decided on Sixth Amendment, not Fifth Amendment, doctrine, but it does turn on whether Williams voluntarily waived his right to counsel (for which there are a special set of rules). And see Yale Kamisar, who in *Police Interrogations and Confessions* (Ann Arbor: University of Michigan Press, 1980), argues that *Brewer* should have been decided as a *Miranda* doctrine, rather than a *Massiah* doctrine case.

The question of whether Williams voluntarily waived his right to counsel points to a continuing difficulty in *Miranda* doctrine: how can we know if a waiver is voluntary? If counsel is necessary to avoid unwitting self-incrimina-tion, isn't counsel necessary knowingly to waive the right to counsel? Note that the statement "I waive [my right to . . .]" is another performative.

29. See Italo Calvino, *If on a Winter's Night a Traveller* [*Se una notte d'inverno un viaggiatore*], trans. William Weaver (New York: Harcourt Brace Jovanovich, 1981).

30. See, for instance, *United States v. Doe,* 465 U.S. 605 (1984) (tax records) and *Gilbert v. California,* 388 U.S. 263 (1967) (handwriting samples); see also *New York v. Quarles,* 467 U.S. 649, 666 (1984), where Justice O'Connor, concur-ring in part and dissenting in part, claims: "Only the introduction of a defen-dant's own *testimony* is proscribed by the Fifth Amendment's mandate that no person 'shall be compelled to be a witness against himself.' That mandate does not protect an accused from being compelled to surrender *nontestimonial* evi-dence against himself." On many of these questions, see Akhil Reed Amar, *The Constitution and Criminal Procedure* (New Haven: Yale University Press, 1997).

31. *Schmerber v. California,* 384 U.S. 757, 761 (1966).

32. *Holt v. United States,* 218 U.S. 245, 252–53 (1910).

33. It is not certain that those "lifeless papers" still would be protected to-

day, given the Court's decisions in *Fisher v. United States,* 425 U.S. 391 (1976), and *Andresen v. Maryland,* 427 U.S. 463 (1976); even private diaries were held to be unprotected by the U.S. District Court for the District of Columbia in *Senate Select Committee v. Packwood,* 845 F. Supp. 17 (D.C. 1994).

34. *Griswold v. Connecticut,* 381 U.S. 479 (1965).

35. *United States v. Ceccolini,* 435 U.S. 268, 277 (1978) (citing *Smith v. United States,* 117 U.S. App. D.C. 1 [1963]).

36. See Kamisar, *Police Interrogation,* 187. One finds versions of this hypothetical in cases involving jailhouse informants.

37. *Miller v. Fenton,* 474 U.S. 104, 110 (1985); but see *Colorado v. Connelly,* 479 U.S. 157 (1986).

38. Seidman, "*Brown* and *Miranda,*" 719. Seidman also characterizes Frankfurter's opinion in *Culombe* as a "disaster." For a critical examination of the philosophical analysis of the problem, see Joseph D. Grano, *Confessions, Truth, and the Law* (Ann Arbor: University of Michigan Press, 1993).

Kamisar argues in *Police Interrogation and Confessions* that "trustworthiness" is a better test than "voluntariness," though it, too, presents problems.

39. Jan Hoffman, "Questioning *Miranda:* Police Tactics Chipping Away at Suspects' Rights," New York *Times* 29 March 1998, 1 and 40; "Police Refine Methods So Potent, Even the Innocent Have Confessed," 30 March 1998, A-1 and B-4.

40. See, among many relevant cases: *Frazier v. Cupp,* 394 U.S. 731 (1969); *Oregon v. Elstad,* 470 U.S. 298 (1985); *Withrow v. Williams,* 507 U.S. 680 (1993); I shall discuss *Oregon v. Elstad* in chapter 6.

41. *Dickerson v. United States,* 120 S.CT. 2326 (2000).

Chapter Two

1. Cited in Vitaly Shentalinsky, *The KGB's Literary Archive,* translated, abridged, and annotated by John Crowfoot (London: Harvill Press, 1995), 53. I have also consulted the French (unabridged) translation: Vitali Chentalinski, *La Parole ressucitée: Dans les archives littéraires du K.G.B.* (Paris: Robert Laffont, 1993), and the account of Meyerhold's interrogation in Edward Braun, *Meyerhold. A Revolution in Theatre* (Iowa City: University of Iowa Press, 1995). Meyerhold's first interrogator was Kasbulov, Head of the NKVD Special Investigative Section; when his first confession fell short of what the NKVD wanted, he was turned over to Voronin, who with his assistants, Rodos and Shvartsman, augmented "psychological attack" with "physical methods."

2. *Brown v. Mississippi,* 297 U.S. 278, 285 (1936), citing *Snyder v. Massachusetts,* 291 U.S. 97 (1934), and *Rogers v. Peck,* 199 U.S. 425 (1905).

3. On false confessions, see especially Richard J. Ofshe and Richard A. Leo, "The Social Psychology of Police Interrogation: The Theory and Classification of True and False Confessions," *Studies in Law, Politics and Society* 16 (1997): 189–251. I shall discuss the case of Paul Ingram in chapter 5, and that of Peter Reilly—and the issue of false confessions generally—in chapter 6.

4. This quotation is from page 112 of the pre-*Miranda* edition of O'Hara (1956). The post-*Miranda* version reproduces this passage verbatim, but now in appendix 1, which is preceded by a discussion of the fact that the ACLU *amicus* brief in *Miranda* singled out such tactics for critique and that the Court largely incorporated the brief into its Opinion. Yet O'Hara keeps the passage, since "the Court did not state that the use of these techniques was illegal or express an opinion as to their use in circumstances where the suspect has waived his right to the presence of counsel. . . . [T]he legality of their use would probably depend on the manner in which they were used and the subject to whom they were applied." O'Hara continues, "The examples . . . are negative." Then he writes, in a curious sentence: "They are presented here to implement the Court's recommendations by indirection." Charles E. O'Hara, *Fundamentals of Criminal Investigation,* 2d ed. (Springfield, Ill.: Charles C. Thomas, 1970), 817.

5. O'Hara, *Fundamentals* (1970), 107.

6. Fred E. Inbau, John H. Reid, and Joseph P. Buckley, *Criminal Interrogation and Confessions,* 3d ed. (Baltimore: Williams & Wilkins, 1986), 24. This is the post-*Miranda* edition of Inbau and Reid's manual; the 1956 version was the one cited in the Court's Opinion in *Miranda.*

7. O'Hara, *Fundamentals* (1970), 109.

8. O'Hara, *Fundamentals* (1970), 819–21 (appendix 1). One can find more detailed scenarios for the same techniques throughout Inbau and Reid.

9. See *Frazier v. Cupp,* 379 U.S. 731 (1969). The confession ruled admissible here occurred between *Massiah* and *Miranda.* See *State v. Kelekolio,* 849 P.2d 58 (Haw. 1993). I am indebted to Ed Schiffer for bringing these cases to my attention in his essay for my seminar, "Narrative & Rhetoric in the Law," Yale Law School, spring 1998.

10. C. Brian Jayne and Joseph P. Buckley, "Criminal Interrogation Techniques on Trial," *The Prosecutor* (fall 1991): 23–32. The authors are "members of the staff of John E. Reid and Associates, a firm that specializes in the interview and interrogation of suspected criminal offenders and of employees in the investigation of acts of misconduct. It also conducts regional and national training seminars on that subject."

11. O'Hara, *Fundamentals* (1970), 107–8.

12. Inbau and Reid, *Interrogation* (1986), 170.

13. David Simon, *Homicide* (1991; New York: Ivy Books, 1993).

14. Alec Wilkinson, "The Confession," *The New Yorker* 4 October 1993, 162.

15. It is not altogether clear to me how fully aware author Wilkinson is of the dependencies and complicities he records. He seems admiring and deferential toward Mr. Apology and leaves his motives unanalyzed. One senses a certain complicity on his part with his subject. But perhaps this is the artful reticence of the journalist.

16. Theodor Reik, *The Compulsion to Confess: On the Psychoanalysis of Crime and Punishment* (New York: Farrar, Straus & Cudahy, 1959).

17. J. M. Coetzee, "Confession and Double Thoughts: Tolstoy, Rousseau,

Dostoevsky" (1985), in *Doubling the Point* (Cambridge: Harvard University Press, 1992), 274.

18. Jean-Jacques Rousseau, *Confessions, Autres textes autobiographiques,* ed. Bernard Gagnebin (Paris: Bibliothèque de la Pléiade, 1962), 89. Translations from Rousseau are my own. I have discussed this episode from the *Confessions* in a different context, in my book *Body Work* (Cambridge: Harvard University Press, 1993), 41–42. Rousseau's exhibitionism is well analyzed by Jean Starobinski in *Jean-Jacques Rousseau: la transparence et l'obstacle* (Paris: Plon, 1971); in English, *Jean-Jacques Rousseau: Transparency and Obstruction,* trans. Arthur Goldhammer (Chicago: University of Chicago Press, 1988).

19. See especially Freud, *Three Essays on the Theory of Sexuality,* in *Standard Edition,* vol. 7; and Juliet Mitchell, "From King Lear to Anna 'O' and Beyond: Some Speculative Theses on Hysteria and the Traditionless Self," *Yale Journal of Criticism* 5 (2) (1992): 93.

20. See *Confessions,* 175.

21. Freud, "Constructions in Analysis," in *Standard Edition* 23:260–61.

22. Henry James, Preface to *The American* (New York: Scribners, 1907), xvi.

23. Fyodor Dostoevsky, *The Brothers Karamazov,* trans. Richard Pevear and Larissa Volokhonsky (1990; Vintage Books, 1991).

24. See Freud, "Criminals from a Sense of Guilt," part of "Some Character-Types Met with in Psychoanalytic Work," in *Standard Edition* 14:332–33, where Freud argues that crimes are committed in order to realize a preexisting sense of guilt and to invite punishment.

25. Stendhal, *Le Rouge et le noir* (Paris: Garnier/Flammarion, 1964), 476. My translation.

26. On the "monster" identity and on the legitimation through illegitimacy, see my longer discussion of these issues, complete with textual references, in Peter Brooks, *Reading for the Plot* (1984; Cambridge: Harvard University Press, 1992), chap. 3.

Chapter Three

1. *Culombe v. Connecticut,* 367 U.S. 568 (1961), is a 6–3 decision with a complicated set of opinions: Frankfurter announced the judgment of the Court and an opinion in which Justice Potter Stewart joined; Warren wrote a concurring opinion; Justice William O. Douglas wrote another concurring opinion, joined by Justice Hugo Black; Justice William Brennan wrote another opinion, concurring in the result, this one joined by Warren and Black; Justice John Marshall Harlan wrote the dissenting opinion, joined by Justices Tom Clark and Charles Evans Whittaker. The lack of any majority opinion in the case itself points to the complexities of "due-process voluntariness" analysis.

Arthur Culombe's conviction on first-degree murder was reversed by the decision; he later pleaded guilty to second-degree murder, was sentenced to life in prison, became a model prisoner, and he died in prison of a probable brain tumor at age forty-six.

2. Robert Weisberg, "Criminal Law, Criminology, and the Small World of Legal Scholars," *University of Colorado Law Review* 63 (1992): 521, 538–39.

3. Frankfurter's argument reposes on the Fourteenth Amendment due process clause. At the time of *Culombe,* the Fifth Amendment had not yet been made applicable to criminal procedure of the several states; this occurred in *Malloy v. Hogan,* 378 U.S. 1 (1964). But Frankfurter argues, in the lines leading up to the "twisted until he breaks" quotation, that English and American courts have long insisted on "the rigorous demand that an extra-judicial confession, if it was to be offered in evidence against a man, must be the product of his own free choice." In a long footnote glossing this assertion, Frankfurter argues that "the conceptions underlying the rule excluding coerced confessions and the privilege against self-incrimination have become, to some extent, assimilated" (583 n. 25). Thus he includes the concept of the Fifth Amendment privilege if not the Amendment itself.

That is to say, we do not exclude coerced confessions simply on unreliability grounds, but also on the basis of methods and contexts in which they were obtained if these appear to violate the subject's free volition. One wonders what Frankfurter would have thought of the Court's decision in *Colorado v. Connelly,* 479 U.S. 157 (1986), when it accepted as voluntary—without any confirmatory evidence—the confession of a delusional schizophrenic who confessed because "voices" told him to do so.

4. See Blaise Pascal: "La justice et la vérité sont deux pointes si subtiles que nos instruments sont trop mousses pour y toucher exactement." *Pensées,* ed. Michel le Guen (Paris: Gallimard/Folio, 1977), #41.

5. Joseph D. Grano, *Confessions, Truth, and the Law* (Ann Arbor: University of Michigan Press, 1993), 82.

6. Maimonides, *The Code of Maimonides: Book Fourteen, The Book of Judges 52–53,* trans. Abraham M. Hershman (New Haven: Yale University Press, 1949), quoted in Leonard W. Levy, *Origins of the Fifth Amendment,* 2d ed. (1968; New York: Macmillan, 1986), 438. Frankfurter himself cites the eighteenth-century treatise on evidence by Sir Geoffrey Gilbert:

> our Law in this differs from the Civil Law, that it will not force any Man to accuse himself; and in this we do certainly follow the Law of Nature, which commands every Man to endeavor his own Preservation; and therefore Pain and Force may compel Men to confess what is not the Truth of Facts, and consequently such extorted Confessions are not to be depended on. (582 n. 24)

7. *Garrity v. New Jersey,* 385 U.S. 493, 497 (1967).

8. Rousseau, *Confessions* (Paris: Bibliothèque de la Pléiade, 1962), 18.

9. Fyodor Dostoevsky, *The Brothers Karamazov,* trans. Richard Pevear and Larissa Volokhonsky (New York: Vintage, 1991), 40–41.

10. Theodor Reik, *The Compulsion to Confess* (New York: Farrar, Straus & Cudahy, 1959), 208; see my discussion of Reik's view in chapter 2.

11. See, e.g., Henry J. Friendly, "The Fifth Amendment Tomorrow: The Case for Constitutional Change," *University of Cincinnati Law Review* 37 (1968): 671; Grano, *Confessions*. See also the following essays in R. H. Helmholz, *The Privilege Against Self-Incrimination* (Chicago: University of Chicago Press, 1997): Helmholz, "The Privilege and the *ius commune*"; John H. Langbein, "The Privilege and Common Law Criminal Procedure: The Sixteenth to Eighteenth Centuries"; Eben Moglen, "The Privilege in British North America: The Colonial Period to the Fifth Amendment." The essays in this volume offer useful correctives to the classic but historically somewhat skewed account by Leonard W. Levy in *Origins of the Fifth Amendment*.

12. Helmholz, "The Privilege and the *ius commune*," 27.

13. Coke's Rep. 9, at 10, 77 Eng. Rep. 1421, 1422 (1609), cited in Levy, *Origins,* 246.

14. "*Mea culpa* belongs to a man and his God. It is a plea that cannot be exacted from free men by human authority. To require it is to insist that the state is the superior of the individuals who compose it, instead of their instrument." Abe Fortas, "The Fifth Amendment: *Nemo Tenetur Seipsum Prodere,*" *The Journal* 25 (Cleveland Bar Association, 1954): 91, 98, cited in Levy, *Origins,* 431. See, on the other hand, proposals for "reform" that would eliminate the privilege in pretrial questioning before a magistrate; an example of such procedure is given in Albert W. Alschuler, "A Peculiar Privilege in Modern Perspective," in Helmholz et. al., *The Privilege Against Self-Incrimination,* 203–4.

15. See John Milton, *Paradise Lost* 2:557–61.

16. See *United States v. Rutledge,* 900 F.2d 1127, 1129 (7th Cir. 1990); see Grano, *Confessions, Truth and the Law,* 63–64. Posner continues his critique of the "voluntariness" analysis:

> Taken seriously it would require the exclusion of virtually all fruits of custodial interrogation, since few choices to confess can be thought truly "free" when made by a person who is incarcerated and is being questioned by armed officers without the presence of counsel or anyone else to give him moral support. The formula is not taken seriously. . . . In any event, very few incriminating statements, custodial or otherwise, are held to be involuntary, though few are the product of a choice that the interrogators left completely free.

This statement echoes Justice Jackson's view in *Ashcraft v. Tennessee,* but it strikes me as too complacently resigned to an acceptance of the involuntary. Posner claims that, particularly in the light of *Colorado v. Connelly,* 479 U.S. 157 (1986)—which I shall discuss in chapter 6—the test should be "whether the government has made it impossible for the defendant to make a rational choice as to whether to confess. . . ." Does this really help in our understanding of how criminal suspects are to be treated?

17. Lieutenant Sam Rome became a legendary, or infamous, figure in Connecticut investigations. To cite Donald S. Connery (who wrote a book about the Peter Reilly case, discussed in chapter 6): "From the 1950s to the late 1970s, during and after the reign of Sam Rome as Connecticut's most feared and famous detective, the state police focused on confessions as the fastest way to solve crimes." "Justice Unserved?" *The Hartford Courant,* 3 July 1994.

18. *Escobedo v. Illinois,* 378 U.S. 478, 483 (1964).

19. See Herman Melville, *Bartleby the Scrivener,* in *Billy Budd and Other Tales* (New York: NAL/Signet, 1979), 123–24.

20. Grano, *Confessions, Truth, and the Law,* 110.

21. *Miller v. Fenton,* 474 U.S. 104 (1985).

22. *Arizona v. Fulminante,* 499 U.S. 279 [1991].

23. Simon, *Homicide,* 213.

24. O'Hara, *Fundamentals of Criminal Investigation,* 2d ed. (Springfield, Ill.: Charles C. Thomas, 1970), 817.

25. Thomas N. Tentler, *Sin and Confession on the Eve of the Reformation* (Princeton: Princeton University Press, 1977), xvi. See also the interesting analyses by Matthew Senior, *In the Grip of Minos: Confessional Discourse in Dante, Corneille, and Racine* (Columbus: Ohio State University Press, 1994).

26. Michel Foucault, *Histoire de la sexualité, I: La volonté de savoir* (Paris: Gallimard, 1976), 78–79. My translation. In English, *The History of Sexuality,* trans. Robert Hurley (New York: Pantheon, 1978).

27. Alschuler, "A Peculiar Privilege," 184.

28. See the trenchant article by John H. Langbein, "Torture and Plea Bargaining," *University of Chicago Law Review* 46 (1978): 3. Langbein writes:

we have moved from an adjudicatory to a concessionary system. We coerce the accused against whom we find probable cause to confess his guilt. . . . we make it terribly costly for an accused to claim his right to the constitutional safeguard of a trial. We threaten him with a materially increased sanction if he avails himself of his right and is thereafter convicted. This sentencing differential is what makes plea bargaining coercive (12).

29. *North Carolina v. Alford,* 400 U.S. 25, 29 n. 2 (1970).

30. Grano, *Confessions, Truth, and the Law,* 118. The quotation is from Mark Berger, "Legislating Confession Law in Great Britain: A Statuatory Approach to Police Interrogation," *University of Michigan Journal of Law* 24 (1990): 64. England and Scotland have paid more attention to legislating the rules of police interrogation, though the most recent amendments to the rules in England would seem to have dangerously restricted the suspect's rights. The old English warning by the police to the suspect said: "You do not have to say anything unless you wish to do so, but what you say may be given in evidence." The new warning, per the Police and Magistrates Bill of 1994, says: "You do not have to say anything. But if you do not mention now something which you later use in your defense, the court may decide that your failure to mention it now strength-

ens the case against you. A record will be made of anything you say and it may be given in evidence if you are brought to trial."

I note this defense of the much-criticized new warning: "Former Law Lord Lord Ackner described the right of silence as an 'odd quirk of the law' and declared that the onus of proof was not going to be altered by the proposed changes. Police had a duty to investigate and it was 'repugnant to common sense' that they should be frustrated by 'archaic laws and practices.' He made clear that police interviews should be taped and preferably placed on video and demanded how that was unfair to the accused." *Parliamentary News* 25 April 1994.

Among recent proposals for reform of the American system of police interrogation, see Akhil Reed Amar, *The Constitution and Criminal Procedure: First Principles* (New Haven: Yale University Press, 1997), for instance his recommendation that "The best way to [rein in unsupervised police officers] is to shift interrogation from police stations to magistrates' hearing rooms" (76), using depositions as in civil procedure. This may, however, beg the question of whether the resulting procedure would constitute "interrogation" in the sense that the police practice it and want it.

In a recent article, William J. Stuntz argues that the development of constitutional criminal procedure by the Court in the 1960s and after has encouraged legislatures to "pass overbroad criminal statutes and underfund defense counsel": thus a vicious circle, in which courts and legislatures seek to undermine each other. "The Uneasy Relationship between Criminal Procedure and Criminal Justice," *Yale Law Journal* 107 (1997): 1, especially 53.

Chapter Four

1. James Joyce, *A Portrait of the Artist as a Young Man* (New York: Viking, 1964), 159.

2. Sigmund Freud, "On the History of the Psycho-analytic Movement" (1914), in *Standard Edition* 14:13.

3. Thomas N. Tentler, *Sin and Confession on the Eve of the Reformation* (Princeton: Princeton University Press, 1977), 52.

4. The story is recounted by Eusebius, *Historia Ecclesiastica* 5:28, and cited in Oscar D. Watkins, *A History of Penance,* 2 vols. (1920; New York: Burt Franklin, 1961), 1:108–9.

5. See Henry Charles Lea, *A History of Auricular Confession and Indulgences in the Latin Church,* 3 vols. (1896; New York: Greenwood Press, 1968), 1:171.

6. See Michel Sot, "Introduction" to Groupe de la Bussière, *Pratiques de la Confession* (Paris: Editions du Cerf, 1983), 13–21.

7. See, among other sources, A. Esmein, *Cours élémentaire du droit français* (14th ed; Paris: Sirey, 1921), especially 88–89; and also Esmein, *A History of Continental Criminal Procedure* (Boston: Little, Brown and Co., 1913).

8. The history of the various inquisitions promulgated by the Church is complex, and the image of "the Inquisition" has often been provided, for our

time, by the Spanish Inquisition, which comes later and has a separate history. There were inquisitions before Lateran IV, but Lateran IV makes the significant step of creating papal control of the inquisition. Lateran IV (canon 8, *Qualiter et quomodo debeat*) also establishes procedures for inquests, that is, for inquisitorial procedures in ecclesiastical courts—procedures that would have a strong influence on secular justice as well.

9. Edward Peters, *Inquisition* (New York: The Free Press, 1988), 50. On Lateran IV, see also, among other sources: Joseph R. Strayer, ed., *Dictionary of the Middle Ages* (New York: Scribner's, 1982–1989), 3:640; Raymonde Forville, *Latran I, II, III, et Latran IV* (Paris: Editions de l'Orante, 1965); Jane Sayers, *Innocent III* (London: Longman, 1994).

10. See Norman P. Tanner SJ, ed., *Decrees of the Ecumenical Councils,* 2 vols. (Washington, D.C.: Georgetown University Press, 1990), 1:245.

11. Matthew Senior, *In the Grip of Minos: Confessional Discourse in Dante, Corneille, and Racine* (Columbus: Ohio State University Press, 1994), 35. Senior's book, the product of a literary scholar well-versed in Church history and also in modern literary theory, is a most helpful study of the issues that concern me here.

12. See Philippe Boutry, "Réflexions sur la confession au XIXe siècle: Autour d'une lettre de Soeur Marie-Zoé au curé d'Ars (1858)," in *Pratiques de la confession,* 227. On the importance of the verbal versus the written, James A. Brundage cites the remark of Pope Innocent IV that it seemed contrary to nature "to trust the skin of a dead animal more than the voice of a living man." *Medieval Canon Law* (London: Longman, 1995), 133.

13. Saint Bonaventure, as cited in *Dictionnaire de Théologie Catholique* (Paris: Letonzey et Ané, 1911), s.v. "Confession: Du Concile de Latran au Concile de Trente," 3:920; Joyce, *Portrait,* 142.

14. See Emile Benveniste, "De la subjectivité dans le langage," *Problèmes de linguistique générale* (Paris: Gallimard, 1966), 258–66; in English, *Problems in General Linguistics,* trans. Mary Elizabeth Meek (Coral Gables, Fla.: University of Miami Press, 1971).

15. See Jacques Lacan, "Intervention sur le transfert," *Ecrits* (Paris: Editions du Seuil, 1966), 216; in English, *Ecrits,* trans. Alan Sheridan (New York: Norton, 1977).

16. On the intersection of religious and legal models of confession, see Jacques Chiffoleau, "Sur la pratique et la conjoncture de l'aveu judiciaire en France du XIIIe au XVe sièlce," in *L'Aveu: Antiquité et moyen-âge,* Collection de l'Ecole Française de Rome, 88 (Rome: Ecole Française de Rome, 1986), 341–80.

17. See Caroline Walker Bynum, "Did the Twelfth Century Discover the Individual?" in *Jesus as Mother* (Berkeley: University of Callifornia Press, 1982), 82–109. Bynum refers in particular to the very interesting book by Colin Morris, *The Discovery of the Individual, 1050–1200* (London: S.P.C.K., 1972); see also the highly informative essay by John F. Benton, "Consciousness of Self and Perceptions of Individuality," in Benton, *Culture, Power and Personality in Medieval*

France, ed. Thomas N. Bisson (London and Rio Grande: Hambledon Press, 1991), 327–56. See also the very interesting connections between legal discourse and literary forms discussed by R. Howard Bloch in *Medieval Literature and the Law* (Berkeley and Los Angeles: University of California Press, 1977).

18. See the discussion of Paolo and Francesca by Jeremy Tambling, *Confession: Sexuality, Sin, the Subject* (Manchester: Manchester University Press, 1990), 48–49.

19. Dante Alighieri, *The Inferno of Dante,* trans. Robert Pinsky (New York: Noonday, 1994) 5:120–23. The "teacher" is Virgil, and Francesca is here echoing the famous lines with which Aeneas begins to tell his tale of the destruction of Troy to Dido: a tale that will have dire amorous consequences for Dido, as the story of Lancelot does for Francesca, but which is of course in another realm— the epic realm—from Francesca's narrative of private life.

20. Michel Foucault, *Histoire de la sexualité, 1: La volonté de savoir* (Paris: Gallimard, 1976), 80.

21. Paolo Segneri, *Il confessore istruito* (Venezia: Appresso li Prodotti, 1685), 16.

22. See Tentler, *Sin and Confession;* and Hervé Martin, "Confession et contrôle social à la fin du Moyen Age," in *Pratiques de la Confession,* 117–36. Steven Ozment suggests that the obsession with sexuality is evidence of the "domination of lay piety by clerical ideals." See Ozment, *The Age of Reform* (New Haven: Yale University Press, 1980), 219.

23. Senior, *In the Grip of Minos,* 78.

24. See Erich Auerbach, *Mimesis: The Representation of Reality in Western Literature,* trans. Willard Trask (Garden City, N.Y.: Anchor Books, 1957), chap. 1.

25. See Natalie Zemon Davis, *The Return of Martin Guerre* (Cambridge: Harvard University Press, 1983). I have also consulted the first edition of Coras's account, *Arrest Memorable, du Parlement de Tolose . . .* (Lyons: Antoine Vincent, 1561).

26. Rousseau, *Rêveries du promeneur solitaire,* in *Confessions, Autres textes autobiographiques* (Paris: Bibliothèque de la Pléiade, 1959), 1098.

27. Philippe Ariès, *L'Enfant et la vie familiale sous l'ancien régime* (Paris: Plon, 1960).

28. Stephen J. Greenblatt, "Psychoanalysis and Renaissance Culture," in *Learning to Curse: Essays in Early Modern Culture* (New York and London: Routledge, 1990), 131. Greenblatt states later in his essay that "psychoanalysis was, in effect, made possible by (among other things) the legal and literary proceedings of the sixteenth and seventeenth centuries," an argument I of course find very much consonant with my own.

29. See Coras, *Arrest memorable:* "Grande fut certainment l'astuce, de ce paillard, d'entretenir ladite Rols, en cet erreur trois ans & davantage, qu'elle infailliblement cuidoit estre sa femme . . . " [Great certainly was the deception of this seducer to maintain the said Rols in this error three years and more, such that she believed indubitably to be his wife . . .], 20.

In her novel, *The Wife of Martin Guerre* (San Francisco: Colt Press, 1941)—
a novel written without recourse to Coras and other source material—Janet
Lewis creates a Bertrande who after three years with the new Martin decides he
is an impostor and takes legal action against him, from anger and fear for her
soul. If the first element of this scenario might be plausible, I find the second—
her instigating legal action against him—less than convincing.

30. Coras, *Arrest memorable:* "les lieux, temps & heures, des actes secretz de
mariage (plus aisez, beaucoup à comprendre, qu'honnestes à réciter ou escrire) &
les propos, qu'avant, après, & en l'acte, ils avoient tenuz," 17.

31. The requirement of annual confession may indeed be closely linked to
the Church's drive to regularize and control marriage: as Jeremy Tambling
writes, "it is tempting to link the confessional requirement to the desire to bring
marriage into the public domain, to make it not merely a matter of people living
together, but licensed; not secret; a matter of consent and not cohabitation." *Confession: Sexuality, Sin, the Subject,* 41. Lateran IV, in canon 51, indeed inveighs
against "clandestine marriages."

32. See Davis, *The Return of Martin Guerre,* 47–50.

33. Michel de Montaigne, "Des Boyteux," *Essais* (Paris: Bibliothèque de la
Pléiade, 1961), livre 3, chapitre 11, p. 1156.

34. Montaigne, "Du Repentir," *Essais* livre 3, chapitre 2, p. 900.

35. Rousseau, *Confessions,* 5.

36. A couple of well-publicized recent examples: Albert Talmo, 52, turned
himself in to the Toms River, New Jersey police in 1996 for the killing of Julie
Linzmeyer in 1968. He said his guilty conscience had led to a life of alcoholism,
drug dependency, and despair; police said he had never been a suspect in the
killing and would never have been caught. He tried to confess to his wife and to
friends, but they did not believe him. Katherine Anne Power, formerly a member of a radical political group, turned herself in to the Boston, Massachusetts
police after twenty-three years as a fugitive—living under an assumed name—
and confessed that she drove the "switch car" in a bank robbery that involved
the killing of Boston policeman Walter Schroeder.

A search of newspaper files reveals a number of such Raskolnikovian cases:
"A man whose conscience troubled him for twenty years walked into a police
station to confess to killing a pedestrian in a hit-and-run accident (*Times* (London), 12 September 1997); "A man tormented by his conscience confessed to a
twenty-five-year-old killing he said he committed as a teen-age gang member,
and he told police that another man served time for the crime (*Los Angeles
Times,* 20 November 1986).

Chapter Five

1. On the mutes of nineteenth-century melodrama, see Peter Brooks, *The
Melodramatic Imagination* (1976; New Haven: Yale University Press, 1995),
chap. 3, "The Text of Muteness."

2. Freud, "The Question of Lay Analysis" (1926), in *Standard Edition* 20:189.

3. Freud, *Standard Edition* 23:265–66.

4. Lawrence Wright, *Remembering Satan* (1994; New York: Vintage Books, 1995).

There is also an extensive discussion of the Ingram case in Elizabeth Loftus and Katherine Ketcham, *The Myth of Repressed Memory* (New York: St. Martin's Press, 1994), 227–63. The proliferation of confessions in Ingram's case—extending eventually to his wife and a son as well as Ingram and his daughters—reminds one of the case of a sixteenth-century family of vagrants accused of murder and witchcraft, who under torture confessed to at least ten murders committed per year, replete with satanic rituals and so forth. See Michael Kunze, *Highroad to the Stake* [*Strasse ins Feuer: Vom Leben und Sterben in der Zeit des Hexenwahns*], trans. William E. Yuill (1982; Chicago: University of Chicago Press, 1987).

5. See Richard Ofshe and Ethan Watters, *Making Monsters: False Memories, Psychotherapy, and Sexual Hysteria* (New York: Scribner's, 1994), 165–75.

6. *Franklin v. Duncan,* 884 F. Supp. 1435 (N.D. Cal. 1995).

7. See the accounts of the case by: Harry N. Maclean, *Once Upon a Time* (New York: HarperCollins, 1993); Lenore Terr, *Unchained Memories* (New York: Basic Books, 1994), 32–60; Loftus and Ketcham, *The Myth of Repressed Memory,* 38–72; Ofshe and Watters, *Making Monsters,* 253–72.

8. See Freud, *From the History of an Infantile Neurosis* (1918), in *Standard Edition* 17:60; for further discussion of the problem of primal scenes versus primal fantasies, see Freud, *Introductory Lectures on Psychoanalysis,* in *Standard Edition,* vols. 16–17.

9. See *Fragment of the Analysis of a Case of Hysteria* (1905), in *Standard Edition* 7:104. For a sampling of responses to this case-history, see the essays collected in Charles Bernheimer and Claire Kahane, *In Dora's Case* (New York: Columbia University Press, 1985).

10. See Frederick Crews, *The Memory Wars* (New York: New York Review, 1995), 171. While I agree with Crews's dim view of this and other recovered memory litigation, I see no justification in his claim that such a misuse of psychotherapy invalidates the whole of psychoanalysis and somehow proves Freud to be a charlatan. On the contrary, Freud's view of repression—once he had abandoned the notion of "seduction" as a literal fact—seems to invalidate such claims at law. On the role of Terr's testimony, see also MacLean, *Once Upon a Time.* Judith Herman, a psychiatrist whose work has tended to bolster the claims of recovered memory therapy, nonetheless puts us on guard concerning the incompatible ends of therapy and legal adjudication: "The therapist has to remember that she is not a fact-finder and that her role is to be an open-minded, compassionate witness, not a detective." *Trauma and Recovery* (New York: Basic Books, 1992), 135. For a judicious assessment of research on memory, see Daniel L. Schachter, *Searching for Memory* (New York: Basic Books, 1996); Schacter discusses "The Memory Wars" in chap. 9, at 248–79.

11. On repression in Freud, see Freud, "Repression" [Die Verdrängung]

(1915), in *Standard Edition* 14:146–58; and the useful discussion in Jean Laplanche and J.-B. Pontalis, *Le Vocabulaire de la psychanalyse* (Paris: Presses Universitaires de France, 1971), 392–96. "Traumatic amnesia," too, can cause the loss of direct recall.

12. The decision of the district court granting Franklin a retrial was upheld by the U.S. Court of Appeals for the Ninth Circuit in 1995. Franklin meanwhile remained in jail for several years, unable to raise his one million dollar bail. In 1996, California abandoned the retrial and dismissed charges against him.

13. *Tyson v. Tyson,* 727 P.2d 226 (Wash. 1986).

14. Marianne Wesson, "Historical Truth, Narrative Truth, and Expert Testimony," *Washington Law Review* 60 (1985): 331. Wesson's article is largely indebted to Donald P. Spence, *Narrative Truth and Historical Truth* (New York: Norton, 1982), a book which has been highly influential but which also suffers from some confusions: see, for example, the comments of Janet Malcolm in "Six Roses ou Cirrhose?" *The New Yorker,* 24 January 1983, 96.

15. See Spence, supra, who argues an opposition between "narrative truth" and "historical truth," whereas I tend to think that for Freud these are allied and opposed to what he calls "material truth." That is, I don't think Freud claims that "historical truth," whether in his patients' lives or in the life of civilization, is ever verifiable. See Freud in "Constructions in Analysis" and *Moses and Monotheism,* in *Standard Edition,* vol. 23.

The majority and dissenting opinions in *Tyson* have been much cited in subsequent cases, with varying outcomes. Some courts have argued that since all memory is subject to distortion, it is unfair to single out repressed or "delayed" memories for exclusion, and therefore the statute of limitations should be tolled in such cases. Yet this argument could cut the other way: statutes of limitations exist precisely because memories are unreliable and commonsensibly judged to be more so with the passage of time. On these arguments, see Daniel Brown, Alan W. Scheflin, and D. Corydon Hammond, *Memory, Trauma Treatment, and the Law* (New York: W. W. Norton, 1998), especially 578–612. The authors cite with approval the opinion of Judge Linda Dalianis in *State of New Hampshire v. Walters,* Nos. 93-S-2111 and 93-S-2112 (Super. Ct., Hillsborough S. Dist. 1995), admitting "repressed memory" evidence on the grounds that it is subject to the same lay evaluation as any memory. I note, however, that the Supreme Court of New Hampshire recently reversed Walters' conviction. *State v. David Walters,* 698 A.2d 1244 (N.H. 1997).

Some courts seem to have argued themselves into the strange position that wholly repressed or delayed memories (called "Type 2") can lead to tolling the statute of limitations, whereas continuing memories from the deep past ("Type 1") will still be subject to the statute of limitations. One can see the legal but not the psychological or moral justification for such a position.

16. See Moira Johnston, *Spectral Evidence: The Ramona Case* (Boston: Houghton Mifflin, 1997). See the argument against permitting such suits in Cynthia Grant Brown and Elizabeth Meertz, "A Dangerous Direction: Legal

Intervention in Sexual Abuse Survivor Therapy," *Harvard Law Review* 109 (1996): 549, in which the authors argue the father should have sued his daughter, not her therapist.

Franklin v. Duncan also led to a suit by George Franklin against Lenore Terr and others, but it was dismissed.

17. For a good discussion of these issues, see Paul Gewirtz, "Victims and Voyeurs: Two Narrative Problems at the Criminal Trial," in Peter Brooks and Paul Gewirtz, eds., *Law's Stories* (New Haven: Yale University Press, 1996), 135–61. For a summary of the Victims Rights Movement and its outcomes, see Andrew Karmen, *Crime Victims: An Introduction to Victimology* (Monterey, Cal.: Brooks/Cole, 1984). I recall the advertisements for a Victims' advocate group carried on New Haven buses in the 1980s, which read: "He gots his rights, I got 20 stitches."

18. Martha Minow, "Surviving Victim Talk," *UCLA Law Review* 40 (1993): 1411, 1415–16. See also Lynne N. Henderson, "The Wrongs of Victim's Rights," *Stanford Law Review* 37 (1985): 937; Michael Ira Oberlander, "The *Payne* of Allowing Victim Impact Statements at Capital Sentencing Hearings," 45 *Vanderbilt Law Review* 45 (1992): 1621; Susan Bandes, "Empathy, Narrative, and Victim Impact Statements," *University of Chicago Law Review* 63 (1996): 361.

19. *Booth v. Maryland,* 482 U.S. 496, 499 (1987); *Payne v. Tennessee,* 501 U.S. 808 (1991). Between *Booth* (decided by a 5–4 majority) and *Payne* (6–3), Justices Powell and Brennan left the Court and were replaced by Kennedy and Souter, who joined the four *Booth* dissenters to create the majority of *Payne.*

20. *South Carolina v. Gathers,* 490 U.S. 805 (1989).

21. Minow, "Surviving Victim Talk," 1417.

22. See Roland Barthes, *S/Z* (Paris: Editions du Seuil, 1970), 145–46, 157–58; in English, *S/Z,* trans. Richard Miller (New York: Hill and Wang, 1974).

23. *California v. Brown,* 479 U.S. 538 (1987).

24. *Woodson v. North Carolina,* 428 U.S. 280, 304 (1976).

25. David Marshall, *The Surprising Effects of Sympathy* (Chicago: University of Chicago Press, 1988), 5.

26. Adam Smith, *The Theory of Moral Sentiments,* ed. D. D. Raphael and A. L. Macfie (Oxford: Clarendon Press, 1976), 9.

27. See Jean-Jacques Rousseau, *Lettre à M. d'Alembert sur les spectacles,* in *Du Contrat social* (Paris: Garnier, 1962); Denis Diderot, *Paradoxe sur le comédien* in *Oeuvres esthétiques* (Paris: Garnier, 1959); see the discussion of these texts in Marshall, *Surprising Effects of Sympathy,* and also the discussion of "empathy" in Bandes, "Empathy, Narrative, and Victim Impact Statements."

28. On Anna O., see Josef Breuer and Sigmund Freud, *Studies on Hysteria,* in *Standard Edition* 2:21–47. Some proponents of victim testimony have argued their "cathartic" value: see Henderson, "The Wrongs of Victim's Rights," 979.

29. Jorge Luis Borges, "The Shape of the Sword," trans. D. A. Yerby, in *Labyrinths* (New York, New Directions, 1954), 68.

Chapter Six

1. See in particular *Harris v. New York,* 401 U.S. 222 (1971) and *Michigan v. Tucker,* 417 U.S. 433 (1974).

2. In a 1990 California training videotape, "Questioning 'Outside *Miranda,'*" Devallis Rutledge, assistant district attorney, Orange County, gives this advice to the police: "All of these cases have said there's legitimate uses that a Miranda-violative statement can be put to. The only use it can't be put to is to prove the person's guilt in a trial. But it can be used to prove he's a liar when he gets on the stand and tells a different story. It can be used to discover other evidence that will prove his guilt in trial." Jan Hoffman, "Questioning Miranda," *New York Times,* 29 March 1998, 40.

3. *Oregon v. Elstad,* 470 U.S. 298 (1985).

4. *Wong Sun v. United States,* 371 U.S. 471 (1963).

5. Citing *Taylor v. Alabama,* 457 U.S. 687 (1982), which in turn is citing *Brown v. Illinois,* 422 U.S. 590 (1975).

6. *United States v. Bayer,* 331 U.S. 532, 540 (1947).

7. Citing Arthur S. Aubry Jr. and Rudolph R. Caputo, *Criminal Interrogation,* 3d ed. (Springfield, Ill.: Thomas, 1980), 291.

8. Citing Robert F. Royal and Steven R. Schutt, *The Gentle Art of Interviewing and Interrogation: A Professional Manual and Guide* (Englewood Cliff, N.J.: Prentice-Hall, 1976), 143.

9. Rousseau, *Confessions,* 156–57.

10. I quote from the very detailed presentation of the Reilly case by Donald S. Connery, *Guilty Until Proven Innocent* (New York: Putnam, 1977), 42.

11. Richard J. Ofshe and Richard A. Leo, "The Social Psychology of Police Interrogation: The Theory and Clasification of True and False Confessions," in *Studies in Law, Politics and Society* 16 (1977): 215.

12. See Ofshe and Leo, "Social Psychology of Police Interrogation," 231–34. In a later essay, Leo writes of "*Miranda*'s utter irrelevance, as well as our own blindness, to the ongoing and tragic problem of false confessions." Richard A. Leo, "*Miranda* and the Problem of False Confessions," in Richard A. Leo and George C. Thomas III, *The Miranda Debate* (Boston: Northeastern University Press, 1998), 277.

13. See John H. Langbein, "Torture and Plea Bargaining," *University of Chicago Law Review* 46 (1978): 21–22.

14. M. G. Lewis, *The Monk* (1796; Oxford: Oxford Univ. Press, 1998), 423.

15. Edward Peters, *Inquisition* (New York: The Free Press, 1988), 91. See also Henry Kamen, *The Spanish Inquisition: A Historical Revision* (New Haven: Yale University Press, 1998).

16. I cite from Nicolau Eymerich and Francisco Peña, *Le Manuel des Inquisiteurs,* trans. Louis Sala-Molins (Paris: Mouton, 1973), 162. The Dominican Eymerich wrote his *Directorium* in Avignon in 1376; it was printed in 1503; Peña's revision was published in Rome in 1585.

17. See, for instance, the work of historian Carlo Ginzburg, in, among

other books, *Il formaggio e i vermi* (Torino: Einaudi, 1976), trans. *The Cheese and the Worms* (Baltimore: Johns Hopkins University Press, 1980) and "Stregoneria e pietà popolare," in *Miti emblemi spie* (Tornio: Einaudi, 1986), 3–28.

18. See Jacques Chiffoleau, "Sur la pratique et la conjoncture de l'aveu judiciaire en France du XIIIe au XVe siècle," in *L'Aveu: Antiquité et moyen-âge,* Collection de l'Ecole Française de Rome, 88 (Rome: Ecole Française de Rome, 1986), 361.

19. Literary representations of the Inquisition are studied by Peters in *Inquisition.*

20. Victor Hugo, *Torquemada,* in *Oeuvres complètes: Théâtre,* II (Paris: Robert Laffont, 1985), partie 2, acte 2, scène 5. My translation.

21. Fyodor Dostoevsky, *The Brothers Karamazov,* trans. Richard Pevear and Larissa Volokhonsky (New York: Vintage, 1991), 258.

22. Arthur Koestler, *Darkness at Noon,* trans. Daphne Hardy (1941; New York: Bantam Modern Classic, 1968), 73. This passage is also discussed by Louis Michael Seidman in "Rubashov's Question: Self-Incrimination and the Problem of Coerced Preferences," *Yale Journal of Law and the Humanities* 2 (1990): 149.

23. See Michel Foucault, *Surveiller et punir* (Paris: Gallimard, 1975), 47.

24. See P. Linebaugh, "The Ordinary of Newgate and His Account," in *Crime in England, 1550–1800,* ed. J. S. Cockburn (Princeton: Princeton University Press, 1997), 246–69.

25. *The True Confession of Margaret Clark* (London: Joseph Collier, 1680), 1.

26. Rousseau, *Julie, ou la Nouvelle Héloïse* (Paris: Garnier, 1960), part 5, letter 3, page 546. Any commentary on transparency in Rousseau owes a large debt to the classic study by Jean Starobinski, *Jean-Jacques Rousseau: la transparence et l'obstacle* (Paris: Gallimard, 1971).

27. Rousseau, "Lettre à M. d'Alembert sur les spectacles," in *Du Contrat social* (Paris: Garnier, 1962), 225.

28. Louis de Saint-Just, *Oeuvres choisies* (Paris: Gallimard, 1968), 327. On Rousseau and the Jacobins, see Carol Blum, *Rousseau and the Republic of Virtue* (Ithaca: Cornell University Press, 1986) and Caroline E. Weber, "The Limits of 'Saying Everything': Terrorist Suppressions and Unspeakable Difference in Rousseau, Sade, Robespierre, Saint-Just, and Desmoulins," unpublished doctoral dissertation, Yale University, December 1998. On the contemporary American demand for transparency, see Sarah Boxer, "Transparent Enough to Hide Behind," *New York Times,* 19 December 1998.

29. Albert Camus, *La Chute* (Paris: Gallimard/Folio, 1972), 116; my translation. In English: *The Fall,* trans. Justin O'Brien (New York: Alfred A, Knopf, 1956), 110. I give in the text page number references to the French and the English.

30. Jacques Lacan, "Intervention sur le transfert," *Ecrits* (Paris: Editions du Seuil, 1966), 216.

31. See Richard Sennett, *The Fall of Public Man* (New York: Alfred A. Knopf, 1977), especially part 4, "The Intimate Society."

32. *Colorado v. Connelly,* 479 U.S. 157 (1986).

33. The majority in *Connelly* consists of Rehnquist, White, Powell, O'Connor, and Scalia; and, in part, Blackmun; Stevens concurred in the judgment but dissented on the major issue of "voluntariness"; Brennan and Marshall dissented.